C000205208

CHANCERY LITIGATION HANDBOOK

CHANCERY LITIGATION HANDBOOK

Vivian Chapman
General editor

Lynne Counsell
Precedents editor

JORDANS

2005

Published by
Jordan Publishing Limited
21 St Thomas Street
Bristol BS1 6JS

British Library Cataloguing-in-Publication Data

A catalogue record for this book is available from the British Library.

ISBN 0 85308 904 3

Typeset by Jordan Publishing Limited
Printed In Great Britain by MPG Books Ltd, Bodmin, Cornwall

FOREWORD

In many respects this book is a second edition of *Chancery Practice and Procedure* (Jordans, 2001). In my foreword to that work I pointed out that, following the introduction of the Civil Procedure Rules, the practice and procedure was the same in both the Chancery Division and the Queen's Bench Division. I stressed the need for up-to-date textbooks to guide and instruct the busy practitioner as to how to apply those rules to familiar types of Chancery Proceedings.

Now, some 4 years and many Rules, Practice Directions and decisions later, the need remains. As in the case of its predecessor the book focuses on the practical aspects of litigation at all its stages, a point emphasised by its new description as a 'litigation handbook'. In the pages that follow the reader is guided by experienced practitioners in the field through all the steps involved in the various claims and applications commonly pursued in the Chancery Division.

The biographical details of the editors and contributors, which have also been updated, confirm their expertise in the areas of which they write. In this book they generously share that expertise with their readers. I have no doubt that all who have occasion to litigate in the Chancery Division or to bring equivalent claims in the county court will benefit from it.

Andrew Morritt
Vice-Chancellor of the Supreme Court
January 2005

PREFACE

Litigation in the Chancery Division of the High Court has changed. The emphasis has shifted towards modern business disputes. Procedure has been modernised by the Civil Procedure Rules. However, Chancery litigation retains its own distinctive character and expertise. There are still many specialised areas of Chancery practice which have their own unique procedures, such as the areas of corporate and personal insolvency, contentious probate and charity litigation.

This handbook is written and edited by a team of barristers who are all members of 9 Stone Buildings, Lincoln's Inn and who are all experienced Chancery practitioners. The purpose of the handbook is to give clear, practical and up-to-date guidance to all who embark on Chancery litigation.

Part 1 of the handbook begins by dealing with the progress of Chancery proceedings from commencement to the execution of Chancery judgments. It then deals with the important specialised Chancery jurisdictions.

Part 2 contains detailed procedural guides.

The accompanying CD-ROM contains Chancery forms and precedents and the Chancery Guide.

Vivian Chapman
January 2005
Lincoln's Inn

BIOGRAPHICAL DETAILS

GENERAL EDITOR

Vivian Chapman
Vivian Chapman specialises in property litigation and advice. He was called to the bar in 1970 after taking a double first in law at Christ's College, Cambridge. He is head of chambers. He has appeared in numerous reported cases. Recent cases include: *R (Richards) v Pembrokeshire County Council* [2004] EWCA Civ 1000 (Court of Appeal: judicial review: ECHR Art 6 and 1st Protocol Art 1); *Crest Nicholson Residential (South) Ltd v McAllister* [2004] 2 All ER 991 (Court of Appeal: restrictive covenants); *Fraser v Canterbury Diocesan Board of Finance (No 2)* [2004] EWCA Civ 15 (Court of Appeal: School Sites Acts); *Massey v Boulden* [2003] 2 All ER 87 (Court of Appeal: rights of way); *Crest Nicholson Residential (South) Ltd v McAllister* [2003] 1 All ER 46 (restrictive covenants); *Padgham v Rochelle* [2003] WTLR 71, [2002] WTLR 1483 (undue influence); *Bettison v Langton* [2002] 1 AC 27 (House of Lords: rights of common); *Carapeto v Good* [2002] WTLR 801, 1305 and 1311 (probate); *Fitzpatrick v Sterling Housing Association Ltd* [2001] 1 AC 27 (House of Lords: landlord and tenant); *Fraser v Canterbury Diocesan Board of Finance (No 1)* [2001] Ch 669 (Court of Appeal: Schools Sites Acts); *Barclays Bank Trust Co Ltd v McDougall* (2001) 2 WTLR 23 (trusts: construction of settlement); *R v National Assembly of Wales ex parte Robinson* (2000) 80 P&CR 348 (public rights of way: deletion from definitive map); *Price Meats Ltd v Barclays Bank plc* [2000] 2 All ER (Comm) 346 (Banking: constructive notice of forgery). He has a special interest in and is an acknowledged expert on the law relating to commons and greens and was described by Lord Hoffmann in *R v Oxfordshire County Council ex parte Sunningwell PC* [2000] AC 335 as 'a barrister with great experience in this branch of the law' and by Lightman J in *Oxfordshire County Council v Oxford City Council* [2004] 2 WLR 1291 as 'a senior barrister with wide experience in this field'. He has taken part as Inspector or counsel in over 40 public inquiries into village green applications. He is a bencher of Lincoln's Inn and a Recorder, in which capacity he regularly sits as a part time judge. He is described as a Leading Chancery Junior in *Chambers Guide to the Legal Profession 2005*. He is General Editor of *Chancery Practice and Procedure* (Jordans, 2001). He has also written numerous articles and regularly speaks on property law and litigation at conferences and seminars.

PRECEDENTS EDITOR

Lynne Counsell
Lynne Counsell BA (London); Dip Law (City University) was called to the Bar in 1986. There are two distinct aspects to her practice. The first being general Chancery, particularly wills, trusts, probate, family provision, land and landlord and tenant. The second aspect is commercial law, particularly the law relating to investments and companies, shareholder matters, partnership, financial services and the regulation of money laundering. She has a specific expertise in interim remedies. She is joint editor of *Halsbury's Laws on Injunctions*; co-author of *Insider Trading* (Tolley, 1993). She has

contributed to various volumes of *Atkin's Court Forms*, including contract, money, easements, limitation and financial services. She has also contributed the chapter on Injunctions to Ashe and Rider *International Tracing of Assets* (Sweet & Maxwell).

CONTRIBUTORS

Daniel Bromilow

Daniel Bromilow studied law at Robinson College, Cambridge and joined Chambers after completing pupillage, having been called to the Bar in November 1996. He has a wide-ranging practice covering most areas of Chancery and general civil/commercial work, but specialises in real property, landlord and tenant, wills, trusts and company law.

Edward Denehan

Edward Denehan LLB (Warwick) was called to the Bar at Lincoln's Inn in July 1981. His practice is exclusively real property, both contentious and non-contentious including landlord and tenant (both commercial and residential), land and conveyancing, restrictive covenants, easements, boundaries, property valuation, mortgages, housing and professional negligence arising from these areas. He was once a tutor in property law at the University of Warwick, and tutor in landlord and tenant law, and planning and local government law at the Inns of Court School of Law. He lectures extensively on property matters and is a panel lecturer for Jordans on conveyancing and landlord and tenant matters. He was the author of 'Guide to Possession Actions' *Advocacy Manual* (Inns of Court School of Law), and the joint author of *Landlord and Tenant Manual* (Inns of Court School of Law). He is a member of the Chancery Bar Association, the Property Bar Association, and the South Eastern Circuit. Identified as a Star of the Chancery Bar and as 'a solicitors' favourite' at the Landlord and Tenant Bar by *Lawyer Magazine*. Recommended by the *Legal 500* (2004 edn) as a leading junior in property litigation. He has appeared in numerous reported cases concerning property matters including, in the field of commercial landlord and tenant law, *Mount Eden Land Limited v Folia Limited* [2003] PLSCS 188, *Hart Investments plc v Burton Hotel Limited* [2002] L&TR 93, *Basch v Stekel* [2001] L&TR 1, *The Prudential Assurance Company Limited v Eden Restaurants (Holborn) Limited* [2000] L&TR 480, *Mean Machine Limited v Blackheath Leisure (Carousel) Ltd* (1999) 78 P&CR D36, *Sight & Sound Education Limited v Books Etc Limited* [1999] 3 EGLR 45, *Bacchiocchi v Academic Agency Limited* [1998] 1 WLR 1313, *Kened Limited v Connie Investments Limited* [1997] 1 EGLR 21, *Estates Gazette Limited v Benjamin Restaurants* [1995] 1 All ER 129, *Wandsworth London Borough Council v Singh* [1991] 2 EGLR 71 and *Capital & Counties plc v Hawa* [1991] 2 EGLR 133.

Sheila Foley

Sheila Foley BA was called to the Bar in 1988. Her practice encompasses all aspects of corporate, partnership and personal insolvency. She also specialises in company law including formations, nature and constitution, shares and debentures administration, enforcement of directors' duties, directors' disqualification, shareholder disputes, liquidation and receiverships. She is a member of the Chancery Bar Association.

James Hanham

James Hanham (MA (Oxon), LLB (London)) was called to the Bar in 1996. He specialises in all aspects of real property (including mortgages) and both residential and commercial landlord and tenant law (areas upon which he regularly lectures). His expertise extends to company and insolvency matters (a recently reported case of his being that of *Woodbridge v Smith* [2004] BPIR 247) and general chancery/commercial litigation. He is a member of the Chancery Bar Association and the Property Bar Association.

Cenydd I Howells

Cenydd Howells MA, LLM (Cantab) was called to the Bar by Lincoln's Inn in 1964. Since finishing pupillage he has practised at 9 Stone Buildings (formerly 11 Stone Buildings) in general Chancery with particular emphasis on Land Law and Trusts. Member of the Chancery Bar Association, the Property Bar Association and the Society of Trust and Estate Practitioners. Member of the Wales & Chester Circuit and, since 1992, a Recorder (Civil, Chancery and Family work). Member of the Panel of Judges accepted to try cases involving evidence and proceedings in Welsh. Fellow of the Chartered Institute of Arbitrators, he sits from time to time as an arbitrator. He is an Examiner of the Court (approved to take evidence requested by foreign courts).

Constance Mahoney

Constance Mahoney was called to the Bar in 2000, and has been a tenant at 9 Stone Buildings since December 2001. She has a general Chancery/commercial practice including real property, landlord and tenant, media and entertainment, constructive trusts/proprietary estoppel, company, insolvency, probate (contentious and non-contentious), trusts, contract, negligence and other torts. Reported cases in which she has appeared include *Carapeto v Good* [2002] WTLR 801 (contentious probate); *Khiaban v Beard* [2003] 1 WLR 1626 (Court of Appeal: whether court could require claimant to increase value of claim); *Cityb@se plc v Memery Crystal* [2003] All ER (D) 01 (Nov) (solicitors' negligence); *Re OT Computers Ltd* [2004] All ER (D) 361 (May) (Court of Appeal: application for disclosure of policy under Third Parties (Rights against Insurers) Act 1930). She has also appeared in the High Court and the Court of Appeal in the Turks & Caicos Islands.

Helene Pines Richman

Helene Pines Richman is a specialist and recognised expert in the fields of commercial, property and private client litigation and is named as a Leading Junior in both the *Legal 500* (2005) and *Legal Experts 2005*. A graduate of the University of Pennsylvania (Ivy League) with a degree in bioengineering and a Juris Doctor in Law, she began practising law in 1983 in New York City for a large international firm. In 1992 she was called to the English Bar and has since maintained a practice with domestic as well as international focus. She continues to be a member of the NY Bar and takes on cases with a cross-border element. In England, she appeared in the House of Lords in the leading case on undue influence and mortgages. *Etridge* [2001] 4 All ER 449, the Vice-Chancellor's court in *Clegg v Andersson t/a Nordic Marine* [2003] 1 Comm All ER 721 (seminal case on the Sale of Goods Acts), *Buggs v Buggs* [2003] 147 SJLB 111 (constructive trusts and proprietary estoppel), and numerous other reported cases. She routinely acts in large-scale group litigation and was Lead Counsel for the wives in the *BCCI* cases, and high-value claims. She is an editor of Butterworths' Older Client Law Service, and author of *Atkins Court Forms (Mortgages) and (Partnerships)* and many other published articles. She is a past lecturer at the University of Westminster School of Law and now frequent lecturer in property and private client litigation for CLT and other course providers. She is a member of the Chancery Bar Association, the Commercial Bar Association and sits as a panel judge in the Council of the Inns of Court Bar Disciplinary Tribunals. She is a Past Chairwoman of the Association of Women Barristers (having served two terms) and is now Vice-President, along with Baroness Hale of Richmond who sits as President.

David Rowell

David Rowell LLB Hons (Oxon) was called to the Bar in 1973 and joined 9 Stone Buildings in 2001. His practice covers the whole field of Chancery work but he specialises mainly in private client work, personal taxation, trusts, property law, landlord and tenant and charities. Notable cases include include: *Hambro v Duke of Marlborough* [1994] Ch. 158 (where he drafted a scheme for the future management of Blenheim Palace); *Challock Parish Council v Shirley* [1995] 2 EGLR 137 (easements and land valuation); *Rabin v Gerson Berger* [1986] 1 All ER 374 (trusts); *Re Evans deceased* [1986] 1 WLR 101 (claims against estates of deceased persons); *Re Box Hill Common* [1980] Ch 109 (commons registration).

Peter Shaw

Peter Shaw was a solicitor for 9 years before being called to the Bar in 1995. His principal areas of practice include all aspects of corporate and personal insolvency, company law (including directors disqualification), insurance coverage litigation, sale and leasing of goods, professional negligence, trusts of land, commercial fraud and Chancery/commercial litigation. Notable cases include: *Re Nordictrack (UK) Limited* [2000] 1 BCLC 467, Arden J (voluntary winding up following discharge of Administration; deemed date of winding up – s 86 of the Insolvency Act 1986); *Carter-Knight v Peat* [2000] BPIR 968, Neuberger J (remedied default in Individual Voluntary Arrangement – court's discretion to make a Bankruptcy Order; decision of district judge remitted due to failure to give reasons); *Moore Large & Co Ltd v Hermes Credit & Guarantee Plc* [2003] 1 Lloyd's Rep 163 (credit insurance; variation of cover; material misrepresentation; affirmation of policy); *Pantone 485 Ltd* [2002] 1 BCLC 266 (limitation periods for breach of judiciary duty); *Conquest v Fox* [2003] All ER (D) 360 (liquidator's claims for misfeasance; preference; void charge in favour of director); *Boyden v Stern* [2004] BCC 599 (limitation period applicable to claims to recover unlawful loans to directors). He is a member of the Insolvency Lawyers Association, and the Chancery Bar Association.

Timothy Sisley

Timothy Sisley BA (London) is a former solicitor, admitted in 1985. His work embraces solicitors' and other professional negligence, landlord and tenant, land and conveyancing, planning, sale of goods, leasing and consumer credit, commercial arrangements, employment, suretyship, insolvency and civil recovery in fraud.

John Smart

John Smart BSc (Bristol), Dip Law (City University) was called to the bar in 1989. He is recommended by the *Legal 500* as a leading junior in the areas of personal tax, trusts and probate. He also undertakes company, partnership, property and insolvency work and, from time to time, work involving intellectual property law, private international law and professional negligence. Notable cases include: *IRC v McGuckian* [1997] 1 WLR 991 (HL) (income tax avoidance); *Re Bremner (a Bankrupt)* [1999] FLR 912 (trustee in bankruptcy bringing application for sale of home of discharged bankrupt who had inoperable cancer); *Hitch v Stone (Inspector of Taxes)* [2001] STC 214 (CA) (capital gains tax avoidance, whether agreement for lease was a sham); *R. (on the application of Werner v IRC* [2002] STC 1213 (challenge to notice under s 20(1) of the Taxes Management Act 1970); *Robson v Mitchell* [2004] STI 1605 (s 253 of the TCGA 1992 loss relief for payment under guarantee). He is a member of the Chancery Bar Association, Revenue Bar Association and the Society of Trust and Estate Practitioners.

Richard Wilson
Richard Wilson LLB (Sheffield) LLM (London) was called to the Bar in 1996. He joined 9 Stone Buildings in 1999 where he specialises in trusts, tax, probate and charity law. He is the author of numerous articles and books and lectures widely on private client subjects. He is a member of the Chancery Bar Association, Revenue Bar Association and the Society of Trust and Estate Practitioners (STEP).

Lana Wood
Lana Wood MA (Cantab) BCL (Oxon) was called to the Bar in 1993 and joined 9 Stone Buildings in 1999. She specialises in Land and Property Law and advises on a wide spectrum of land and property matters including conveyancing, easements and restrictive covenants, boundaries, commons, adverse possession, property contracts, co-habitation and mortgages. She is frequently instructed to provide advice for title indemnity insurance purposes and more general advice for developer clients. She undertakes landlord and tenant work including both commercial and residential and has a particular expertise in enfranchisement (flats and houses), right to manage and rights of first refusal. Her advocacy experience extends from the High Court and Court of Appeal, through County Courts to the Lands Tribunal and Leasehold Valuation Tribunal. She also lectures on real property and landlord and tenant matters for CLT and other course providers and is a deputy district judge.

CONTENTS

Contents of the accompanying CD-ROM

Forms and precedents

The Chancery Guide 2002

TABLE OF CASES

TABLE OF STATUTES

TABLE OF STATUTORY INSTRUMENTS

References are to paragraph numbers and to Procedural Guides.

TABLE OF OTHER MATERIALS

TABLE OF ABBREVIATIONS

the Act	Insolvency Act 1986
AJA 1985	Administration of Justice Act 1985
CA 1993	Charities Act 1993
CCA 1984	County Courts Act 1984
CEA 1995	Civil Evidence Act 1985
CPR	Civil Procedure Rules 1998
CPR PD	Civil Procedure Rules Practice Direction
CVA	company voluntary arrangement
EA 2002	Enterprise Act 2002
HA 1988	Housing Act 1988
IA 1986	Insolvency Act 1986
ICTA 1988	Income and Corporation Taxes Act 1988
I(PFD)A 1975	Inheritance (Provisions for Family and Dependants) Act 1975
IR 1986	Insolvency Rules 1986
ITA 1984	Inheritance Tax Act 1984
IVA	individual voluntary arrangement
LPA 1925	Law of Property Act 1925
LP(R)A 1938	Leasehold Property (Repairs) Act 1938
LRA 1967	Leasehold Reform Act 1967
LTA 1927	Landlord and Tenant Act 1927
LTA 1954	Landlord and Tenant Act 1954
LTA 1987	Landlord and Tenant Act 1987
PA 1890	Partnership Act 1890
RA 1977	Rent Act 1977
the Rules	Insolvency Rules 1986
SCA 1981	Supreme Court Act 1981
SLA 1925	Settled Land Act 1925
TA 1925	Trustee Act 1925
TA 2000	Trustee Act 2000
TLATA 1996	Trusts of Land and Appointment of Trustees Act 1996
TMA 1970	Taxes Management Act 1970
VTA 1958	Variation of Trusts Act 1958

Part 1

NARRATIVE

Chapter 1

INTRODUCTION

Constance Mahoney & David Rowell

STRUCTURE OF THE HIGH COURT

1.1   The High Court of Justice forms part of the Supreme Court of England and Wales, together with the Court of Appeal and the Crown Court.[1] For administrative purposes, there are three divisions of the High Court: the Chancery Division, the Queen's Bench Division and the Family Division.

1.2   The judges of the Chancery Division are the Lord Chancellor,[2] the Vice-Chancellor and such of the puisne judges of the High Court as are for the time being attached to the Chancery Division.[3] The Lord Chancellor is both president of the Supreme Court[4] and president of the Chancery Division.[5] The Vice-Chancellor[6] is vice-president of the Chancery Division. Judges from other Divisions may also act as judges in the Chancery Division,[7] as may an acting or retired judge of the Court of Appeal, a retired puisne judge of the High Court, a circuit judge and a recorder (provided they are under the age of 75).[8]

1.3   Most interim and procedural applications are dealt with by masters (in Chancery Chambers at the Royal Courts of Justice[9]) or by appointed district judges (in a district registry). They control the progress of cases and deal with many matters arising in the course of litigation, whether or not these are

---

[1]   Supreme Court Act 1981 (SCA 1981), s 1(1).

[2]   On 12 June 2003 the Prime Minister announced the creation of a new Department for Constitutional Affairs, which has assumed most of the responsibilities of the former Lord Chancellor's Department. It is not clear at the time of writing what effect the reforms will have upon the Chancery Division, save that Lord Falconer, the current Lord Chancellor, will operate as a conventional Cabinet minister, and does not intend to sit as a judge in the House of Lords before the new Supreme Court is established.

[3]   SCA 1981, s 5(1)(a).

[4]   Ibid, s 1(2).

[5]   Ibid, s 5(1)(a).

[6]   The Vice-Chancellor usually sits for part of the year in the Court of Appeal and for the rest of the year in the Chancery Division.

[7]   SCA 1981, s 5(3).

[8]   Ibid, s 9(1) and (1A).

[9]   The Royal Courts of Justice, Strand, London WC2A 2LL. See also Chancery Guide, Section A, paras 5.35–5.40 as to how to make an application to a master. The Chancery Guide 2002 can be viewed on the CD which accompanies this book.

contentious. Certain matters may not be dealt with by a master or district judge without the Vice-Chancellor's consent.[1] Of these, the majority are substantive rather than procedural matters, with the exception that a master or district judge may only give directions for early trial after consulting the judge in charge of the relevant list.[2]

1.4　　There is a High Court district registry in most major county court centres.[3] Chancery Division cases may be commenced in any district registry, but 'should normally be transferred to the appropriate Chancery District Registry upon the first occasion the case comes before the court'.[4]

BUSINESS OF THE CHANCERY DIVISION

1.5　　The Chancery Division has much of its own distinct business which is derived from the following four sources.

(1)　Statute

1.6　　Some statutes specifically provide that claims under those statutes must be issued in the Chancery Division, for example matters under the Law of Property Act 1925[5] and the authorisation (if the Charity Commissioners have refused it) of 'charity proceedings' under the Charities Act 1993.[6]

(2)　Civil Procedure Rules 1998

1.7　　The Civil Procedure Rules 1998 (CPR) assign certain business to the Chancery Division. Examples of such assignment are numerous. They include High Court mortgage possession cases,[7] probate claims,[8] claims relating to the administration of estates and trusts and charity proceedings,[9] revenue appeals to the High Court,[10] applications under the Commons Registration Act 1965[11] and proceedings under the Financial Services and Markets Act 2000.[12]

---

[1]　CPR, PD2B, para 5.1.
[2]　CPR, PD2B, para 5.2.
[3]　For a list of district registries, see Civil Courts Order 1983, SI 1983/713, as amended.
[4]　Chancery Guide, Section A, para 12.7.
[5]　Law of Property Act 1925 (LPA 1925), s 203(4).
[6]　Charities Act 1993 (CA 1993), s 33(5).
[7]　CPR, PD55, para 1.6.
[8]　CPR, r 57.2.
[9]　CPR, r 64.1(3).
[10]　CPR, Sch 1, RSC Ord 91, r 1.
[11]　RSC Ord 93, r 16.
[12]　RSC Ord 93, r 22.

(3) Specific assignment under SCA 1981, Sch 1

1.8 Business is distributed between the Divisions of the High Court in accordance with Sch 1 to the SCA 1981.[1] Under Sch 1, causes and matters relating to the following are assigned to the Chancery Division:

(a) the sale, exchange or partition of land, or the raising of charges on land;
(b) the redemption or foreclosure of mortgages;
(c) the execution of trusts;
(d) the administration of the estates of deceased persons;
(e) bankruptcy;
(f) the dissolution of partnership or the taking of partnership or other accounts;
(g) the rectification, setting-aside or cancellation of deeds or other instruments in writing;
(h) probate business, other than non-contentious or common form business;
(i) patents, trade marks, registered designs, copyright or design right;
(j) the appointment of a guardian of a minor's estate, and all causes and matters involving the exercise of the High Court's jurisdiction under the enactments relating to companies.

1.9 A claim based upon any of these listed causes of action *must* be issued in the Chancery Division, if issued in the High Court.[2] However, in a few cases, the court may transfer the case to another Division, applying the general principle that any High Court judge of any Division has jurisdiction to hear any action which is within the jurisdiction of the High Court.[3]

(4) Matters not specifically assigned to any Division

1.10 There are many causes of action which cannot be found in the three Division lists in Sch 1 to the SCA 1981. These include general landlord and tenant cases, disputes involving contracts (other than for the sale, exhange or partition of land or proceeding in the Commercial Court), professional negligence claims and other tort cases. A claim based upon any such unlisted cause of action *may* be issued in the Chancery Division (although it may be transferred to another Division by the court).

1.11 If a claim issued in the Chancery Division comes within the definition of 'commercial claim' under CPR, r 58.1(2), the court will usually adopt the practice of the Commercial Court (to the extent that it is consistent with the

---

[1]   SCA 1981, s 61(1).
[2]   Chancery Guide, Section A, para 1.5.
[3]   SCA 1981, s 5(5).

CPR and any relevant practice direction).[1] Practitioners should consult the Admiralty and Commercial Courts Guide 2002 for guidance.

CHANCERY BUSINESS OUTSIDE LONDON

Chancery proceedings in the county court

1.12 The county court has jurisdiction under Part II of the County Courts Act 1984 (CCA 1984) to hear and determine certain cases which would generally be regarded as Chancery business.

1.13 The county court's jurisdiction includes:

(a)   any action founded on contract or tort (except actions for libel or slander, and any action in which the title to any toll, fair, market or franchise is in question);[2]

(b)   any action for the recovery of a sum recoverable by virtue of any enactment for the time being in force;[3]

(c)   any action for the recovery of land;[4]

(d)   any action in which the title to any hereditament comes into question.[5]

This jurisdiction is subject to the monetary limits set out in the High Court and County Courts Jurisdiction Order 1991.[6] Under this Order, the county court has jurisdiction under several specific statutory provisions *whatever* the amount involved in the proceedings and *whatever* the value of any fund or asset connected with the proceedings. The same Order has also abolished the jurisdiction limits of the county court in respect of a wide range of cases of contract and tort.

1.14 The county court has 'all jurisdiction of the High Court' to hear and determine:

(a)   proceedings for the administration of the estate of a deceased person, where the estate does not exceed in amount or value the county court limit;[7]

(b)   proceedings:

(i)   for the execution of any trust; or

---

[1]   Chancery Guide, Section A, para 1.6.
[2]   CCA 1984, s 15. As to whether any particular case is 'founded on contract', see *Hutchinson v Islington London Borough Council* [1998] 3 All ER 445, CA.
[3]   CCA 1984, s 16.
[4]   Ibid, s 21(1).
[5]   Ibid, s 21(2).
[6]   SI 1991/724.
[7]   CCA 1984, s 23(a).

(ii) for a declaration that a trust subsists; or

(iii) under s 1 of the Variation of Trusts Act 1958 (VTA 1958);

where the estate or fund subject, or alleged to be subject, to the trust does not exceed in amount or value the county court limit;[1]

(c) proceedings for foreclosure or redemption of any mortgage or for enforcing any charge or lien, where the amount owing in respect of the mortgage charge or lien does not exceed the county court limit;[2]

(d) proceedings for the specific performance of, or for the rectification, delivery-up or cancellation of any agreement for the sale, purchase or lease of any property, where, in the case of a sale or purchase, the purchase money, or in the case of a lease, the value of the property, does not exceed the county court limit;[3]

(e) proceedings relating to the maintenance or advancement of a minor, where the property of the minor does not exceed in amount or value the county court limit;[4]

(f) proceedings for the dissolution or winding-up of any partnership (whether or not the existence of the partnership is in dispute), where the whole assets of the partnership do not exceed in amount or value the county court limit;[5]

(g) proceedings for relief against fraud or mistake, where the damage sustained or the estate or fund in respect of which relief is sought does not exceed in amount or value the county court limit.[6]

1.15 The 'county court limit' is currently £30,000.[7]

1.16 Outside London, proceedings in bankruptcy must be issued in the relevant county court, rather than in the district registries.[8]

1.17 The county court also has jurisdiction under s 24 of the CCA 1984 to hear and determine certain equity proceedings where the parties have agreed by memorandum that a particular county court shall have jurisdiction in the proceedings. These proceedings include all those within s 23 of the CCA 1984 (listed in **1.14** above), together with those detailed in s 24(2) of the CCA 1984, but not proceedings under s 1 of the VTA 1958. In other words, parties can agree that a county court shall have jurisdiction in a s 23 case where the monetary value of the claim exceeds £30,000.

---

1 CCA 1984, s 23(b).
2 Ibid, s 23(c).
3 Ibid, s 23(d).
4 Ibid, s 23(e).
5 Ibid, s 23(f).
6 Ibid, s 23(g).
7 County Courts Jurisdiction Order 1981, SI 1981/1123.
8 Chancery Guide, Section A, para 12.2.

1.18   Where the county court has jurisdiction and the monetary value of a claim exceeds £15,000,[1] a claimant may have a choice as to where to issue the claim.[2] The advantage of issuing in a local county court is that it is usually much more convenient for the parties and the witnesses (and possibly also for the court if a site visit is necessary) than the High Court. It is sometimes possible to negotiate with the court and circuit listing authorities so that a Chancery case in an ordinary county court is tried by a circuit judge or recorder with Chancery experience. However, a claim with an estimated value of less than £50,000 'will generally be transferred to a county court' unless it is within a specialist list.[3]

1.19   Chancery masters, at their discretion,[4] transfer certain cases pending in the Chancery Division to the Chancery list at the Central London County Court, regardless of the county court monetary limit. Where such a transfer is likely, the claim can be issued in the Central London County Court (if appropriate to be issued there), with a request for transfer to the Chancery list.[5]

District registries

1.20   Most Chancery cases heard outside London which are not issued in a county court are heard in the district registries. Chancery judges sit regularly in Birmingham, Bristol, Cardiff, Leeds, Liverpool, Manchester and Newcastle-upon-Tyne, and occasionally in Preston.[6] At these courts, there are specially appointed circuit judges who have Chancery experience and who act as High Court judges of the Chancery Division. At Preston, however, attendance by such judges does not occur regularly. Certain High Court Chancery judges from London sit from time to time at these places and other courts outside London.[7]

1.21   If a Chancery case is proceeding in any district registry other than a Chancery district registry, the case should normally be transferred to the appropriate Chancery district registry upon the first occasion the case comes before the court.[8] However, in many circumstances (for example, because of

---

[1]   A claim for money in which the county courts have jurisdiction may only be commenced in the High Court if the financial value of the claim is more than £15,000: High Court and County Courts Jurisdiction Order 1991, Art 4A.

[2]   Ibid, Art 4.

[3]   Chancery Guide, Section A, para 13.5.

[4]   This discretion will generally involve weighing up the complexity of facts involved in the case and the legal issues, remedies and procedures involved.

[5]   Chancery Guide, Section A, para 13.10.

[6]   Ibid, para 12.1.

[7]   Ibid, para 12.10. It is by no means always impossible to have a case tried by a High Court judge at courts other than at the Royal Courts of Justice or at one of the Chancery district registries.

[8]   Chancery Guide, Section A, para 12.7.

the inability of witnesses to travel far or because of the necessity of a site visit), arrangements can be made for the Chancery court to sit elsewhere.[1]

1.22 It is also possible to arrange for a case of exceptional difficulty or importance to be heard by a High Court judge, instead of a circuit judge. High Court judges will also, in exceptional circumstances, deal with matters excepted from the jurisdiction of an authorised circuit judge.[2]

1.23 Interim applications in cases issued outside London should normally be made to a district judge (provided that a district judge has jurisdiction to hear and determine the application).[3] If the parties consider that a High Court judge or circuit judge should hear the application, they should arrange for it to be listed on one of the ordinary application days.[4]

1.24 If the parties are not sure how to manage any procedural matter, they should be able to consult a district judge by post or telephone.

1.25 Practitioners should be aware that listing arrangements[5] and standard forms of directions differ amongst the district registries. There may even be varied practice in respect of which court forms should be used for a particular application. It is therefore recommended that practitioners either enquire with the relevant court before taking any formal procedural step, or that each step is taken well in advance of its deadline, so that there is time to remedy any noted defect in the documents to be filed.

---

[1]   Chancery Guide, Section A, para 12.8.
[2]   Ibid, para 12.9.
[3]   Ibid, para 12.11. See further Chapter 3.
[4]   Ibid, para 12.13.
[5]   Individual listing arrangements are set out in ibid, paras 12.19–12.24.

Chapter 2

COMMENCEMENT OF PROCEEDINGS

Constance Mahoney & David Rowell

PRE-ACTION PROTOCOLS

2.1   Before a claim is issued, it is necessary to consider whether any relevant pre-action protocol has been complied with. The onus is on all proposed parties to litigation to ensure that a relevant approved protocol has been complied with in substance before litigation is commenced. There are currently eight pre-action protocols.[1]

2.2   However, practitioners should also be aware that para 4 of the Practice Direction on Protocols states that:

> 'In cases not approved by any approved protocol, the court will expect the parties, in accordance with the overriding objective and the matters referred to in CPR 1.1(2)(a), (b) and (c), to act reasonably in exchanging information and documents relevant to the claim and generally in trying to avoid the necessity for the start of proceedings.'[2]

2.3   The Practice Direction then sets out details of the steps which should normally be taken by proposed parties where an existing protocol does not apply. These include (in summary) the following.

(a)   The proposed claimant should write a letter setting out details of the proposed claim, enclosing copies of relevant documents, requesting copies of any relevant documents in the proposed defendant's possession, and drawing attention to the court's powers to impose sanctions for failing to comply with the Practice Direction (enclosing a copy of the Practice Direction if the proposed defendant is not legally represented).[3]

---

[1]   The eight existing pre-action protocols cover: personal injury; disease and illness at work claims; resolution of clinic disputes; defamation; construction and engineering disputes; professional negligence; housing disrepair; and judicial review.

[2]   Practice Direction on Protocols, para 4.1.

[3]   See full details of steps to be taken in ibid, paras 4.2–4.3.

(b)   The proposed defendant should acknowledge this letter in writing within 21 days of its receipt, and state when a full written response will be given.[1]

(c)   The proposed defendant's full written response should either accept the claim in whole or in part (making proposals for settlement and if necessary stating which parts are or are not accepted), or state that the claim is not accepted. If any of the claim is not accepted, the proposed defendant should give detailed reasons why, enclosing copies of documents on which the proposed defendant relies and copies of documents requested by the claimant (or giving reasons for not providing them).[2]

2.4   'If the claim remains in dispute, the parties should promptly engage in appropriate negotiations with a view to settling the dispute and avoiding litigation.'[3]

2.5   If any party to litigation does not comply either with a relevant pre-action protocol or with the Practice Direction (where no existing protocol applies), the court will have an absolute discretion as to whether sanctions should be applied to the non-complying party.[4] Such sanctions are rarely imposed in practice unless the infringement is more than minor and has adversely affected the other party, or unless the litigation could have been avoided by compliance with the relevant protocol.

2.6   Practitioners who practice in the fields of probate and trusts should also be aware of the existence of a draft pre-action protocol for the resolution of probate and trust disputes.[5] Although it is understood that the draft protocol will not be adopted formally, it provides useful guidance of best practice in these areas, together with templates for pre-action correspondence.

DECIDING WHERE TO ISSUE PROCEEDINGS

2.7   Certain claims should be issued only in the Chancery Division (if in the High Court) or should be listed as being Chancery business (if in a county court).[6] However, many claims are not defined as Chancery business in the county court and are not necessarily assigned to any particular division in the High Court. In such cases, where proceedings are brought in the High Court,

---

[1]   See full details of steps to be taken in Practice Direction on Protocols, para 4.4.
[2]   See full details of steps to be taken in ibid, paras 4.5–4.6.
[3]   Ibid, para 4.7.
[4]   Ibid, para 3.3.
[5]   The Association of Contentious Trust and Probate Specialists has drafted the protocol, which may be viewed by visiting the Association's website at www.actaps.com.
[6]   For a list of causes of action for which claims *must* be issued in the Chancery Division, see **1.8**. For guidance as to the county courts' Chancery jurisdiction, see **1.13** et seq.

it is a matter of judgment whether or not the Chancery Division is the most appropriate division.

2.8   The county courts have exclusive jurisdiction over certain claims. For example, where a mortgagee is seeking possession of a residential property outside Greater London, the claim may only be brought in the relevant county court.[1] In a wide range of cases where proceedings are brought under the Rent Act 1977 (RA 1977), if the claimant starts the claim in the High Court, he will not be entitled to recover any costs.[2] In the case of proceedings for possession under the Housing Act 1988, a claimant who issues the claim in the High Court will only be entitled to such costs as he would have been entitled to if he had started the claim in the county court.[3] The clear policy behind these rules is to ensure, as far as possible, that possession actions for the recovery of residential premises are brought in the county court.

2.9   In relation to most claims, there is no requirement that the claim must be issued in a particular county court. However, there are two exceptions to this rule.

2.10   The first exception applies where a claim is for one of the following:

(a)   the recovery of land;[4]
(b)   the foreclosure or redemption of any mortgage or, subject to CPR, r 73.10, for enforcing any charge or lien on land;[5] or
(c)   the recovery of moneys secured by a mortgage or charge on land.[6]

Such a claim may only be commenced in the court for the district in which the land or any part of the land is situated.

2.11   The second exception applies where a claim satisfies one of the following criteria:

(a)   the claim is listed in Table 2 in CPR PD8B, Section B;
(b)   the claim in the county court is for, or includes a claim for, damages for harassment under s 3 of the Protection from Harassment Act 1997;
(c)   the claim would have been brought before 26 April 1999:
    (i)   in the High Court, by originating motion,
    (ii)   in the county court by originating application or by petition, and

---

[1]   CCA 1984, s 21(3).
[2]   RA 1977, s 141.
[3]   Housing Act 1988 (HA 1988), s 40.
[4]   See CPR, r 55.3(1). This rule does not apply if the claim is issued in the High Court and a certificate is included in the claim form stating the reasons for bringing the claim in that court (CPR, r 55.3(2)), or an enactment provides that the claim does not have to be issued in the local county court.
[5]   See CPR, Sch 2, CCR Ord 4.
[6]   Ibid.

no other procedure is prescribed in an Act, a rule or a practice direction.

Where this exception applies, the claim (if it is to be issued in a county court at all), may only be started:

(a)   in the county court for the district in which:
      (i)   the defendants or one of the defendants lives or carries on business, or
      (ii)   the subject matter of the claim is situated; or
(b)   if there is no defendant named in the claim form, in the county court for the district in which the claimant or one of the claimants lives or carries on business.[1]

CLAIM FORMS

2.12   Claims should be issued using either an N1 claim form (where the claim is issued under CPR Part 7) or an N208 claim form (where the claim is issued under CPR Part 8),[2] except where a Practice Direction requires a special practice form to be used for a particular type of proceeding or proceedings in particular courts.[3]

2.13   All claim forms should be marked in the top right-hand corner 'Chancery Division' in the High Court and 'Chancery Business' in the county court, except where a specialist form is used (in which case the court should automatically place it in the appropriate list). The title of the claim should contain only the names of the parties to the proceedings, save in the following instances:[4]

(a)   proceedings relating to the administration of an estate should also be entitled 'In the estate of AB deceased';
(b)   contentious probate proceedings should be entitled 'In the estate of AB deceased (probate)';
(c)   proceedings under the Inheritance (Provision for Family and Dependants) Act 1975 should be entitled 'In the Matter of the Inheritance (Provision for Family and Dependants) Act 1975';
(d)   proceedings relating to pension schemes *may* be entitled 'In the Matter of the [   ] Pension Scheme';

---

[1]   CPR, PD8B, para B.6.
[2]   The majority of court forms can be downloaded from the Court Service website at www.courtservice.gov.uk, or from the Insolvency Service website at www.insolvency.gov.uk.
[3]   CPR, PD7, paras 3.1–3.4.
[4]   Chancery Guide, Section A, para 2.3. NB. Some cases relating to the estates of deceased Lloyd's names require additional wording: see Chancery Guide, Section B, para 26.53.

(e)   proceedings in the Companies Court are entitled 'In the matter of the [relevant legislation] and of [the relevant company or person]'.[1]

2.14   The majority of claims proceed as Part 7 claims and are governed by the general rules set out in the CPR. However, the CPR provide for exceptions from the general rules in respect of some specialist claims and claims issued under Part 8.

SPECIALIST PROCEEDINGS

2.15   'Specialist proceedings' were formerly governed by CPR Part 49. However, Part 49 applies now only to proceedings under the Companies Act 1985 and the Companies Act 1989 (in relation to which reference should be made to the Practice Direction on Applications (PD23) under the Companies Act 1985). Rules relating to other 'specialist proceedings' are now to be found in CPR Part 57 (probate claims, rectification of wills, substitution and removal of personal representatives), Part 58 (commercial court claims), Part 59 (mercantile court claims), Part 60 (technology and construction court claims), Part 61 (admiralty claims) and Part 62 (arbitration claims).

2.16   Of particular relevance to Chancery practitioners will be the special rules for possession claims in CPR Part 55, for landlord and tenant claims in Part 56, for intellectual property claims in Part 63, and for claims relating to estates, trusts and charities in Part 64. An examination of these special procedures is beyond the scope of this chapter; however, reference is made to them in other chapters in this work covering specialist topics.

PART 8 CLAIMS

2.17   The general rule is that a claim should only be issued under CPR Part 8 where use of a Part 8 claim form is prescribed by the CPR or where there is unlikely to be any substantial dispute of fact, such as where the only issues before the court are questions of construction of a document or a statute.[2] This rule will not apply where a Practice Direction states that a particular type of claim should not be brought under the Part 8 procedure.[3] Many particular types of claim are also issued under Part 8 pursuant to the Practice Direction to CPR Part 8. Of these, the most relevant to Chancery practitioners are applications to enforce charging orders, applications with respect to funds in court and proceedings relating to solicitors. Applications to enforce charging orders should be issued in the court in which the charging order was made

---

[1]   Chancery Guide, Section B, para 20.5.
[2]   CPR, r 9.1(2)(a) and CPR, PD8, para 1.1. See also the Chancery Guide, Section A, para 2.13.
[3]   CPR, r 8.1(4).

(provided that that court has jurisdiction).[1] Where a claim is issued under Part 8 inappropriately, a court officer may refer the claim to a judge for the judge to consider the point,[2] and the judge may give such directions as he considers appropriate.[3]

2.18   In some circumstances, and where prescribed by a Practice Direction, it may be necessary to seek the court's permission to issue a Part 8 claim form without naming a defendant.[4] Examples of such claims include applications for payment or transfers of money in court. An application should be made to the court *before* the claim is issued, attaching a copy of the claim form to be issued and draft directions for consideration by the master.

2.19   Part 8 claims do not require particulars of claim to be filed,[5] and a defendant to a Part 8 claim need not file a defence.[6] Neither party may seek judgment in default.[7] A Part 8 claimant should file a witness statement in support of his claim at the same time as he issues the claim.[8] Both should be served simultaneously on the defendant. The defendant then has 14 days in which to decide how to respond, and to file a witness statement in response (if necessary), together with an acknowledgment of service.[9] The claimant then has 14 days in which to file evidence in response.[10] It is recognised that particularly in complex cases, these time periods may be onerous or impossible to comply with; they may be extended by agreement, provided any such agreement is filed with the court.[11]

2.20   Once the period for the defendant to acknowledge service (or to file evidence, if later) has expired, the court will review the file. If the papers are in order, the court may not require a hearing, but may be able to make a final determination in the case. Usually, however, the case will be listed either for a substantive hearing before a judge or for a case management hearing.

PARTICULARS OF CLAIM

2.21   When drafting particulars of claim, particular attention should be had to the requirements of CPR, r 16.2 and to the guidelines in the Chancery Guide.[12]

---

[1]   CPR, r 73.10(2).
[2]   CPR, PD8, para 1.5.
[3]   CPR, PD8, para 1.6.
[4]   CPR, r 8.2A.
[5]   CPR, PD7, para 6.2.
[6]   CPR, PD8, para 3.1.
[7]   CPR, PD8, para 3.5.
[8]   CPR, r 8.5(1).
[9]   CPR, rr 8.3, 8.5(3) and (4).
[10] CPR, r 8.5(5) and (6).
[11] Chancery Guide, Section A, para 2.17.
[12] Ibid, paras 2.6–2.12 and Appendix 1.

2.22 Where a claim includes an allegation of fraud, dishonesty, malice or illegality, the particulars of claim must include the facts on the basis of which the inference is alleged. Practitioners are responsible for ensuring that no such allegation is made unless there is admissible material to support the allegation. If this is not the case, the allegation may be struck out and a wasted costs order may be made against the practitioner responsible.[1] In the case of barristers, pleading such an allegation without proper foundation may be a disciplinary offence under their professional conduct rules.[2]

CONSTRUCTION CLAIMS

2.23 Claims for the construction of documents will usually be issued under CPR Part 8 (unless there is a dispute as to the facts of the case).

2.24 Construction claims often arise from uncertainty on the part of personal representatives or trustees as to the construction of the terms of a will or trust. In order to resolve this uncertainty without the costs of a hearing, personal representatives or trustees may make an application to the High Court seeking determination of the construction issue under s 48 of the Administration of Justice Act 1985 (AJA 1985).[3] Section 48 states that the court may determine the matter without a hearing, provided the court has been given a written opinion on the relevant issues by a person who has a 10-year High Court qualification.[4]

2.25 Applications under s 48 of the AJA 1985 may be issued using a Part 8 claim form without naming a defendant, under CPR, r 8.2A. No separate application for permission under r 8.2A need be made.[5] The application should be made in the Chancery Division of the High Court.

2.26 The claim form should be supported by a witness statement or affidavit to which the following must be exhibited:[6]

(a)   copies of all relevant documents;
(b)   instructions to a person with at least a 10-year High Court qualification ('the qualified person');
(c)   the qualified person's opinion; and
(d)   draft terms of the desired order.

---

[1]   Chancery Guide, Section A, paras 2.6–2.7.
[2]   See Code of Conduct of the Bar Council, Part VII, para 704.
[3]   As amended by the Courts and Legal Services Act 1990, Sch 10.
[4]   Ie a person who has had rights of audience in relation to all proceedings in the High Court for 10 years: see Courts and Legal Services Act 1990, s 71.
[5]   CPR, PD64, para 5.
[6]   Chancery Guide, Section B, para 26.37.

2.27 The witness statement or affidavit (or exhibits thereto) must state:[1]

(a) the names of all persons who are, or may be, affected by the order sought;

(b) all surrounding circumstances admissible and relevant in construing the document;

(c) the date of qualification of the qualified person and his or her experience in the construction of trust documents;

(d) the approximate value of the fund or property in question; and

(e) whether it is known to the applicant that a dispute exists and, if so, details of such dispute.

2.28 The application will be placed before the master, who will consider whether the evidence is complete. If it is complete, he will send the file to the judge[2] (because a master does not have power to make a final determination in such a case without the permission of the Vice-Chancellor[3]). The judge will consider the file and, if necessary, direct service of notices on non-parties under CPR, r 19.8A, or request such further information as he may desire. If the judge is satisfied that the order sought is appropriate, the order will be made and sent to the applicant.[4]

2.29 If, following service of notices under CPR, r 19.8A, any acknowledgement of service is received, the applicant *must* apply to the master (on notice to the parties who have so acknowledged service) for directions.[5] If the applicant desires to pursue the application to the court, the master will usually direct that the case proceeds as a Part 8 claim.

2.30 If, on the hearing of the application, the judge is of the opinion that any party who entered an acknowledgment of service has no reasonably tenable argument contrary to the qualified person's opinion, in the exercise of his discretion he may order such party to pay all or part of any costs thrown away.[6]

---

1   Chancery Guide, Section B, para 26.38.
2   Ibid, para 26.39.
3   CPR, PD2B, para 5.1(i).
4   Chancery Guide, Section B, para 26.40.
5   Ibid, para 26.41.
6   Ibid, para 26.42.

Chapter 3

INTERIM APPLICATIONS

Constance Mahoney & David Rowell

INTRODUCTION

3.1   From a very early stage in proceedings it may be necessary for a litigant to seek directions from the court as to how to manage the litigation, or to seek interim relief from the court, or to seek to terminate the litigation altogether by seeking judgment in default, summary judgment, or to strike out the other party's statement of case. It is outside the scope of this chapter to discuss the multitude of forms of relief sought by interim application. Particular rules relating to some interim applications may be found in CPR Part 12 (default judgment), Part 13 (setting aside default judgment), Part 24 (summary judgment) and Part 25 (interim remedies). Practitioners should also ensure that they are familiar with the provisions of CPR Part 23 (general rules about applications) and its Practice Direction.

3.2   The court expects parties to co-operate from the start of the litigation. Parties should endeavour to agree proposals for the management of the case at the allocation stage.[1] If the parties do not agree or attempt to agree case management directions, the costs of a case management conference are unlikely to be recoverable by any party.[2] If agreement proves impossible, each party should put forward its own proposals for the future management of the case. Such proposals should be based upon the draft case management directions contained in Appendix 6 of the Chancery Guide.

3.3   It is often convenient to hear an interim application during a case management hearing, provided appropriate notice has been given to the other party, the application is in the proper form required by CPR Part 23 and the court has been notified of the extended time estimate for the hearing, if necessary.[3] The court is highly unlikely to hear an interim application at a case management hearing unless the applicant party has complied with these requirements (or the other party consents).

---

1   Chancery Guide, Section A, para 3.3.
2   Ibid, para 3.4.
3   Ibid, para 3.8.

APPLICATIONS FOR INFORMATION AND DISCLOSURE

3.4   Before making an application for further information or specific disclosure by another party, the applicant *must* communicate directly with the other party in an attempt to reach agreement or narrow the issues before the matter is raised with the court. If the applicant cannot satisfy the court that it has taken such steps, the court will usually require such steps to be taken before hearing the application.[1]

ISSUING THE APPLICATION

3.5   An interim application should be made to the court in which the proceedings were started, or (if applicable) to the court to which the proceedings were transferred. In the High Court, an application should be made to a judge only if it needs to be heard and determined by a judge (in practice, this will include most applications for an injunction).[2] Most procedural applications should be made to a master (or district judge) unless there is some special reason for making it to a judge.

3.6   When deciding to which level of judge to apply, practitioners should refer to the Practice Direction on Allocation of Cases to Levels of Judiciary,[3] which sets out in detail the restrictions on the jurisdiction of a master or a district judge. Reference should also be made to the arrangements for listing of particular business set out at paras 6.17–6.27 of the Chancery Guide.

3.7   The general rule is that applications should always be made with notice to the respondent. The length of the notice should normally be 3 clear days before the hearing. However, applications made without notice or at short notice will usually be heard in the following cases:[4]

(a)   where the giving of notice might frustrate the order (for example, a search order);

(b)   where the application is so urgent that there is insufficient time to give proper notice (although the applicant should attempt at the very least to give informal notice to the respondent);

(c)   where the application relates to matters which are merely procedural. Examples of such matters include service out of the jurisdiction, extension of the validity of claim forms, permission to issue writs of possession etc. Orders made on such applications will usually give the

---

[1]   Chancery Guide, Section A, para 3.10.
[2]   Ibid, para 5.1.
[3]   Which may be found at CPR, PD2B.
[4]   Chancery Guide, Section A, para 5.4.

respondent a certain number of days in which to apply to set aside or vary the order;

(d)   where the application is for permission to serve the substantive application at short notice[1] (such an application can be made without notice to the interim applications judge);

(e)   where all parties consent;

(f)   where the court permits;

(g)   where the overriding objective is best furthered by doing so.

3.8   When applying to a judge in the High Court in London, applications should be filed before 10 am on the working day before the date for which notice of the application has been given. The applicant should file two copies of the claim form in the proceedings, two copies of the application notice (of which one will bear a stamp to show that the appropriate fee has been paid) and a completed 'Judge's Application Information Form'.[2] Bundles of documents may also need to be prepared and filed at the same time as the application.[3] Where the applicant seeks a freezing injunction or a search order, he should also file two copies of the order sought.[4]

3.9   In most applications before a judge, the applicant (and the respondent if he has received notice of the application) should also file a skeleton argument. Where the application is without notice, the skeleton argument should be filed with the papers which the judge is asked to read on the application.[5] Where the application is with notice, the parties' skeleton arguments should be filed as soon as possible, and not later than 10 am on the day before the hearing.[6] The only excusable reasons for not providing a skeleton argument for an interim application before a judge are:[7]

(a)   that the application is likely to be so short that it does not warrant one (in practice, this would apply to only a handful of applications, and, if in doubt, a brief skeleton argument should be filed);

(b)   that the application is so urgent that there is no time to prepare a skeleton argument;

(c)   that the application is ineffective and the order is agreed by all parties.

---

[1]   Chancery Guide, Section A, para 5.7.

[2]   See form at Chancery Guide, Appendix 5, Part 1.

[3]   Chancery Guide, Section A, para 7.16. See also the guidelines at ibid, paras 7.9 and 7.16, Appendix 2 of the Chancery Guide, and CPR, PD39, para 3.

[4]   Chancery Guide, Section A, para 5.18.

[5]   Ibid, para 7.22.

[6]   Ibid, para 7.23.

[7]   Ibid, para 7.20.

URGENT APPLICATIONS

3.10   Where a party wishes to make an urgent application without notice, he should notify the clerk to the interim applications judge by telephone.[1] Two copies of the order sought and an electronic copy on disk (in Word for Windows) and a completed 'Judge's Application Information Form' should be handed to the judge's clerk.

3.11   If the interim applications judge is not able to hear the application immediately and the application is very urgent, it may be heard by any available judge. A request for a very urgent hearing in such circumstances should be made to the clerk to the interim applications judge, or, in default, to the Chancery listing officer.

3.12   A party making an urgent application must make every effort to issue a claim form before the application is made. If he is not able to do so, he will usually be required to undertake to the court to issue the claim form forthwith even if no order is made at the hearing of the application.[2]

3.13   It is possible to have a very urgent application determined outside usual court hours or during the legal vacation.[3] The details of the procedure to be followed are set out in the Chancery Guide.[4] For out-of-hours hearings, the applicant must be able to satisfy the court as to why the application was not made or could not be made during normal court hours. For vacation hearings, the applicant must be able to satisfy the court that the application generally qualifies as 'vacation business', ie that it requires to be heard immediately or promptly.

HEARINGS BEFORE THE JUDGE

3.14   The Daily Cause List and the Chancery Division Term List will specify which judge is the interim applications judge on any particular day.

3.15   If the case has been listed for trial, any application should be made to the interim applications judge only if a hearing before a master cannot be obtained in time for the application not to delay the hearing of the case.[5] Parties should first consult the masters' clerk as to the availability of the

---

1   Chancery Guide, Section A, para 5.17.
2   Ibid, para 5.17.
3   Term dates are set out in the Practice Direction on Court Sittings, annexed to CPR, Part 39.
4   Chancery Guide, Section A, paras 5.29–5.32 (emergency arrangements), para 5.35f (vacation arrangements).
5   Ibid, para 6.15.

master or, in an appropriate case, apply to the master himself. Sometimes an urgent application can be heard by the Chief Master or a deputy.[1]

3.16 If the hearing of the application is before the interim applications judge in the High Court, parties should try to arrive at court at least 10 minutes before the hearing so that they have an opportunity to agree a time estimate, and possibly an order or issues with other parties to the application. All applicants in the day's list of interim applications should be in court at the beginning of the day (usually 10.30 am). The judge will run through the list to ascertain which cases are effective (contested) or ineffective (agreed) and obtain a time estimate for each. Applicants should be ready to give a time estimate (agreed if possible), and to provide the judge with all relevant information as to their state of readiness, whether the parties are in agreement or negotiating to agree an order and whether the matter is urgent. After hearing from all applicants, the judge will decide in what order to hear the applications and give any directions necessary.[2]

3.17 Any application which is likely to take longer than two hours will be dealt with as an application by order (interim application by order) which means that the hearing of the application will not be dealt with in the applications list but the judge will direct that it shall be heard on a date to be fixed by the Listing Office. It will be placed on the Interim Hearings List, and arrangements should be made with the Chancery listing officer by the parties (usually by counsel's clerk or by solicitors) for a fixed or floating date.[3] The applicant should provide to the listing officer a written time estimate for the hearing signed by the advocates for all parties.[4] The parties may wish to consider instead seeking a direction for a speedy trial, which may obviate the need for a hearing of the interim application, thereby minimising their costs burden.

3.18 The parties may agree to adjourn an application, but for no longer than 14 days, and there can be no more than three successive adjournments by agreement.[5]

HEARINGS BEFORE THE MASTERS

3.19 If the hearing of the application is to be before a master, the application should be made with notice to the respondent. If a case management conference has been listed in the proceedings, the applicant should ensure that

---

[1]   Chancery Guide, Section A, para 6.28.
[2]   Ibid, para 5.10.
[3]   Ibid, para 5.11.
[4]   Ibid, para 7.5.
[5]   Ibid, para 5.13.

the application is listed to be heard at the case management conference.[1] If the hearing is estimated to last for more than two hours, the directions of the master should be obtained before the matter is listed.[2]

3.20 The parties to the application have a duty to try to agree directions before the hearing and to provide a draft of the order sought for the master's consideration. Draft orders for directions should, where possible, follow the draft case management directions at Appendix 6 of the Chancery Guide. Skeleton arguments[3] should be provided for the hearing of the application if it is estimated to last for one hour or more,[4] and should be delivered together with a bundle of documents for the hearing, to the master's room no later than 10 am on the day before the hearing.[5]

3.21 Oral applications without notice can be made to masters between 2.15 pm and 2.45 pm on working days.[6] Such applications should be made in the usual way prescribed by CPR Part 23, and not by way of letter.[7] Any correspondence between a party and the master *must* be copied to other parties in the litigation. When making such an informal application, the applicant should ensure that he notifies the clerk to the Chancery masters by 4.30 pm on the previous day so that the file is obtained for the master. If the application is very urgent, notice may be given at any time to the masters' clerk.

3.22 There is no distinction between term time and vacation for hearings before a Chancery master.

INTERIM APPLICATIONS OUTSIDE LONDON

3.23 Any application should normally be made to a district judge (provided he has power to hear it).[8] The district judge may of his own initiative direct that the application be referred to a High Court judge or to an authorised circuit judge (for example, because of the complexity of the matter or the need for specialist attention).[9] Alternatively, if any of the parties considers that the matter is appropriate to be heard by a High Court judge or a circuit judge, one

---

[1] Chancery Guide, Section A, para 5.35.
[2] Ibid, para 5.36.
[3] For the form and content of skeleton arguments, see Chancery Guide, Appendix 3. Photocopies of any authorities to be relied upon should be attached to the skeleton argument, or provided in a separate indexed bundle.
[4] Chancery Guide, Section A, para 7.43.
[5] Ibid, para 7.41.
[6] Ibid, para 6.31.
[7] Ibid, para 5.39.
[8] Ibid, para 12.11.
[9] Ibid, para 12.12.

or all of the parties may arrange for the application to be listed on one of the ordinary application days.[1]

3.24 Usually, one day a week is reserved for all interim matters, applications and short appeals.[2] As with hearings before the interim applications judge in London, all matters will be called into court at the beginning of the day in order to work out in which order the cases will be heard. Application days in the various district registries are detailed in para 12.15 of the Chancery Guide.

3.25 The general rules concerning interim applications will apply to applications made in the district registries. The only exception to this outside London is that a judge is unlikely to agree to more than two adjournments by consent (as opposed to the usual three).[3] Further, applications to vacate a trial date will require substantial justification and a hearing (even if by consent), normally before the trial judge. In the case of applications out of hours or by telephone, the applicant should contact the relevant court office.[4]

HEARINGS IN PRIVATE

3.26 The general rule is that hearings will be in public.[5] However, if publicity would defeat the object of the hearing (as with applications for freezing or search orders), the judge may hear an application in private.[6] If an application for a freezing or search order is to be made in private, it will be listed as an 'Application without notice' without naming the parties. An application is also likely to be heard in private if it involves confidential information,[7] the interests of a child or patient[8] or uncontentious matters arising in the administration of trusts or in the administration of a dead person's estate.[9] The court can also order the non-disclosure of the name of a party or witness if it considers that non-disclosure is necessary in order to protect the interests of that party or witness.[10]

---

[1] Chancery Guide, Section A, para 12.13. Guidance may be sought by telephone from the district judge as to, for example, whether a hearing is necessary, or which level of judge should determine the matter.
[2] Ibid, para 12.14.
[3] Ibid, para 12.18.
[4] Ibid, para 12.16.
[5] CPR, PD39, para 1.2.
[6] Chancery Guide, Section A, para 5.18.
[7] CPR, r 39.2(3)(c).
[8] CPR, r 39.2(3)(d).
[9] CPR, r 39.2(3)(e).
[10] CPR, r 39.2(4).

NON-ATTENDANCE OF A PARTY

3.27 A party may consent to the relief being sought on an application, rather than attend. If the relief is wholly covered by the application notice this is not a problem. The court may proceed in the absence of any party.[1] An appropriate letter or draft statement of agreed terms signed by the party or the party's solicitor will suffice.[2]

3.28 However, if the agreed relief is more extensive than that sought in the application notice, or if there are undertakings to be given, parties must follow a prescribed procedure to obtain an order of the court in accordance with their agreed terms.[3]

3.29 In some cases (and often in respect of applications which are procedural in nature), the application can be processed without a hearing where the parties have either consented to the order sought, or have made their representations to the court in writing, or where the court considers that a hearing is not necessary.[4] Where the parties have agreed directions or the order sought by the applicant, the court should be informed as soon as possible and provided with a draft order signed, if possible, by the parties to the application. If a hearing has been listed, parties should then check with the court as to whether they are still required to attend the listed hearing.

ORDERS

3.30 At the conclusion of the hearing of the application, the judge or master will often direct the parties to agree the form of order to reflect his decision. The parties should then attempt to do so, and deliver an original of their agreed draft (often called a 'minute of order') to the judge or master, signed by each party's representative. The applicant is usually responsible for drafting the minute of order and will then submit it to the other parties for comments and/or agreement. If the parties are unable to agree the form of order, they should each send to the judge or master their preferred version, with a written

---

[1] CPR, r 23.11(1).
[2] Chancery Guide, Section A, para 5.24.
[3] The procedure is set out in full at ibid, para 5.26.
[4] CPR, r 23.8.

explanation of the reasons for their failure to agree. The judge or master will then either recall the parties for a further hearing or simply determine the form of order himself.

Chapter 4

PREPARATION FOR TRIAL

Constance Mahoney & David Rowell

LISTING ARRANGEMENTS

4.1   Trials in the High Court which involve witnesses are listed in the Trial List.[1] At an early stage in the proceedings the court will give directions with a view to fixing the period during which the case will be heard ('the trial window'). The majority of CPR Part 8 claims will not be listed in the Trial List because they are usually determined on written evidence alone.

4.2   The court will direct that one party (usually the claimant) attends the listing officer by appointment to fix a date for the trial within the trial window, and gives notice of that appointment to all other parties.[2] When attending the listing appointment, the claimant will need to have details of any dates on which his or her counsel, experts or witnesses will not be available. Once fixed, the trial date will rarely be altered.[3] If it appears at the listing appointment that it is impracticable to list the trial within the trial window, the listing officer will fix the trial date outside the trial window at the first available date.

4.3   When attending a listing appointment for a trial before a judge, the claimant should also file with the listing officer a written time estimate for the hearing, signed by the advocates for all parties.[4] The time estimate should include sufficient time for reading documents, hearing advocates' speeches, examining witnesses (if any), giving judgment (if appropriate), assessing costs (if likely) and making an application for permission to appeal (if appropriate).[5]

---

[1]   Chancery Guide, Section A, para 6.4. The other two main lists are the Interim Hearings List (comprising interim applications and appeals from masters) and the General List (other matters, including revenue, bankruptcy and pension appeals, Part 8 proceedings, applications for judgment and all company matters). There is also a separate Patents List.

[2]   Ibid, para 6.8.

[3]   Ibid, para 6.11.

[4]   Ibid, para 7.5.

[5]   Ibid, para 7.4.

4.4   On each Friday of term[1] and on such other dates as may be appropriate, the Clerk of the Lists publishes a Warned List, which shows which cases are likely to be heard in the following week. Parties in cases in the Warned List may agree to offer a particular date in that week for the hearing. Any matters for which no date has been arranged are liable to appear in the list for hearing with no warning, except that they will be listed in the next day's list of cases, which is available every afternoon.[2]

4.5   If the parties' or the court's time estimate for the length of the hearing needs to be varied after the case has been listed, or if the case is settled, withdrawn or discontinued, the parties *must* immediately inform the listing officer *in writing*,[3] otherwise they risk an adverse costs order, particularly if the trial has to be adjourned.[4]

4.6   Seven days before the date fixed for the hearing, the claimant's solicitors[5] *must* inform the listing officer whether there is any variation in the time estimate for the hearing, and whether the case is likely to be disposed of summarily. The listing officer should generally be kept informed of any development in the case which is likely to affect the length of the hearing.

4.7   Special listing arrangements for particular business are set out in paras 6.17–6.27 of the Chancery Guide. Details of assignment of particular business amongst the masters are set out in paras 6.28–6.30 of the Chancery Guide.

4.8   Special listing arrangements for each district registry are set out in paras 12.20–12.24 of the Chancery Guide.

APPLICATION TO ADJOURN TRIAL

4.9   The need to apply for an adjournment of a trial should arise only where there has been a change of circumstances which was unknown or unforeseeable when the trial date was fixed.[6] If such an application is necessary, the applicant must inform the listing officer as soon as possible.

4.10   If the application is agreed, the parties should apply jointly in writing to the listing officer, who will then consult the appropriate judge. Despite the

---

[1]   Term dates are set out in the Practice Direction on Court Sittings (CPR, PD39B).

[2]   Chancery Guide, Section A, para 6.12. The daily list of cases (Daily Cause List) can be viewed at www.courtservice.gov.uk.

[3]   Ibid, para 6.13.

[4]   Ibid, para 7.8.

[5]   If the claimant is a litigant in person, this task must be performed by the solicitors for the first-named defendant who has instructed a solicitor.

[6]   Chancery Guide, Section A, para 7.38.

parties' agreement, the judge may decide that the trial should take place on the fixed date, or he may grant the adjournment subject to conditions, and give directions for the fixing of a new hearing date. If the application is opposed, the applicant should arrange through the listing officer for a hearing of the application to take place before the appropriate judge. By 12 noon on the day before the hearing, the applicant should deliver a short statement (not necessarily a witness statement or affidavit) of the reasons for the adjournment to the listing officer. If the reasons include a failure to take reasonable steps in the litigation, the court may disallow costs between the solicitor and the client, or otherwise make an adverse costs order, or dismiss the application.

4.11   An application to adjourn a trial may be heard by a master if, for example, it becomes clear on the hearing of an interim application or at a case management conference that failure to adjourn the trial will cause injustice to one or both parties.[1]

BUNDLES

4.12   Great emphasis is laid on the proper preparation of trial bundles, so as to save time and costs and to promote a better understanding of the case. It is therefore essential to ensure that the rules and directions set out in Appendix 2 of the Chancery Guide and in para 3 of the Practice Direction to CPR Part 39 are followed as closely as possible. Failure to do so may result in rejection of the bundles by the court and/or adverse costs orders.[2]

4.13   CPR, r 39.5 provides that unless the court orders otherwise, the *claimant* must file a trial bundle not more than 7 clear days and not less than 3 clear days before the start of the trial. This rule does not apply to cases whose documents consist of fewer than 25 pages. When filing the trial bundle, the claimant should also file a further agreed time estimate for the trial and an agreed reading list for the judge (including a time estimate for reading the documents on the reading list), both of which documents should be signed by the advocates for all parties.[3] If these documents cannot be agreed, the parties should each file their own signed time estimate and reading list.

4.14   A bundle should be provided for any hearing before a master which is listed for one hour or more, or where a bundle would assist.[4] Bundles for trials

---

1   Chancery Guide, Section A, para 6.11.
2   Ibid, para 7.10.
3   Ibid, para 7.17.
4   Ibid, para 7.40.

or similar hearings before a master should be filed at least 2 clear days before the date fixed for the hearing.[1]

4.15 All parties have a duty to co-operate in agreeing bundles for use in court,[2] and should ensure that they record the nature of their agreement in correspondence so that it is clear whether they agree:

(a)   only on the composition and preparation of the bundle;

(b)   that the documents in the bundle are authentic;[3] and

(c)   that the documents may be treated as evidence of the facts stated in them.[4] If agreement on this point is impossible, the party not willing to agree should write to the court at the time of filing the bundles to explain his reasons for refusing to agree.

It is important to begin the process of agreeing bundles (which can take months) early enough to allow for all possible agreement between the parties as to their contents, for references to bundles to be included in skeleton arguments, and for the bundles to be delivered to the court on time.[5]

4.16 Originals of all documents in the trial bundle should be available in court during the trial.[6]

SKELETON ARGUMENTS

4.17 Each party should always prepare a skeleton argument for a trial, unless the court orders otherwise.[7] Skeleton arguments should be filed with the Listing Office or with the judge's clerk (if the case has been assigned to a particular judge) at least two clear days before the date fixed for the trial (or the first day of the trial window if the trial is floating).[8] If the facts of the case involve more than a few persons, it is advisable to file a list of those persons (a *dramatis personae*) together with the skeleton argument. In most cases, the parties should also file a chronology and a list of issues (both of which should be agreed if possible).[9]

4.18 The parties should negotiate between themselves (usually between counsels' clerks) as to how and when skeleton arguments and any

---

[1]   Chancery Guide, Section A, para 7.41.
[2]   Ibid, para 7.12.
[3]   See CPR, r 32.19.
[4]   Chancery Guide, Section A, para 7.13.
[5]   Ibid, para 7.11.
[6]   CPR, PD39, para 3.3.
[7]   Chancery Guide, Section A, para 7.20.
[8]   Ibid, para 7.21.
[9]   Ibid, para 7.28.

accompanying documents should be exchanged. If no arrangements exist (which may arise, for example, where one party is a litigant in person), all such documents should be given to the other parties in sufficient time before the hearing for their consideration.[1]

4.19 When preparing a skeleton argument, reading list or chronology, practitioners should have regard to the relevant guidelines in Appendix 3 to the Chancery Guide. If these guidelines are not followed, it is unlikely that a skeleton argument will have the maximum persuasiveness. Practitioners should also ensure that they demonstrate in a skeleton argument that they have complied with para 8.1 of *Practice Direction (Citation of Authorities)*.[2]

AUTHORITIES

4.20 All practitioners should familiarise themselves with *Practice Direction (Citation of Authorities)*.[3] In particular, it should be noted that it is the duty of advocates to draw the attention of the court to any authority not cited by an opponent which is adverse to the case being advanced.

4.21 Where it is intended to rely on any authority to support legal argument at the trial, parties must ensure that the court usher receives a list of authorities by 9 am on the day of the hearing.[4] The list should indicate which authorities are to be provided by photocopy.

4.22 In practice, advocates will often prepare a separate indexed bundle of authorities and file it at the same time as the skeleton argument, thus ensuring that the judge has the relevant cases to hand when reading the skeleton argument. It is often helpful to the judge if all authorities are included in one agreed bundle. Authorities or extracts from textbooks should always be photocopied so that they can be read vertically from the page (ie not two pages of original to one A4 page).[5] If extracts are in small type, they should be enlarged if possible when photocopied. Where only a short passage from a long case is needed, the headnote and key pages only should be copied and placed in the bundle, and the usher should be asked to have the full volume of the relevant law report in court. There is no need to paginate a bundle of authorities, although care should be taken that the photocopies of authorities include the page numbers from the law report for ease of reference during submissions.

---

1   Chancery Guide, Section A, para 7.29.
2   [2001] 1 WLR 1001.
3   Ibid, para 4.
4   Chancery Guide, Section A, para 7.32.
5   Ibid, Appendix 2, para 32.

4.23 If authorities are not clearly set out in the skeleton arguments, parties should exchange lists of authorities by 4 pm on the day before the trial, or otherwise face the risk of an adverse costs order if the trial is lengthened or delayed due to their failure to do so.[1]

4.24 Any bundle or list of authorities *must* bear a certification by the advocate responsible for arguing the case that the requirements of para 8 of the Practice Direction have been complied with. Parties should ensure that they do not make excessive use of authority: see the directions in the Practice Direction. In particular, citation of authority should be restricted to the expression of legal principle rather than the application of such principle to particular facts.[2]

4.25 When citing authorities, practitioners should have regard to *Practice Direction (Judgments: Form and Citation)*[3] and *Practice Direction (Judgments: Neutral Citations)*.[4] In particular, practitioners should ensure that where a case has been reported in the official law reports, that report is cited in preference to any report.[5]

WITNESS STATEMENTS

4.26 It is beyond the scope of this chapter to discuss the rules in the CPR in relation to the evidence of witnesses of fact and experts (see CPR Parts 32–35). However, there are particular practices for preparing and filing evidence in the Chancery Division, which are summarised below.

4.27 Appendix 4 to the Chancery Guide provides supplementary guidance on the drafting of witness statements. In particular, it is stated that:

(a)   the evidence of the witness should be expressed, so far as possible, in the witness's own words (unless the witness's perception or recollection of the events in question is not in issue);

(b)   the witness statement should be in numbered paragraphs;

(c)   the witness statement should be as concise as possible;

(d)   the witness statement should be signed by the witness and contain a statement of truth;

(e)   the witness statement should cover only those issues on which the party serving the statement wishes that witness to give evidence-in-chief.

---

[1] Chancery Guide, Section A, para 7.33.
[2] Ibid, para 7.34.
[3] [2001] 1 WLR 194.
[4] [2002] 1 WLR 346.
[5] *Practice Direction (Judgments: Form and Citation)* [2001] 1 WLR 194, para 3.1.

4.28 Any party who objects to the relevance or admissibility of any part of the witness statement should notify the other party of his objection within 28 days of service. The parties should attempt to resolve the issue. If resolution is impossible, the objecting party should apply at the pre-trial review (if there is one) or at the trial for the judge to strike out or ignore that part of the evidence to which he objects.[1]

4.29 When filing a witness statement, parties should also file a written evidence lodgment form.[2]

4.30 Exhibits and backsheets to witness statements should *not* be included in the trial bundle immediately behind the relevant statement.[3] Instead, exhibits should usually be arranged in the bundle in chronological order. Then, once the bundle has been paginated, references to the page numbers of the exhibited documents should be inserted into the witness statements (in manuscript if necessary) by the reference to that document.[4]

---

[1]   Chancery Guide, Appendix 4, para 25.
[2]   Ibid, Appendix 5, Part 2.
[3]   Ibid, Appendix 2, paras 25 and 26.
[4]   Ibid, para 24.

Chapter 5

TRIAL

Constance Mahoney & David Rowell

PUBLIC OR PRIVATE

5.1 The general rule is that trials before a judge are held in public. The usual exceptions in CPR, r 39.2 apply in the Chancery Division. Where the court decides to exclude evidence on the basis of public interest immunity there is no discretion to admit such evidence on condition that the court sits in private.[1]

5.2 Certain hearings are to be listed in the first instance by the court as hearings in private, namely:

(a)   a claim by a mortgagee against one or more individuals for an order for the possession of land;

(b)   a claim by a landlord against one or more tenants or former tenants for repossession of a dwelling house based on non-payment of rent;

(c)   an application to suspend a warrant of execution or warrant of possession, or to stay execution where the court is being invited to consider the ability of a party to make payments to another party;

(d)   a redetermination under CPR, r 14.13 or an application to vary or suspend the payment of a judgment debt by instalments;

(e)   an application for a charging order (including an application to enforce a charging order), third party debt order, attachment of earnings order, administration order, or the appointment of a receiver;

(f)   an order to attend court for questioning;

(g)   the determination of the liability of an LSC-funded client under regs 9 and 10 of the Community Legal Service (Costs) Regulations 2000,[2] or of an assisted person's liability for costs under reg 127 of the Civil Legal Aid (General) Regulations 1989;[3]

(h)   an application for security for costs under s 726(1) of the Companies Act 1985;

---

[1]   *Powell v Chief Constable of North Wales Constabulary* [2000] TLR 91, CA.

[2]   SI 2000/441.

[3]   SI 1989/339.

(i)   proceedings under the Consumer Credit Act 1974, the Inheritance
        (Provision for Family and Dependants) Act 1975 or the Protection
        from Harassment Act 1997;

(j)   an application by a trustee or personal representative for directions as
        to bringing or defending legal proceedings.[1]

5.3   In practice, applications by trustees relating to the management
of private trusts and by personal representatives (for example to authorise a
sale to one of the trustees or to extend trustees' powers under s 57 of the
Trustee Act 1925) are usually heard in private. Applications under the
Variation of Trusts Act 1958 where the object is simply to lift protective trusts
are normally dealt with by a master in private. Other applications under that
Act are usually heard in public unless there are special circumstances justifying
a hearing in private, for example where the trial involves sensitive information
relating to a beneficiary who is a child or mental patient.

PROCEDURE AT TRIAL: EVIDENCE

5.4   The procedure at trial in the Chancery Division is essentially the same
as in other divisions of the High Court, and the same rules of evidence apply
as in other civil proceedings. Nevertheless, a few points may be made.

5.5   An important aim of the CPR is to ensure that court time is used as
efficiently as possible. Unless notified otherwise, it is assumed that the judge
will have read the skeleton arguments and the principal documents referred to
in the reading list. He will state at an early stage how much he has read and
what arrangements are to be made for reading any documents not already
read. An adjournment after the opening speeches may be appropriate for this
purpose.[2]

5.6   The burden of proof is the normal civil standard of a balance of
probabilities. However, it is always difficult for a party to go behind a written
document. In cases where a party is seeking rectification of an instrument,
there must be 'convincing proof' of the mistake and the fact that the
document does not represent the true intention of the parties when it was
executed.[3] Therefore, an insistence by the defendant that the written
agreement does represent the agreement between the parties is often fatal to a
claim for rectification, but it may be possible to undermine the defence by
reliance on documentary evidence which proves the common intention of the
parties at the date of execution. It is particularly difficult to discharge the

---

[1]   CPR, PD39, para 1.5.
[2]   Chancery Guide, Section A, para 8.5.
[3]   *Joscelyne v Nissen* [1970] 2 QB 86, at 98.

burden of proof in cases where the claimant is trying to rectify a deed of settlement, and even more so a voluntary settlement.[1] A court will hesitate to act on the oral evidence of the settlor, many years after the event, that the settlement does not represent his true intention; but if that evidence is supported by contemporaneous written instructions, there is a greater likelihood that relief will be granted. Often, however, rectification proceedings are brought without any real opposition because a third party, such as the Inland Revenue, will not accept a document as corrected without a court order. In such cases the judge must still be persuaded by convincing evidence that the instrument as executed did not represent the true intention of the parties at the time.

5.7   Where a will is to be construed the probate must be in court at the opening of the case. The court is entitled to send for the original will, the form of which may give clues to the testator's intention which are not apparent from the probate copy. When any other document is to be construed, the original should similarly be available. The court should not be asked to construe a document by reference to a copy.[2]

5.8   It is usually convenient for the evidence of experts to be taken all together at the same time following the giving of factual evidence. This should be agreed between the parties before the trial and raised at the pre-trial review or with the judge at the start of the trial.[3]

5.9   Under the CPR, if two or more parties want to submit expert evidence on a particular issue, the court may direct that evidence on this issue should be provided by a single expert jointly instructed.[4] This procedure is encouraged in suitable cases, such as where expert evidence is necessary on questions of expert fact rather than opinion, or on the issue of quantum where the main dispute concerns liability. It is wholly wrong for one party to have a conference with the joint expert in the absence of the other party.[5] Many cases, however, will turn primarily upon expert opinion (such as allegations of professional negligence) where it will be appropriate for each side to instruct its own expert.[6] In *Daniels v Walker*[7] the Court of Appeal held that in substantial cases the correct approach is to regard the instruction of a joint expert as the first step in obtaining expert evidence; but that if a party, for reasons which are not fanciful, wishes to obtain further information before

---

[1]   *Mortimer v Shortall* (1842) 2 Dr & War 363; *Bohote v Henderson* [1895] 1 Ch 742; *affirmed* [1895] 2 Ch 202.

[2]   Chancery Guide, Section A, para 8.20.

[3]   Ibid, para 8.17.

[4]   CPR, r 35.7.

[5]   *Peat v Mid-Kent Healthcare Trust* [2002] 1 WLR 210.

[6]   Chancery Guide, Section A, para 4.11.

[7]   [2000] 1 WLR 1382.

making a decision whether to challenge part or all of that expert's report, he should, subject to the court's discretion, be permitted to obtain that evidence.

5.10   It should be remembered that a party is always free to instruct his own expert, and this may be essential to enable the party to formulate his case properly. The only questions are whether the expert will be allowed to give evidence, and whether his costs will be allowed as costs of the action.

5.11   Section 9 of the Civil Evidence Act 1995 (CEA 1995) makes provision for the proof of records of business or public authorities. A document shown to be part of such records may be received in evidence without further proof. It is taken to form part of such records if a certificate to that effect is produced to the court signed by an officer of the business or public authority to which the records belong.[1] The absence of an entry in the records of a business or public authority may be proved by affidavit of an officer of the relevant business or authority.[2]

JUDGMENT

5.12   At the end of the trial the judge will either give an extempore judgment or reserve judgment. If a written judgment is handed down before delivery in court, the legal representatives of the parties will not normally be allowed to reveal the contents to their clients until one hour before judgment is formally delivered in court. Arguments on costs generally follow judgment but, in a straightforward case, it is not unusual for costs arguments to be heard at the conclusion of speeches before a reserved judgment is given.

5.13   Costs in the Chancery Division, as elsewhere, usually follow the event. However, in a dispute over a will or the construction of a trust deed costs are frequently ordered to be paid out of the estate or trust fund, especially where the testator or settlor can be regarded as responsible for the problem. Similarly, where trustees or personal representatives apply to the court for directions, the costs of all parties are normally paid out of the fund or estate.

5.14   In such cases the trustees or personal representatives will be entitled to their costs on the indemnity basis unless they have been guilty of misconduct.[3] Practice varies as to whether the other parties receive their costs on the standard or indemnity basis. Where trustees or personal representatives are litigating with strangers to the trust or estate the normal rules as to costs apply between the parties, but if the trustees or personal representatives have acted properly in bringing or defending the proceedings they will be entitled to their

---

[1]   CEA 1995, s 9(2).

[2]   Ibid, s 9(3).

[3]   CPR, r 48.4(3).

costs, so far as not otherwise recovered, out of the trust or estate on the indemnity basis.[1]

5.15 Permission to appeal is required in all Chancery cases except for (a) appeals against committal orders, (b) certain insolvency appeals and (c) certain cases where a right of appeal is provided by statute.[2] Permission to appeal should be sought from the court against whose decision the appeal is to be brought or, if that court refuses permission, from the court to which the appeal is to be made.[3] Permission will be given only if the court considers that the appeal has a real prospect of success or that there is some other compelling reason why it should be heard.[4] The appellant's notice must be filed at the appeal court within such period as the lower court directs or, in the absence of such a direction, within 14 days of the date of the decision appealed against.[5]

---

[1]   CPR, r 48.4(3).
[2]   Chancery Guide, Section A, para 10.4.
[3]   CPR, r 52.3(2) and (3).
[4]   CPR, r 52.3(6).
[5]   CPR, r 52.4.

Chapter 6

ORDERS

Constance Mahoney & David Rowell

INTRODUCTION

6.1   Chancery orders tend to be complicated. In many cases the court will direct the advocates to agree and sign a statement of the terms of the order (commonly called a minute of order). If the proceedings are in the Royal Courts of Justice the statement should, when agreed and signed, be delivered to Chancery Chambers Registry and Issue Section. If the parties are unable to agree the terms, the matter will need to be referred back to the judge who heard the original application.[1]

6.2   This inevitably causes delay and extra expense. It is therefore advisable for the applicant to prepare a draft of the order before the hearing and provide copies to the court and the other parties. This usually ensures that any queries about the wording are raised and resolved at the original hearing. It also enables the court to prepare and seal the order more quickly.[2]

6.3   An order is enforceable from the time it is sealed, although effective from the date it is made.

WORKING OUT THE ORDER

6.4   Another characteristic feature of Chancery orders is that they usually contain detailed provisions concerning their effect.

Accounts and inquiries

6.5   Unless otherwise specified by an order, accounts and inquiries will be taken by a master or district judge in the High Court, or by a district judge in the county court.[3] When making the order the court will usually give directions in relation to such matters as:

---

[1]   Chancery Guide, Section A, para 9.5.
[2]   Ibid, para 9.4.
[3]   CPR, PD40, para 9.

(a)	the manner in which any account or inquiry is to be prosecuted;

(b)	the evidence to be adduced in support of any such account or inquiry;

(c)	the preparation and service on the parties to be bound thereby of the draft of any deed or other instrument which is directed by the judgment to be settled by the court and the service of any objections to the draft;

(d)	the parties required to attend all or any of the proceedings; and

(e)	the time within which each proceeding is to be taken.

6.6	If directions are not given in the order itself an application should be made to the appropriate master or district judge asking for such directions as soon as possible. The application notice should specify the directions sought. The applicant should write to the other parties giving details of the directions sought and seeking their response within 14 days. The application should state that the other parties have been consulted, and have copies of the applicant's letter and any responses attached to it.[1]

6.7	The party ordered to account should prepare his account and verify it by an affidavit or witness statement.[2] Any other party may object to any amount received or claimed by another party by informing the accounting party of his objection in writing. The notice of objection must specify its grounds and contain a statement of truth unless it is verified by an affidavit or witness statement.[3]

6.8	The court can intervene in the inquiry or taking of the account where it is considered that there has been a delay. It may make such directions as it thinks appropriate, including that the Official Solicitor take over the conduct of the proceedings.[4]

6.9	The court may allow distribution of some of the shares from a fund, even when the identities of individuals entitled to other shares in the fund are unknown.[5]

6.10	The taking of an account in Chancery chambers (for example, between partners or trustees and beneficiaries) is a notoriously long-drawn-out and expensive procedure. Unless the accounting party has kept very full records it may be difficult to establish whether or not particular items are properly claimed. Proceedings usually end in a compromise rather than in the master signing off the account. Parties should bear this in mind and plan their tactics accordingly. Once the accounting party has prepared his account, the other party is well-advised not to challenge everything which is merely questionable,

---

[1]	Chancery Guide, Section A, para 9.19.

[2]	CPR, PD40, para 2.

[3]	CPR, PD40, para 3.

[4]	CPR, PD40, para 6.

[5]	CPR, PD40, para 7.

but to concentrate instead on items which are improper on the face of it or important enough to make attacking them worthwhile.

Sale of land by court order

6.11 In relation to orders for the sale of land a draft order should be prepared which deals with the mechanics of the proposed sale. If a draft order is not prepared the court will make an order for sale in general terms requiring a further application to work out the details if the parties cannot agree. Matters which require careful consideration in drafting an order for sale of land are as follows:

(a) conduct of the sale;

(b) choice of agent;

(c) mode of sale;

(d) commission;

(e) permission to purchase;

(f) title;

(g) contract;

(h) viewing the property;

(i) obtaining vacant possession;

(j) completion; and

(k) protection of proceeds of sale.

6.12 The conduct of the sale is normally given to the solicitors for one of the parties, or to an independent solicitor. It is advisable that the solicitors of the party seeking sale are given the conduct since they can prevent possible delays by a party reluctant to sell and exercise better control over costs. Committing the conduct to an independent solicitor tends to increase costs and delay by involving a three-way correspondence between the parties' solicitors and the independent solicitor.

6.13 The choice of agent is affected by a number of factors. The property may be of a nature requiring a specialist agent (eg a hotel). A very expensive property may require an agent who has national or even international coverage. The choice of mode of sale is normally between auction and private treaty although other methods (eg sale by sealed bids) are possible. Which is preferable depends on such factors as the type of property and the urgency to sell. If the sale is to be by auction, an agent who holds regular and substantial auctions is preferable. The court will usually set a reserve.

6.14 One or both of the parties to the proceedings may wish to buy. A party wishing to do so should seek an order giving him permission to do so.[1] Permission to bid at auction is readily granted, as the price paid should reflect

---

[1]   *Nugent v Nugent* [1908] 1 Ch 546.

the market value. In the case of a sale by private treaty, the court will be more cautious in giving permission to the party whose solicitor has conduct of the sale. There should be evidence that the property has been duly exposed to the market and that the price is fair and reasonable.

6.15   If one party has obtained an order for the sale of a property occupied by another party, the occupier may try to cause difficulties. It is a good idea to incorporate in the order provision requiring the occupier to allow prospective purchasers (accompanied by estate agents) to view the property at all reasonable times. If the sale is to be with vacant possession, it is prudent to incorporate into the order a provision that vacant possession must be given on completion.

6.16   Unless the parties agree the terms of the proposed contract and any conveyance or transfer to be made under it, the terms will have to be settled by the court or by reference to conveyancing counsel. The prudent practice on sales under court direction is for the terms of any conveyance, lease or transfer to be settled at the same time as the contract.

Reference to conveyancing counsel

6.17   Both the High Court and the county court have power to direct conveyancing counsel to investigate and report on the title to any land or to draft any document.[1] Any party to the proceedings may object to counsel's report, the dispute thereby arising being settled by a judge.[2] The issue by the Land Registry of standard forms, which merely require the parties to complete certain information, has greatly reduced the scope for disputes over conveyancing documents. Such documents may be used not only when the title is already registered, but also when the transaction will necessitate first registration.

Execution of documents

6.18   Chancery orders often require the execution of an instrument such as a contract, conveyance or lease. If any party neglects or refuses to execute the instrument, or cannot after reasonable inquiry be found, the High Court may nominate a person to execute on such terms and conditions, if any, as may be just. The instrument then operates as if it had been executed by the person originally directed to do so.[3]

6.19   The application will be made by application notice in accordance with CPR Part 23 but should not be made in anticipation of a failure to execute, unless the person in question has already shown by his conduct that he refuses

---

[1]   CPR, r 40.18.
[2]   CPR, r 40.19.
[3]   SCA 1981, s 39.

to execute.[1] Masters and district judges are normally appointed to execute documents, but a solicitor has on occasion been appointed.

Delivery-up of documents

6.20 If a document is void or voidable the court has an inherent jurisdiction to order its delivery-up. This prevents the document remaining at large and a further claim being based on it, or a third party relying on the document. The order will not be made where:

(a)   the document is not wholly void, eg where it is void only against creditors;[2] or

(b)   the party seeking the order has been guilty of laches or acquiescence or has adopted the document[3] or refuses to submit to equitable terms imposed by the court.[4]

Delivery-up has also been refused on the ground that the instrument is invalid on its face,[5] although it may be doubted whether this would be followed where there is any chance of a third party being misled.

---

[1]   *Savage v Norton* [1908] 1 Ch 290.
[2]   *Ideal Bedding Co Ltd v Holland* [1907] 2 Ch 157.
[3]   *Franco v Bolton* [1797] 3 Ves 368, 30 ER 1058.
[4]   *Lodge v National Union Investment Co* [1907] 1 Ch 300.
[5]   *Gray v Mathias* [1800] 5 Ves 286, 31 ER 591.

Chapter 7

EXECUTION OF CHANCERY JUDGMENTS

Constance Mahoney & David Rowell

INTRODUCTION

7.1   Many judgments require the performance of an act, for example the payment of money, or the delivery-up of property or possession of land. Many also contain a time-limit for compliance. When default occurs the methods for enforcing the payment of money or the delivery-up of chattels are the same in the Chancery Division as in other parts of the High Court. This chapter concentrates on procedures which are particularly relevant in Chancery proceedings.

JUDGMENT FOR POSSESSION OF LAND

7.2   A judgment for the possession of land is enforced in the High Court by a writ of possession. Where the order specifies the time for giving possession it could also in principle be enforced by an order of committal or a writ of sequestration, but that is very unusual in practice.[1] In the county court the order is enforced by a warrant of possession.[2]

7.3   A writ or warrant of possession of land requires the enforcement officer to evict everyone he finds on the premises, whether or not they are a party to the action.[3] All persons in actual possession of all or part of the land must receive notice of the proceedings sufficient to enable them to apply to the court for any relief to which they may be entitled. Therefore, unless the order for possession was made in mortgage proceedings, a writ of possession cannot be issued without the leave of the court. The application for leave is made by a witness statement, which must be lodged in Chancery Chambers.[4] The statement must show that notice of the proceedings has been given to all those in occupation of any part of the land. Similarly, in the county court a person requesting a warrant of possession to be issued must file a request

---

[1]   CPR, Sch 1; RSC Ord 45, r 3(1).
[2]   CPR, Sch 2; CCR Ord 26, r 17.
[3]   *R v Wandsworth County Court ex parte London Borough of Wandsworth* [1975] 3 All ER 390.
[4]   *Practice Direction* [1955] 1 WLR 36.

certifying that the land has not been vacated.[1] The writ or warrant of possession must also contain a proper description of the land of which possession is to be given.[2]

7.4   It is prudent for a representative of the claimant to accompany the enforcement officer to take possession and to secure the premises against any attempt at re-entry by the person evicted.

MANDATORY AND PROHIBITIVE INJUNCTIONS

7.5   If a judgment or order requires a person to do an act within a specified time, or to refrain from doing an act (eg a mandatory or prohibitive injunction) and default occurs, there are basically three methods of enforcement:

(a)   a writ of sequestration against the property of that person;

(b)   if that person is a body corporate, a writ of sequestration against the property of any director or officer of that body;

(c)   subject to the provisions of the Debtors Acts 1869 and 1878, an order of committal against that person or, if that person is a body corporate, against any such officer.[3]

The first two methods of enforcement require the permission of the court.

7.6   A copy of the order must be served personally and endorsed with a warning to the person on whom it is served that disobedience will be a contempt of court punishable by imprisonment or, in the case of a body corporate, by sequestration of its assets and the imprisonment of any individual responsible. Copies of any other relevant order, for example varying or extending the time for compliance, should be served at the same time.[4] However, an order to abstain from doing an act may also be enforced by committal or sequestration, despite non-service, if the court is satisfied that pending service the person against whom it is sought to enforce the order has had notice of it by being present when it was made or by being notified of its terms by telephone, telegram or otherwise.[5]

7.7   An undertaking given to the court is equivalent to an injunction and is enforced in the same way. However, it differs in that the person giving the undertaking is presumed to have knowledge of it, and therefore it is not

---

[1]   CPR, Sch 2; CCR Ord 26, r 17(2).
[2]   *Thynne v Sarl* [1891] 2 Ch 79.
[3]   CPR, Sch 1; RSC Ord 45, r 5.
[4]   CPR, Sch 1; RSC Ord 45, r 7.
[5]   CPR, Sch 1; RSC Ord 45, r 7(6).

necessary for a copy of the order to be served on that person.[1] Nevertheless, the better practice is that such an undertaking should be incorporated as a recital in an order of the court, and a copy of it with a penal notice served on the person giving the undertaking.

7.8 It cannot be stressed too strongly that if an order needs to be enforced by committal or sequestration, it is important that it should tell the defendant as precisely as possible what he must or must not do. If the original judgment or order does not specify a time-limit for doing an act the court may specify the time subsequently.[2]

7.9 An application to enforce an order or undertaking by committal may be made to the county court if the order was made by, or the undertaking given to, a county court. In other cases the application must be to the High Court.[3] The application must be made by CPR Part 8 claim form or an application notice supported by an affidavit stating the grounds of the application. These should be served personally unless the court dispenses with this requirement.[4]

7.10 On lodging the claim form or application notice the applicant must obtain a hearing date from the court, which must be stated in the claim form or application notice, or a notice of hearing attached to it.[5]

7.11 At the hearing the person against whom the order is being sought is entitled to give oral evidence even though he has not filed or served written evidence. With the permission of the court he may call witnesses to give oral evidence on his behalf even though the witness has not sworn an affidavit.[6] On the other hand the person making the application to commit will not be entitled to rely on any grounds except those set out in the claim form or application notice without the leave of the court.[7] This emphasises the need to prepare the claim form or application notice properly and in particular to specify every breach of the injunction or undertaking upon which it may be necessary to rely.

CHARGING ORDERS

7.12 Where a person is required by a court order to pay a sum of money to another person, the appropriate court may make an order imposing on

---

1   *Hussain v Hussain* [1986] Fam 134.
2   CPR, Sch 1; RSC Ord 45, r 6(2).
3   CPR, PDCommittal, paras 1.2 and 1.3.
4   CPR, Sch 1; RSC Ord 52, r 4.
5   CPR, PDCommittal, para 4.2.
6   CPR, PDCommittal, para 3.
7   CPR, Sch 1; RSC Ord 52, r 6(3).

specified property of the debtor a charge for securing payment of the money due or to become due under that order.[1] Broadly, four kinds of property may be charged:

(a)   land;
(b)   securities;
(c)   funds in court; and
(d)   interests under trusts.[2]

In practice, most charging orders are on land. Information on land owned by the judgment debtor may be obtained at a hearing held pursuant to CPR Part 71. Since 1990 leave to inspect the Land Register is not needed and anyone can search against any property. Evidence of the debtor's ownership is usually provided in the form of an office copy of the entry on the Land Register.

7.13   The procedure is now regulated by CPR Part 73 and CPR PD73. Rules for determining the appropriate court are laid down in CPR, r 73.3. The county court has exclusive jurisdiction where the application relates to a county court judgment or a fund lodged in that court. In practice most charging orders are made in the county court.

7.14   The creditor must first apply for an interim charging order by an application notice, which must contain the information required by CPR PD73, para 1. This is made without notice to the debtor and will be dealt with by a judge without a hearing. If the interim order is made the judge will fix a hearing to consider whether to make a final order.[3] Copies of the interim order, the application notice and any documents served in support of it must be served on:

(a)   the judgment debtor;
(b)   such other creditors as the court directs;
(c)   in the case of interests under trusts, such of the trustees as the court directs;
(d)   in the case of stock or units of a unit trust, the keeper of the register in which it is registered; and
(e)   in the case of funds in court, the Accountant General at the Court Funds Office.[4]

---

[1]   Charging Orders Act 1979, s 1(1).
[2]   Ibid, s 2.
[3]   CPR, r 73.4.
[4]   CPR, r 73.5.

Anyone who objects to the making of a final charging order must file and serve on the applicant written evidence stating the grounds of his opposition not less than 7 days before the hearing.[1]

7.15 At the hearing the judge will decide whether to make a final charging order or to discharge the interim order and dismiss the application. In practice a master or district judge will deal with the matter. He can determine any issues between the parties there and then. Only rarely will he direct a trial of such issues although he has power to do so. The making of an order is by no means automatic even if the debt is established and is unpaid. The court takes account of the interests of the other unsecured creditors as well as the debtor, and the order is likely to be refused if the debt appears too small to justify the remedy, or the value of the property sought to be charged is disproportionate.[2] If the creditor wishes to show that the debtor is simply refusing, rather than unable, to pay, or that he has tried to enforce unsuccessfully by other methods, he should provide evidence of this in his application notice under the heading 'further information'.

7.16 A charging order has the same effect and is enforceable in the same courts and in the same manner as an equitable charge created by the debtor under his hand.[3] A charging order affecting land should be registered under the Land Charges Act 1972 or the Land Registration Act 2002 as appropriate. If it relates to an interest in a trust fund, the trustees should be notified as soon as possible and, in the case of stock, the keeper of the appropriate register should similarly be notified.

7.17 Ultimately a person entitled to a charging order may apply to the court to order a sale of the property. The application must be made using the CPR Part 8 procedure and to the court which made the charging order except where that court does not have jurisdiction. It is important to note that this application is a proceeding for the enforcement of a charge and so the county court's jurisdiction is limited by s 23(c) of the County Courts Act 1984.[4] At present the amount owing in respect of the charge must not exceed £30,000. In a significant number of cases therefore, even though the order was made in the county court, proceedings to enforce it must be taken in the High Court.

7.18 The making of an order for sale is by no means automatic. The court has a discretion. An order for sale is seen as an extreme step and all the circumstances must be considered. If the property is the debtor's home his right to respect for private and family life under the European Convention on Human Rights will be engaged. If the debtor's interest is an undivided share in

---

[1] CPR, r 73.8.

[2] *Robinson v Bailey* [1942] Ch 268, at 271.

[3] Charging Orders Act 1979, s 3(4).

[4] CPR, r 73.10.

a house, prior to 1996 the normal rule was that the wish of the chargee would prevail over those of the other co-owners. However, under s 15 of the Trusts of Land and Appointment of Trustees Act 1996 the court has greater flexibility and the interests of the chargee are only one factor to be taken into account.[1]

RECEIVERS: EQUITABLE EXECUTION

7.19 The appointment of a receiver by way of equitable execution is comparatively rare in practice. However, it remains the most convenient way of execution where the judgment debtor has a life or other limited interest under a trust, so that legal execution is not available by reason of the nature of the interest. The receiver is entitled to receive whatever income or other sums are due to the debtor under the terms of the trust.

7.20 Both the High Court and the county court have power to appoint a receiver by way of equitable execution under s 37 of the Supreme Court Act 1981 and s 107 of the County Courts Act 1984 respectively. An injunction may also be granted ancillary to the order for the appointment of the receiver. In practice the order is usually made by a master or district judge. This is one of the exceptional cases where masters and district judges have the power to grant injunctions.[2]

7.21 The application is to be made in accordance with the rules generally applicable to the appointment of receivers by the court, which are now contained in CPR Part 69. The written evidence should generally identify an individual whom the court is asked to appoint as receiver and be accompanied by his consent to act.[3] Before deciding whether to make the appointment the court will consider the amount claimed by the judgment creditor, the amount likely to be recovered by the receiver and the probable costs of his appointment.[4]

---

[1]   *Mortgage Corporation v Shaire* [2001] Ch 743.
[2]   CPR, PD2B, para 2.3(c).
[3]   CPR, PD69, para 4.2.
[4]   CPR, PD69, para 5.

Chapter 8

TRUSTS AND TRUSTEES

Cenydd I Howells

INTRODUCTION

8.1   This chapter concerns court proceedings involving private (as opposed to charitable) trusts and trustees. The reader is directed to the standard books on trusts for detailed treatment of the substantive law of trusts[1] and to Chapter 11 for court proceedings relating to charities.

8.2   Courts of Equity have always been prepared to assist trustees who are in doubt as to how they ought to act by giving them guidance, directions and protection.[2]

8.3   Before going further it is advisable to identify all the actual and potential beneficiaries under a trust. It will be necessary to do so if beneficiaries' interests are likely to be affected, especially unequally. It is also necessary in order to identify all the persons who might sue the trustees for breach of trust and against whom the trustees may wish to seek protection.

8.4   Beneficiaries can be generally classified as:

(a)   those having an interest in possession in the trust property;
(b)   those who have a contingent interest in such property (ie who may have an interest in possession if and when some future event happens); and
(c)   those who have a future interest in such property but one which is certain to vest in possession and free from contingency.

In a different class are persons who are 'objects' of a discretionary trust. None of this class can insist on receiving any benefit at all, but each has the equitable right to insist that the trustees administer the trust properly.

---

[1]   See eg *Snell's Equity* (30th edn, 2000); Underhill and Hayton *The Law Relating to Trusts and Trustees* (16th edn, 2003); Pettit *Equity and the Law of Trusts* (9th edn, 2001); and Keeton and Sheridan *The Law of Trusts* (12th edn, 1993). Hayton *The Law of Trusts* (4th edn, 2003) is a short illuminating outline of the subject.

[2]   *Chapman v Chapman* [1954] AC 429 at 446, per Lord Simmonds LC.

8.5   In any given case there will probably be some persons who are presently in existence and who come within one of the above classes of beneficiaries. Some beneficiaries, however, may be unborn or otherwise unascertained. It is most important to categorise carefully all such persons, whether existing or otherwise. It is commonly not realised that when one is endeavouring to list all the existing and potential beneficiaries under a particular trust, the court will insist (to the puzzlement of many lay clients) on including:

(a)   possible future children of a woman of child-bearing age;[1]
(b)   a possible future husband or wife of a person of any age, even if he or she is at present happily married; and
(c)   possible future children of a man of any age, even if he is at present happily married to a wife who is not capable of having children or any more children.

COURTS WITH JURISDICTION OVER TRUSTS

8.6   The courts with jurisdiction over trusts are the Chancery Division of the High Court and the county courts. The former has unlimited jurisdiction in terms of value of the subject matter and has residual power through having inherited the inherent jurisdiction enjoyed by the old courts of Chancery.[2] County courts, on the other hand, do *not* have inherent jurisdiction, and the limits of their jurisdiction over trusts is precisely limited in terms of the value of the estate or trust fund.[3] It is important to note the difference in jurisdiction *within* the Chancery Division between judges and Chancery masters (in London) and district judges in High Court district registries which have Chancery jurisdiction (outside London).[4] At county court level, the relevant distinction between circuit judges (including recorders) and district judges (including deputy district judges) is not as defined as it is in the High Court.[5]

---

[1]   One must distinguish carefully between (a) the well-established 'administrative jurisdiction' of the Chancery Division to permit trustees to distribute the trust fund 'on the footing that a named woman is incapable of bearing any children (or any further children)' and (b) the inadmissibility of any evidence proving *incapacity to have children* as to the question of who is entitled to the trust fund under the trust. As to (a) see eg *Re Westminster Bank's Declaration of Trust* [1963] 1 WLR 820, Wilberforce J; and *Re Pettifor's Will Trusts* [1966] Ch 257, Pennycuick J. As to (b), see eg *Figg v Clarke* [1997] 1 WLR 603, Blackburne J. As to (a) there seems to be no case authority as to the legal effect on the above of the existence or possibility of hormone-replacement therapy.
[2]   *Letterstedt v Broers* (1884) 9 App Cas 371 (PC), at 385–386 (per Lord Blackburn); *Re Chetwynd's Settlement* [1902] 1 Ch 692, Farwell J.
[3]   See the County Courts Act 1984, s 23 and the County Courts Jurisdiction Order 1981, SI 1981/1123.
[4]   See CPR, PD2B.
[5]   CPR, PD2B. See, generally, Chapter 1.

COURT PROCEEDINGS INVOLVING TRUSTS: LITIGATION BETWEEN TRUSTEES AND NON-BENEFICIARIES

Generally

8.7 Trustees (whether individuals, companies or other bodies corporate) have full legal capacity to sue and be sued.

8.8 A special situation exists where a beneficiary has, under the trust, the actual possession of land comprised in the trust and another person has trespassed on it, eg where there is a tenant for life under a Settled Land Act 1925 (SLA 1925) settlement. That tenant for life is usually in actual possession of the trust land and entitled (rather than the trustees) to sue for trespass to the land.[1] Where there is a trust of land (under the Trusts of Land and Appointment of Trustees Act 1996 (TLATA 1996)) the trustees will be able to sue for trespass only if no beneficiary is in possession of the land under ss 12 and 13 (in which case that beneficiary will be entitled so to sue).[2]

Parties, commencement and procedure

8.9 Nothing special flows from the fact that trustees are litigants except the strict rule that if trustees sue a stranger (ie a non-beneficiary) they must all join as claimants, and any dissenting trustees must be made defendants. If they are not unanimous in wishing to do so, the trustee or trustees who wish to litigate should apply to the court for directions as to whether or not to litigate and, if so, as to their indemnification out of the trust fund.[3] The proper procedure for such application for *directions* is a CPR Part 8 claim joining as defendants the non-consenting trustee or trustees and such of the possible beneficiaries as the claimants think fit, 'having regard to the remedy claimed'.[4] The court will be concerned to see that there is a fair representation of beneficiaries. Such application is in fact the same as or very similar to a *Re Beddoe* application.[5] If the court decides in favour of authorising the litigation, it may simply do so. If necessary, there does not seem to be any obstacle to the court's directing that the trustee or trustees who wish to litigate be authorised to litigate in the names of all the trustees (ie including the non-consenting trustee or trustees) and at the expense of the trust property. If the court considers that the non-consenting trustees are acting improperly, it may remove them from office, appointing new trustees in their place if suitable ones are proposed. Before such removal, it may give the non-consenting trustees some time for reflection. The procedure in this respect is very flexible. The court is

---

[1] See *Clerk and Lindsell on Torts* (18th edn, 2000), at paras 18-10 et seq as to the general principle.
[2] Ibid.
[3] See *Re Beddoe* [1893] 1 Ch 547, CA.
[4] CPR, Part 64 and PD64B.
[5] [1893] 1 Ch 547, CA.

concerned, as always, to see that the interests of the beneficiaries are safeguarded. Of course, the parties to the action between the trustees and a stranger will be chosen according to ordinary principles of causes of action and liability. Whether *these* proceedings are commenced under CPR Part 7 or under Part 8 will depend on ordinary considerations, as will all progress and allocation to a track.

Costs

8.10 Trustees involved in litigation should consider very carefully the possible incidence of costs upon them. Prima facie, where there is adverse litigation between trustees and another party, the incidence of costs as between those parties will lie in the discretion of the court, but the general rule is that the unsuccessful party will be ordered to pay the successful party's costs.[1] In adverse litigation the court will make orders for costs for or against trustees – just as if they were private individuals engaged in personal litigation. On the other hand, as between the trustees and the beneficiaries of the trust, the trustees are entitled to be indemnified out of the trust property in so far as the costs are not recovered from the other party to the litigation, but such indemnity will depend upon whether the costs have been *properly* incurred in the administration of the trust.[2] It is important to bear in mind that whereas the incidence of the trustees' costs of the litigation as between them and the other party are within the discretion of the judge, such costs *as between the trustees and their beneficiaries* are 'costs, charges and expenses' as mentioned above.[3]

8.11 These principles put the trustees in a dilemma. They will not be certain until the end of the case as to which side (if either) will be ordered to pay the costs. Even if they obtain an order for payment by the other party, they will be uncertain as to *recovery* of such costs until they are actually received. The worst possibility is that the trustees will be ordered to pay the other party's costs – in which case they will probably be personally liable and in an embarrassing position. Again, even if the trustees obtain an order for payment of costs and actually recover on that order, they may be liable to pay their solicitors and counsel further costs which were not allowed (as against the other party) on assessment. A typical example of this would be where successful trustees obtain an order for costs against the other party to be assessed on a standard basis. Their costs would be assessed on such basis and recovered from the other party. There may very well be a shortfall between such amount and the higher amount which the trustees would be liable to pay their own solicitors and counsel on an indemnity basis. In all these situations how can the trustees

---

[1]   CPR, r 44.3.

[2]   See *Turner v Hancock* (1882) 20 ChD 303, CA; and *Re Beddoe* [1893] 1 Ch 547, at 558, per Lindley LJ, and at 562 per Bowen LJ.

[3]   *Re Beddoe* [1893] 1 Ch 547, at 554–555, per Lindley LJ, and at 562, per Bowen LJ.

be sure that they will be indemnified by the trust fund against such costs of adverse litigation?

8.12 One possible course is to wait until the conclusion of the adverse litigation and then, if necessary, obtain consent of the beneficiaries to indemnity out of the trust fund. However, this has only to be stated for it to be seen as a very risky course to take. Beneficiaries may object, particularly if the trustees have failed in the adverse litigation. Further, if (on the strict principles applied by Chancery courts in ascertaining the identity of the existing and potential beneficiaries)[1] there are unascertained, future or contingent beneficiaries, or beneficiaries who are children or not of full mental capacity, the trustees cannot safely rely on the consents of the existing adult beneficiaries of full capacity to take their costs out of the trust fund.[2] Another possible course is for trustees to take personal indemnities from existing beneficiaries or other persons. An indemnity is only worth what it will produce if called upon. It may not be very satisfactory, even if it is possible. The trustees could apply to the court (by a separate application to a Chancery master or district judge) by what is in fact a form of *Re Beddoe* application (see below) *after* the conclusion of the adverse litigation.[3] However, if the litigation ended in failure on the part of the trustees, the court may refuse the application!

8.13 Since the general rule is that trustees are entitled to be indemnified out of the trust fund for expenditure properly incurred, the courts have developed an 'exceptional jurisdiction'[4] to allow trustees involved in prospective or actual litigation with other parties to seek a ruling on their right to be indemnified out of the trust fund for the costs of litigation. This amounts to deciding in advance the question of indemnity as between the trustees and their beneficiaries. The current procedural authority for an application as to costs is CPR PD64, para 6.1, but the exercise of this jurisdiction and the seeking of directions are based on CPR PD64B (which must be carefully studied), precedent and especially the decision of the Court of Appeal in *Re Beddoe*.[5]

8.14 Before making an application for directions, trustees should consult those beneficiaries who are ascertained and of full age and capacity.[6] Save in exceptional circumstances, it is always prudent to notify any person before commencing a case in which he is a defendant. Not to do so may incur criticism and, possibly, some reflection in costs awarded. If all possible beneficiaries are ascertained, of full age and capacity, and agree to

---

[1]   See **8.4** and **8.5**.
[2]   This is the principle underlying the jurisdiction in a *Re Beddoe* application.
[3]   *Re Beddoe* [1893] 1 Ch 547, at 557, per Lindley LJ.
[4]   *Alsop Wilkinson v Neary* [1996] 1 WLR 1220, at 1226, Lightman J.
[5]   [1893] 1 Ch 547, CA.
[6]   CPR, PD64B, para 7.7.

indemnification of the trustees out of the trust fund, a *Re Beddoe* application will be pointless and will be dismissed with costs against the trustee claimants. If, on the other hand, beneficiaries are divided in their opinion on the main case, they should be left to fight the case themselves. In these circumstances any *Re Beddoe* application will again be dismissed with costs.[1]

8.15 The procedure for a *Re Beddoe* application is very strict. It is set out clearly by Lightman J in *Alsop Wilkinson v Neary*.[2] Further, the application *must* be made under a CPR Part 8 claim *independently* of the main litigation and to a Chancery master or district judge who is not involved in the main case (if it has started) and who must exclude himself from the main case (if it is merely prospective). Indeed there is no reason whatsoever why the court in the main case should ever know of the trustees' *Re Beddoe* application or of its result. The trustees will be treated as ordinary litigants in the main case as regards costs. There are at least two reasons for this separation.

(1)   In a *Re Beddoe* application the trustees must make full disclosure to the judge of all strengths and weaknesses of their case. If these factors were known to the other side in the main case, or to the judge who tried the case, this could prejudice the case. The disclosure required in the *Re Beddoe* application is greater than ordinary disclosure in litigation.[3]

(2)   Some or even all of the beneficiaries may not be parties to the main case. However, all the available beneficiaries must be joined as defendants in a *Re Beddoe* application. If there is doubt as to which beneficiaries to join, directions may be sought from the court.[4] Views of beneficiaries will be listened to. The beneficiaries who are joined as defendants (apart from any who clearly support the other party to the main case) must be served with the whole of the trustees' evidence (now usually in the form of witness statements).[5] Any beneficiary may adduce his evidence as to whether the trustees should be permitted to litigate the main case at the expense of the trust fund. The court has power to be flexible as to procedure so as to adapt it to the precise facts of the application.[6]

8.16 The evidence of the applicant trustees will be by witness statement exhibiting any necessary documents to be considered, including a written opinion of the barrister or solicitor-advocate actually conducting the main case

---

[1]   *Re Evans Deceased* [1986] 1 WLR 101, CA.

[2]   *Alsop Wilkinson v Neary* [1996] 1 WLR 1220. See CPR, 64, the two Practice Directions appended thereto and Chancery Guide, paras 26.8–26.10 as to evidence to be adduced.

[3]   It would seem that in *Alsop Wilkinson v Neary*, ibid, at pp 1225–1226, Lightman J must be referring to evidence which would not be discoverable (now 'disclosable') in the main case because it is, for example, oral or privileged.

[4]   CPR, PD64B, para 4. As to identification of beneficiaries, see **8.4** and **8.5**.

[5]   See CPR, Part 8, and rr 32.6 and 32.15. See also CPR, PD32, and CPR, PD64B, para 7.1.

[6]   *Re Eaton* [1964] 1 WLR 1269, Wilberforce J.

(or who will so conduct it if it is merely prospective).[1] A barrister or solicitor-advocate should, if possible, appear at any hearing for directions.[2] If the other party to the litigation is a beneficiary, or if a beneficiary supports that other party, the applicant trustees may include sensitive evidence in exhibits to their witness statement (and not in the witness statement itself), which exhibits may not be served upon such a beneficiary who, in addition, may be excluded from court at the time of consideration of such sensitive evidence.[3] In a plain case, the Chancery master or district judge may make the order, otherwise he will adjourn the application to a Chancery judge.[4] It should be noted, however, that the court will always consider the possibility of giving directions without a hearing.[5]

8.17 At whatever level the application is decided, the principles are the same. In *Re Beddoe* itself Lindley LJ inveighed against 'the old Chancery practice of giving costs out of the estate, almost as a matter of course, without the judge exercising any discretion in each particular case, which he ought to do'.[6] The four main points to be considered by the court on a *Re Beddoe* application are:

(a)   the merits of the main case;
(b)   the likely order for costs at trial of the main case;
(c)   the justice of the application; and
(d)   any special factors.[7]

This is intended to be a rigorous test and the object is to protect unwilling, unascertained or future beneficiaries against the costs of main cases which are likely to fail. It is not possible to define exhaustively what may be 'special factors'. One example is where the main litigation is a test case which may influence the result in other cases.[8]

8.18 Even if the court does make an order as sought in the *Re Beddoe* application, it may make an order giving authority to the trustees to proceed in the main case at the expense of the trust fund, but limited until, for example, after the exchange of witness statements, experts' statements (if any) and disclosure in the main case – when the *Re Beddoe* application will be reconsidered.[9] Further, the court has power (on this application) to direct the

---

1   CPR, PD64B, para 7.2.
2   CPR, PD64B, para 7.12.
3   Ibid. See also *Re Moritz* [1960] Ch 251; and *Re Eaton* [1964] 1 WLR 1269.
4   See CPR, PD2B, para 5.1.
5   See CPR, PD64B, para 6.
6   See *Re Beddoe* [1893] 1 Ch 547, at 554.
7   See *Alsop Wilkinson v Neary* [1996] 1 WLR 1220, at 1226.
8   *Re Westdock Realisations Ltd* (1988) 4 BCC 192, Browne-Wilkinson V-C.
9   CPR, PD64B, para 7.8.

trustees as to their conduct of the main case, subject of course to directions given by the main court as between the parties to the main case.

8.19 Provided that trustees conduct the main case properly and in accordance with any directions the court may have laid down on the *Re Beddoe* application, they will have the benefit of an indemnity out of the trust fund *whatever* the outcome of the main case. An exception to this, however, will be where the trustees failed to make proper disclosure (see **8.15**) to the court on the *Re Beddoe* application. Although a *Re Beddoe* application is not made 'without notice', it seems clear that the fullest disclosure must be made by the trustees to the court (possibly beyond what would be disclosable in the main case). If it is found (probably after the main case trial) that proper disclosure was not made on the *Re Beddoe* application, there would seem to be, on analogy with the obtaining of an order without notice and without proper disclosure, grounds for reversing the *Re Beddoe* order.[1]

COURT PROCEEDINGS INVOLVING TRUSTS: LITIGATION BETWEEN TRUSTEES AND BENEFICIARIES

Application by trustees seeking guidance as to true construction of the trust, the interests of beneficiaries or some other question arising in administration of trust

Generally

8.20 The variety of potential questions arising in proceedings concerning trusts is enormous. Questions may relate to whether the trust exists or is valid, the meaning of the trust instrument, the nature and extent of the beneficial interests or the identity of the beneficiaries. Questions may also arise in the course of administration of the trust, such as whether a proposed or actual advancement or appointment of capital is proper, whether trust property may be bought by one of the trustees, whether a particular transaction can be entered into, or whether money may be spent for a particular purpose which is not clearly authorised by the trust. In addition, questions may concern any of the duties and powers of trustees.

8.21 A very particular feature of Chancery jurisdiction over trusts (or over any other fiduciary such as a receiver or, at least as to proceeds of sale, a mortgagee) is the readiness with which the court will entertain an application by a trustee (or other fiduciary) for guidance. The question must be actual (and not merely hypothetical) and should not be capable of too obvious an

---

[1] See *R v Kensington Income Tax Commissioners* [1917] 1 KB 486, at 505, per Cozens-Hardy MR; and see also *Alsop Wilkinson v Neary* [1996] 1 WLR 1220, at 1224.

answer.[1] Trustees are expected to seek competent advice. They will not be penalised for applying to court pursuant to advice which is found to be wrong, provided they had reasonable grounds to believe that the adviser would be competent.

Commencement and procedure

8.22 If trustees seek the court's decision on any question, procedure is governed by CPR Part 64 and the Practice Directions attached thereto. The question should be raised by a CPR Part 8 claim.[2] If the claim is by the trustees, all of them must be parties. Any trustee who dissents must be made a defendant. Beneficiaries may be made defendants as may be appropriate to the order sought.[3] CPR PD64B, para 7 (as to evidence required) must be studied closely. The evidence must refer to any consultation with beneficiaries which has taken place, and with what result.[4]

8.23 Applications may be heard by the Chancery master, district judge or judge in private (formerly 'in chambers').[5] Decisions of High Court or circuit judges, Chancery masters or district judges sitting in private are not publishable unless the court gives permission (usually on the basis that the case is of general importance).[6] It is possible in a case heard in private for judgment to be given in public (with the consequence that publication is permissible).

8.24 An order for the general (or 'full') administration of the estate or trust by the court is still possible, but 'only if it is considered that the issues between the parties cannot properly be resolved in any other way'.[7] Where personal representatives or trustees are accused of malpractice, the usual course (assuming their non-co-operation) is to sue them for compensation,[8] and request their removal and the appointment of new representatives or trustees who are to administer the estate or trust properly. An example where a general administration order will be made is where the personal representatives or trustees of a substantial estate or trust are beset by a variety of difficulties of a pressing nature (whether as to assets or adverse claims).[9] The claim for general administration may be made either by a creditor or a beneficiary. The defendants will be the personal representatives or trustees.

---

[1]   *Re Buckton* [1907] 2 Ch 406.
[2]   CPR, r 64.3.
[3]   CPR, r 64.4.
[4]   CPR, PD64B, para 7.7.
[5]   CPR, r 39.2(3).
[6]   For an example of a Chancery master's reported judgment, see *Re Woolnough* [2002] WTLR 595.
[7]   CPR, PD64, para 3.
[8]   See **8.60**.
[9]   See eg *Re Dickinson* [1884] WN 199, Chitty J.

8.25 The making of an order for general administration (which may be by a Chancery master[1]) means that the *whole* of the administration (including the collection of assets) is under the control of the court (usually, in the first instance, of a Chancery master). All money assets may be required to be paid into court. Following an order for general administration the personal representatives or trustees are bound to seek the directions of the court (ie of the Chancery Division) as to how they should exercise their powers.[2] Creditors and claimants against the estate or trust are bound to proceed with their debts and claims in a strictly controlled way.[3] Advertisement for creditors or claimants (whether adverse or beneficiaries) may be ordered. Creditors and claimants will be given notice to 'prove' their debt or claim. The court will form a view as to each debt or claim and give the personal representatives or trustees directions as to how to deal with each. This does not mean that any action against the estate or trust will necessarily be transferred to the Chancery Division, but claims can be dealt with in an orderly, co-ordinated manner. The court will do little of its own motion in any detail. The secret of an efficient administration action lies in the detail, and in ensuring that each application for directions is well thought out, well focused and as comprehensive as can be managed. The solicitors for the personal representatives or trustees must keep up the momentum and instigate the applications. They (probably with the assistance of specialist Chancery counsel) must keep abreast of the whole spectrum of the administration. The benefit for the personal representatives or trustees is that if they act in accordance with the court's directions, they will be protected from personal liability. The benefit for beneficiaries is that claims and debts will be methodically scrutinised, evaluated and dealt with, and bogus claims may well be deterred. It is not unknown for a large, rambling, 'messy' estate or trust to be resolved over some years into a much more simple and straightforward solvent estate or trust.

Parties

8.26 A notable feature of Chancery procedure is the care taken to establish the correct parties to applications and to actions generally involving trusts. All interested persons should be parties to litigation in Chancery in as much as the court has always been concerned to see that relevant views of beneficiaries are heard. Trustees (as claimants or as defendants) represent the beneficiaries and any judgment binds the beneficiaries (subject to any court order to the contrary).[4] However, the court will be astute to see that the views of relevant beneficiaries are heard, and may direct that any beneficiary be joined as a party (invariably as a defendant). If trustees are in doubt as to which beneficiaries to

---

[1]   See CPR, PD2B.
[2]   *Re Furness* [1943] Ch 415 Morton J.
[3]   CPR, PD64, para 3.3.
[4]   CPR, r 19.7A

join as defendants, they may apply to the Chancery master for directions, even issuing a claim form without any named defendants.[1]

Costs

8.27 In cases of this type the trustees will normally be regarded as raising a proper question for determination. They will join (or be directed to join) as defendants one or more beneficiaries so that all reasonably possible arguments are presented to the court. As is clear from *Re Buckton*[2] the usual order as to costs is that these will come out of the trust property. This, however, does not prevent the court in a proper case, for example where the case has come to the court only because of the unreasonable or improper attitude of some party, from ordering that party to pay the costs of the application, if this is the just result.

Application by beneficiary which could have been initiated by trustees under above situation

8.28 As mentioned in *Re Buckton*, these will be in all respects treated in the same way as applications commenced by the trustees. There is scope here for the claimant beneficiary to apply to court for an order that his costs be paid out of the trust fund.[3] However, the court will be astute to see whether the case is in reality one of hostile litigation. If it is such, it will be dealt with as to costs.[4]

Application by beneficiary against the trustees (or vice versa) which are of a hostile nature

Generally

8.29 An example of a 'hostile' application by a beneficiary would be one alleging breach of trust on the part of the trustees and seeking compensation for any trust property which may have been lost as a result. Another example would be an application seeking an order that the trustees perform their duty to sell property (in the case of a trust for sale) or exercise their discretion to sell the trust property (in the case of a trust of land within TLATA 1996) by selling it. The second example is adverse but not so obviously hostile as the first. Examples of hostile claims by trustees against a beneficiary would be where the beneficiary has failed to account for trust property in his care or

---

1   CPR, PD64B.
2   [1907] 2 Ch 406.
3   See *Re Buckton* [1907] 2 Ch 406. For an extension of this possibility to a minority shareholder bringing a representative claim and to a member of a pension fund suing the trustees, see *Wallersteiner v Moir (No 2)* [1975] QB 373, CA; *Smith v Croft* [1986] 1 WLR 580, Walton J; *Re Westdock Realisations Ltd* (1988) 4 BCC 192, Browne-Wilkinson V-C; and *McDonald v Horn* [1995] 1 All ER 961, CA.
4   See **8.45**.

where he has asserted a tenancy of the trust land when he has actually been in possession of it only as a beneficiary.

Commencement and procedure

8.30   Whether the application is commenced by a CPR Part 7 claim form or a Part 8 claim form will depend on ordinary criteria – without regard to the fact that any party is a trustee.[1] The choice of procedure may be acute. For instance, a trust of land arises in cases of co-ownership. Hence, a large number of domestic homes are subject to a trust. If the claimant (spouse or partner) needs to prove his or her entitlement to a share in equity,[2] there may well be sufficient likelihood of 'a substantial dispute of fact' to exclude Part 8.

Parties

8.31   The claimant (if a beneficiary) will be the beneficiary (or beneficiaries) who alleges the wrongful act or failure to act. The defendants in such a case will be the trustees. In the case of an allegation of failure to sell and where the claimant seeks an order for sale, he must join *all* the trustees as defendants. He may tell any defendant that, in the absence of resistance by such defendant, no order for costs will be sought against him. There is usually no need to join any more beneficiaries, either as claimants or defendants. If, however, the court considers that on the particular facts of a case one or more other beneficiaries ought to be joined as parties, it may do so. The court will always be astute to look at the impact of the case upon other beneficiaries.

Costs

8.32   The position as between the claimant and the defendant is essentially the same as it would be in litigation between a stranger and the trustees. Included in this reference is the position as to the desirability (from the point of view of the trustee defendant) of a *Re Beddoe* application. If the court on a *Re Beddoe* application makes an order giving the trustee an indemnity as to his costs against the trust property, the trustee will be secure in relation to his costs. However, the court will (as usual) scrutinise the merits of the main case very carefully. If the court considers that the trustee is likely to fail in that case, it will refuse the *Re Beddoe* relief.[3] The trustee will then be exposed to personal liability for costs if an order for costs is made against him in the main case. It must be remembered that failure by a trustee in a *Re Beddoe* application will usually mean the trustee paying the costs of *that* application. A *Re Beddoe* application is not appropriate where the only trustee is a beneficiary in dispute with another beneficiary, eg a spouse or partner in a domestic home dispute.

---

[1]   See Chapter 2.

[2]   And this must be claimed on much more precise, factual grounds than merely 'living together'.

[3]   See *Alsop Wilkinson v Neary* [1996] 1 WLR 1220, at 1226.

COURT PROCEEDINGS INVOLVING TRUSTS: EXAMPLES OF COURT INTERVENTION TO APPROVE TRANSACTIONS, EXTEND TRUSTEES' POWERS OR VARY BENEFICIAL INTERESTS

Generally

8.33 What follows are some examples of court assistance in relation to trusts.

Application for approval of particular transaction or disposition

8.34 The court will be critical of an application by trustees seeking approval for a transaction which, on a close inspection of the trust instrument or of statute (or case-law), would have indicated was plainly within their powers to carry out, or which application was plainly a hopeless application. However, there may be cases where there is no clear conclusion without a court decision, where there is opposition from a beneficiary, or where there are minor, unborn or unascertained beneficiaries whose interests may be affected. In all these cases the trustees should apply to the court for approval of the transaction and/or directions.

8.35 It must be emphasised that if *all* the possible beneficiaries (being of full age and capacity, and ascertained) support the transaction, the court is unlikely to entertain any application for its consent to that transaction. The proper course would be for the trustees and the beneficiaries to enter into an agreement for the transaction to be carried out.[1] The following discussion is therefore based on the assumption that the consent of all such beneficiaries is not forthcoming.

8.36 There are several possible heads of jurisdiction for the court to approve a transaction which cannot otherwise be properly carried out by trustees.

Inherent jurisdiction

8.37 The Chancery Division (but not the county court) has always had an inherent power to approve transactions, but only (as *Chapman v Chapman*[2] laid down) in very limited circumstances. The court has jurisdiction in cases of absolute necessity, 'emergency', or where there is a genuine dispute as to beneficial interests.[3] Where a trust is for accumulation of income but the immediate beneficiaries have no funds for their maintenance, the court may

---

1   This is on the traditional basis that in the stated circumstances the parties should carry out the transaction without involving the court. Note especially the need to be careful in the ascertainment of all the beneficiaries.

2   [1954] AC 429, HL.

3   *Re New* [1901] 2 Ch 534, CA; *Re Powell-Cotton's Re-Settlement* [1956] 1 WLR 23, CA.

allow them maintenance out of the income.[1] If, however, a proposed transaction is within s 57 of the Trustee Act 1925,[2] it is better to proceed under that section in the first place, claiming relief under the inherent jurisdiction in the alternative.

8.38 An example of such a 'double-barrelled' approach would be where a child is entitled to certain property, eg shares in a company which is controlled by his parents, the parents being the trustees of the child's shares. The parents wish to agree to a sale of all the shares in the company to strangers. Can they agree in respect of the child's shares? It has been suggested that the parents, having parental responsibility,[3] can make such agreement on behalf of the child. Any purchaser would be well advised to ignore such suggestion. The real point is that there may be so much conflict of interest between the parents' personal positions and their position *vis à vis* their child's interests that there must be grave risk of the sale of the child's shares being voidable by the child when he comes of age or within a reasonable time thereafter. The only proper course must be for the parents (as trustees) to apply to court (ie to a Chancery master) for directions as to whether or not to contract in relation to the child's shares.

8.39 Such application will be under CPR Parts 8, 64 and PD64.

Trustee Act 1925, s 57

8.40 Section 57 of the Trustee Act 1925 envisages an act which:

(a) is not authorised by the trust;
(b) is to be effected by the trustees and in the management or administration of the trust property;
(c) the court thinks 'expedient'; and
(d) the court will empower the trustees to do.

8.41 An application under s 57 will be under CPR Parts 8, 64 and PD64.

SLA 1925, s 64

8.42 Section 64 of the Settled Land Act 1925 (SLA 1925) gives the court the power to authorise the tenant for life under a SLA 1925 settlement to effect a wide variety of transactions 'affecting or concerning the settled land, or any part thereof, or any other land' which would be 'for the benefit of the settled land'. It has been held to authorise alterations in the beneficial interests.[4] No

---

[1] *Re New* [1901] 2 Ch 534, CA; *Re Powell-Cotton's Re-Settlement* [1956] 1 WLR 23, CA.
[2] See **8.40**.
[3] See Children Act 1989, s 3.
[4] *Re Simmons* [1956] Ch 125 Danckwerts J.

new SLA 1925 settlement can be created after 31 December 1996.[1] Thus, s 64 is confined to pre-existing SLA 1925 settlements. Before 1 January 1997 (when the TLATA 1996 came into force) trustees for sale of land had been given the benefit of applying for relief under s 64 by s 28 of the Law of Property Act 1925 (LPA 1925). Following the repeal of s 28 (by the TLATA 1996), trustees of land have had the benefit of s 6 of the TLATA 1996.[2]

8.43 An application under s 64 will be under CPR Parts 8, 64 and PD64.

Variation of Trusts Act 1958

8.44 The jurisdiction under the Variation of Trusts Act 1958 (VTA 1958) is useful where there is no other satisfactory way of varying beneficial interests under trusts. It is a very specialised jurisdiction for both the Bench and advocates and is extremely rarely exercised by the county courts. The monetary limit under the CCA 1984 cannot be extended by agreement in a case under the VTA 1958.[3] Surprisingly, the jurisdiction under this Act is exercisable by Chancery masters only in very limited circumstances.[4]

8.45 Before contemplating any application under the Act, the possible beneficiaries must be ascertained.[5] This is very important and, in view of the complex definition of the persons on whose behalf the court may assent to the variation (see below), almost certainly requires specialist advice from a practitioner experienced in this field.

8.46 By s 1 of the VTA 1958 the court may approve 'any arrangement ... varying or revoking all or any of the trusts, or enlarging the powers of the trustees of managing or administering any of the property subject to the trusts'. Approval may be given on behalf of beneficiaries who come within any of four defined classes:

'(a) any person having, directly or indirectly, an interest, whether vested or contingent, under the trusts, who by reason of infancy or other incapacity is incapable of assenting;

(b) any person (whether or not ascertained) who may become entitled, directly or indirectly, to an interest under the trusts as being at a future date or on the happening of a future event a person of any specified description or a member of any specified class of persons, but not including any person who would be of that description, or a member of that class, as the case may be, if the said date had fallen or the said event had happened at the date of the application to the court;

---

[1] TLATA 1996, s 2(1).
[2] Section 28 was repealed by TLATA 1996, s 25 and Sch 3. A trust for sale, whenever created, is a 'trust of land' for the purposes of the TLATA 1996.
[3] County Courts Act 1984, ss 23 and 24(3).
[4] CPR, PD2B, para 5.1(c).
[5] See **8.4** and **8.5**.

(c)   any person unborn; or

(d)   any person in respect of any discretionary interest of his under protective
       trusts where the interest of the principal beneficiary has not failed or
       determined.'

8.47 'Protective trusts', 'principal beneficiary' and 'discretionary beneficiary'
are defined in terms of s 33 of Trustee Act 1925 (TA 1925).[1] There is a
complete exception for trusts affecting 'property settled by Act of
Parliament'.[2] This refers to estates such as those given by statute to the first
Duke of Marlborough and the first Duke of Wellington respectively in
gratitude for distinguished military service.

8.48 The VTA 1958 does not limit the scope of SLA 1925, s 64 or TA 1925,
s 57.[3]

8.49 The scheme of the VTA 1958 is that the court may approve (on behalf
of actual, future or potential beneficiaries) an 'arrangement' varying or
revoking etc the trusts.[4] The range of possible arrangements is enormous, far
beyond the limits of TA 1925, s 57 or SLA 1925, s 64, and plainly capable of
avoiding any doubts as to the limits in TLATA 1996, s 6(1) or the Trustee Act
2000. The one very obvious restriction on the jurisdiction is found in the
proviso to s 1. This (the prohibition on approval unless the carrying-out of the
arrangement would be for the benefit of the particular beneficiary or class of
beneficiaries concerned) is crucial and needs extremely close attention in
practice. The need for benefit, however, does *not* apply to any beneficiary
within class (d) above.

8.50 A simple example of such a case would be where a substantial trust
fund is held by trustees upon trust for A for life and, subject thereto, for his
children absolutely. A is aged 45 and happily married to B, aged 44. They have
two children, C and D, aged 23 and 16 respectively. A has no other children.
All are in good health and with normal life expectancies. A wishes to split the
trust fund between himself and his children. The crucial point is to ascertain
who are the beneficiaries. A, C and D are all beneficiaries, A being the life
tenant entitled to the income for his life, and C and D each being entitled to a
share of the capital subject to A's life interest. However, in theory, A may
have future children, whether by B or by some hypothetical, future wife after
the equally hypothetical death of B or divorce from her. If the trust
instrument were made after the coming into force of s 14 of the Family Law
Reform Act 1969, any illegitimate children which A may have since such
coming into force will be beneficiaries equally with C and D and any further

---

[1]   VTA 1958, s 1(2).

[2]   Ibid, s 1(5).

[3]   Ibid, s 1(6).

[4]   See the useful reasoning in *Re Holt's Settlement Trusts* [1969] 1 Ch 100, Megarry J.

legitimate children of A. Even a comparatively simple case becomes rather complex.

8.51 The VTA 1958 requires the court's approval for any proposed 'arrangement' on behalf of D (who is a minor) and of hypothetical future children of A (these being 'unascertained' beneficiaries). C is an adult and able to make his own decisions. The proposed arrangement must be positively beneficial for D and for the future children. The sort of arrangement which might be approved would in essence be one in which A would receive a capital sum appreciably less than the actuarial value of his life interest, and the balance of the trust fund would be held on trust for C, D and any future children of A in equal shares. It is possible that a benefit could be provided for the future children by an 'issue risk' insurance policy. The court would need to examine the difference which would be caused by the arrangement in respect of capital gains tax and inheritance tax (ie the difference between the incidence of such taxes if the arrangement were approved and if matters were simply left to take their course without such approval). This could influence the split which would be approved. There might be a requirement that A's life is to be insured to protect the inheritance tax position.

8.52 In the above example, A would be the claimant, the defendants being C, D (D acting by a litigation friend) and the trustees. There would be no objection to the same firm of solicitors acting for all parties. However, separate advocates would represent each of A, D and the trustees. C could be represented by an advocate or could indicate (in his acknowledgment of service) that he does not intend to contest the application. The court will expect to see advocates (probably Chancery counsel) with experience in trust work appearing in this sort of application. Advocates (especially those for the claimant and the trustees) will be expected to explain to the court the trust position and the tax position as they are before and after the implementation of the arrangement.

8.53 An application to court under the VTA 1958 will be under CPR Parts 8, 64 and PD64. The claimant's witness statement filed with the claim form will have exhibited to it the proposed arrangement for which approval is sought. This arrangement will usually have been agreed by the defendants in advance. If minors are defendants, attention must be given to the litigation friend procedure.[1]

Authorising trustees' remuneration

8.54 In exceptional circumstances (and where the Trustee Act 2000 (TA 2000), s 29 does not apply) the Chancery Division has an inherent jurisdiction to award trustees remuneration (if there is no professional

---

[1]   See CPR, Part 21 and Practice Direction thereto.

trustees' charging clause in the trust instrument), or higher remuneration than is authorised (if there is such a clause). The court balances two principles: (a) that the office of trustee is, prima facie, gratuitous and beneficiaries are to be protected against excessive claims by trustees; and (b) that it is of great importance to the beneficiaries that the trust should be well administered.[1]

8.55   Such application will be under CPR Parts 8, 64 and PD64.

COURT PROCEEDINGS INVOLVING TRUSTS: UNAUTHORISED DEPARTURE FROM TERMS OF TRUST

Generally

8.56   Any departure which is not authorised by statute, by *all* the beneficiaries under the trust – or by the court (under one of the above powers) is strictly a breach of trust. The range of possible departures is great. Some, such as misappropriation of trust property by the trustees, are heinous and involve plain liability on the part of the defaulting trustees; others may involve no loss whatsoever and may even produce a gain to the trust. The danger is that even potential liability may have far-reaching consequences, and be actionable in the future by beneficiaries yet unborn or unascertained.[2]

Remedies for breach of trust

8.57   It is important to remember that a beneficiary cannot sue a trustee for breach of trust, if he, being of full age and capacity and with full knowledge of the facts (and, perhaps, of their legal consequences), concurred or acquiesced in the breach.[3] What is discussed below is subject to this fundamental principle.

Injunction

8.58   There is no reason whatsoever why, in a proper case, a beneficiary should not be entitled to an injunction to prevent a trustee from committing a breach of trust. In the ordinary case this is where loss would be or might be anticipated.

8.59   An application for an injunction will be made either as an interim application in an existing claim or by way of a claim (if proceedings have not started). Whether a claim is made under CPR Part 7 or Part 8 will depend on ordinary principles.[4]

---

[1]   *Re Duke of Norfolk's Settlement Trusts* [1982] Ch 61, CA.
[2]   See **8.4** and **8.5** as to ascertainment of beneficiaries.
[3]   *Fletcher v Collis* [1905] 2 Ch 24, CA; *Re Howlett* [1949] Ch 767, at 775, per Danckwerts J.
[4]   See Chapter 2.

Compensation

8.60 If a trustee breaches one of his duties and/or falls below the relevant standard of care, and loss results, he is liable (at the suit of a beneficiary) to recompense the trust fund (or the claimant beneficiary if that beneficiary is absolutely entitled to the trust fund) for any such loss.[1] It cannot be emphasised too strongly that the trustee's liability is *not* one in 'damages'; it is one for (restitutionary) compensation.[2]

8.61 Foreseeability of loss is not necessary. What can be recovered, however, is only compensation for loss which can be said to have been caused by the breach of trust or fiduciary duty.[3] It is debatable whether a trustee is liable to a beneficiary for damages for tort in addition, or alternatively, to being liable for compensation for breach of trust. There can be no double-recovery of compensation/damages.

8.62 If more than one breach occurs, a loss suffered on one breach cannot be offset against profits on others.[4] However, if both loss and profits arise out of the same transaction or result from the same course of breaches, there may be a case for setting losses off against profits (within such transaction or course of dealing).[5]

8.63 An application for compensation may be made by a CPR Part 7 or Part 8 claim. The choice of procedures is made on the usual principles.[6]

Interest

8.64 Equitable interest (not the same as statutory interest on common law damages) was traditionally 4% pa simple interest, or 5% pa.[7] The latter was awarded (on a compound basis and as an alternative, at the claimant's option, to the profits actually earned) where the trustee was presumed to have received more or where he traded with the money.[8] If the money had been employed in a business or profession but not in a normal trading context (eg it was employed in a solicitors' firm's account), the 5% figure would be awarded on a simple, and not on a compound, basis.[9]

1   *Target Holdings Ltd v Redferns* [1996] AC 421, at 434–435, per Lord Browne-Wilkinson, HL.
2   *Target Holdings Ltd v Redferns* [1994] 1 WLR 1089, CA at 1101, per Peter Gibson LJ, CA; [1996] AC 421 at 432–435, per Lord Browne-Wilkinson, HL.
3   *Target Holdings Ltd v Redferns* [1996] AC 421, HL.
4   *Dimes v Scott* (1828) 4 Russell 195.
5   *Fletcher v Green* (1864) 33 Beavan 426; and *Bartlett v Barclays Bank Trust Co Ltd* [1980] Ch 515, at 538, Brightman J.
6   See Chapter 2.
7   *Re Davy* [1908] 1 Ch 61.
8   *Vyse v Foster* (1872) 8 Ch App 309, at 329, per James LJ.
9   *Burdick v Garrick* (1870) 5 Ch App 233.

8.65 There has always been entitlement in cases of breach of trust to award greater interest in the form of profits actually earned or which ought to have been earned with the trust money. The court may award equitable interest at the rate payable on money held by the court on special account.[1] The court may (at least where the party out of pocket is a commercial concern) award simple interest at 1% above the minimum lending rate.[2] A claimant must be careful to claim and to prove (as far as possible) the proper rate of equitable interest to which he may be entitled. If there is any doubt as to the proper rate, it is probably correct to claim interest on a particular basis 'or at such other rate or rates and for such period or periods as the court may think fit'. An inquiry (by a Chancery master or district judge) as to such interest may be ordered by the trial judge if he is unable to decide there and then the proper calculation of interest. Since equitable interest is not statutory, it is *not* sufficient simply to claim 'interest pursuant to statute'.

Impounding a trustee – beneficiary's beneficial interest

8.66 Where a trustee has committed a breach of trust and is liable to account for compensation, he will not be entitled to receive any money or other property to which he may be entitled as a beneficiary (either directly or by acquisition) under the trust until he has fully accounted in respect of his breach.[3]

8.67 An application under this jurisdiction may be made (if any such order is required) after the judge has found that a trustee–beneficiary is in breach of trust and is liable to account.

Relief of trustee from personal liability for breach of trust

8.68 Where it appears to the court that a trustee is or may be personally liable for any breach of trust, the court has a discretion to relieve the trustee wholly or partly from personal liability for such breach.[4] However, this discretion may be exercised *only* where the trustee in question has acted honestly and reasonably and ought fairly to be excused for the breach of trust and for omitting to obtain the directions of the court in the matter. It is important to remember that the jurisdiction is to grant relief against personal liability for *breach of trust* and not simply against personal liability which may arise from the trusteeship. Thus, a trustee will not be entitled to relief if he distributes trust property before paying or making provision for tax due in respect of it. Such distribution is unwise but not a breach of trust.[5] The

---

[1] *Bartlett v Barclays Bank Trust Co Ltd* [1980] Ch 515.
[2] *Re Duckwari Plc (No 2)* [1999] Ch 268, CA; following *Belmont Finance Corporation Ltd v Williams Furniture Ltd (No 2)* [1980] 1 All ER 393, at 393, CA.
[3] *Re Dacre* [1916] 1 Ch 344.
[4] TA 1925, s 61.
[5] *Re Rosenthal* [1972] 1 WLR 1273.

burden of proving that the trustee is entitled to relief lies squarely on him.[1] At the very least the trustee must show that he acted with as much prudence as he would have shown in managing his own affairs.[2] Every case must be looked at in its own circumstances.[3] Amongst other matters the court will consider:

(a)   the size and nature of the estate;
(b)   the circumstances of the defaulting trustee; and
(c)   the trustees' reliance (or otherwise) on legal advice.[4]

Merely taking legal advice is not 'a passport to relief'.[5] Furthermore, the court is less disposed to grant relief to a trust corporation or other paid trustee than to an unpaid trustee.[6]

8.69   An application under TA 1925, s 61 is made by way of counterclaim. This will be either by a CPR Part 20 application (if in response to a Part 7 claim) or by a clearly stated claim in a defendant's witness statement (if in response to a Part 8 claim). If liability has been established without a claim for relief having been made, a trustee should make any claim for relief under CPR Part 8.

---

[1]   *Re Stuart* [1897] 2 Ch 583.
[2]   *Re Turner* [1897] 1 Ch 536.
[3]   *Re Kay* [1897] 2 Ch 518, at 524.
[4]   *Re Evans* [1999] 2 All ER 777.
[5]   *Marsden v Regan* [1954] 1 WLR 423, at 435, per Lord Evershed MR.
[6]   *Bartlett v Barclay's Bank Trust Co Ltd* [1980] Ch 515, Brightman J.

Chapter 9

CONTENTIOUS PROBATE

Lynne Counsell

INTRODUCTION

9.1   This chapter does not deal with non-contentious probate matters governed by the Non-Contentious Probate Rules 1987,[1] which are assigned to the Family Division. Moreover, this chapter does not deal with the substantive law relating to wills and intestacy.[2]

MEANING OF CONTENTIOUS PROBATE ACTION

9.2   Strictly, contentious probate actions can be divided into three categories:

(1)   *Actions for pronouncement for or against a will in solemn form* – these arise in the following circumstances:
   (a)   when a caveat has been entered at the Probate Registry preventing a grant in common form in respect of the last will of the deceased, a warning has been entered to that caveat and an appearance entered to that.[3] The executor of the challenged will (assuming he wishes to prove the will) must then commence proceedings in the Chancery Division to prove the will in solemn form;
   (b)   an executor may have been cited to propound a will[4] by those entitled on intestacy or under an earlier will where the executor has not attempted to prove the later challenged will;
   (c)   a person entitled under an earlier will or on intestacy may challenge the validity of a later will by seeking an order that it be pronounced against in solemn form.
(2)   *Interest actions* – these are more rare and arise when the interest of a party to a grant of letters of administration is disputed or the

---

[1]   SI 1987/2024.
[2]   For the substantive law, see *Williams on Wills* (18th edn).
[3]   Non-Contentious Probate Rules 1987, r 44. See *Peacock v Lowe* (1867) LR 1 P&D 311.
[4]   Ibid, rr 46–48.

entitlement of someone claiming to be a beneficiary under a will. For example, questions may arise as to the legitimacy of a child and the validity of a marriage.[1]

(3)   *Revocations of grant* – these arise where there already exists a grant of probate or letters of administration in common form but there are grounds for challenging the will in respect of which probate has been granted, or a will is discovered indicating that the deceased did not die intestate after all. Application is then made for revocation of the grant and, if appropriate, can be coupled with an application for proof of a will in solemn form.

9.3   Although not strictly a probate action, it is convenient to include in this chapter applications for the rectification of a will under s 20 of the Administration of Justice Act 1982 as these are covered by CPR Part 57 relating to contentious probate proceedings, notwithstanding such an application is not a 'probate claim' within the meaning of the rules.

COMMENCING A PROBATE CLAIM

9.4   Contentious probate proceedings are governed by CPR Part 57 as supplemented by Practice Direction PD57.[2] There are certain peculiarities in such proceedings which to an extent result from the fact that such actions were originally dealt with by the Ecclesiastical Courts.

9.5   A probate claim is defined in CPR, r 57.1(2) as:

> 'a claim for the grant of probate of the will, or letters of administration of the estate, of a deceased person, the revocation of a grant or a decree pronouncing for or against the validity of an alleged will.'

This thereby broadly covers the three categories of proceedings outlined in **9.2**.

9.6   The claim must be brought in the Chancery Division of the High Court, either in London or in one of the Chancery district registries,[3] or in a county court where there is also a Chancery district registry.[4] A county court thereby only has jurisdiction where (i) an application for a grant has been made through the Principal Registry or a district probate registry; (ii) the value

---

1   This head does not include any application for a declaration as to legitimacy, which must be sought by way of petition under the Family Law Act 1986 in the Family Division.

2   See also the Draft Pre-action Protocol for the Resolution of Probate and Trust Disputes, available from the ACTAPS website.

3   Namely at Birmingham, Bristol, Cardiff, Leeds, Liverpool, Manchester, Newcastle-upon-Tyne and Preston. See CPR, PD57, para 2.2. See also Chapter 2 and the Chancery Guide, Chapter 12.

4   CPR, r 57.2 and PD57, para 2.2.

of the net estate after payment of expenses and debts does not exceed the county court limit of £30,000;[1] and (iii) the county court also has a district registry. If it is not brought in the Chancery Division or the appropriate county court, an application should be made to transfer the action forthwith, or the court will do so of its own initiative.[2]

9.7 A probate claim must be commenced using the procedure in CPR Part 7.[3] The claim form should be in Form N2 and its contents must comply with CPR Part 16.[4] Furthermore, it must contain a statement of the nature of the interest of the claimant and the defendant in the estate of the deceased.[5] For example, it should state whether the claimant is the executor of a will, a beneficiary or is entitled on the intestacy of the deceased (in which case, it should also state the relationship he bore to the deceased).

9.8 At this stage, particulars of claim may be served either endorsed on the claim form itself or served with it.[6] There are certain advantages in adopting this course if the claimant has all the information in his possession necessary to set out his case fully. It will speed up the timetable considerably. It is particularly useful where the claimant simply wishes to propound a will where the particulars of claim are very straightforward. However, the disadvantage is that the filing and service of affidavits or witness statements of testamentary scripts[7] is really designed to take place so that the parties know precisely what, if any, earlier wills will have any bearing on the proceedings before any particulars of claim and defence are served. However, if the claimant is confident that he claims under the last will, there is probably nothing to be gained by not endorsing the particulars of claim on the claim form, or by serving them with it.

9.9 The commencement of a probate claim has the effect of preventing the grant of probate or letters of administration unless the court otherwise directs,[8] and on issue of the claim form the relevant office will send a notice to Leeds District Probate Registry[9] requesting that all testamentary scripts and other relevant documents in any probate registry be sent to the relevant office.

---

[1]   See County Courts Act 1984, s 32 and the County Courts Jurisdiction Order 1981, SI 1981/1123.
[2]   For transfer, see CPR, r 30.2.
[3]   CPR, r 57.3(b).
[4]   It must contain a concise statement of the nature of the case and the remedy sought in accordance with CPR, r 16.2. See also Chancery Guide, Appendix 1. See Chapter 2.
[5]   CPR, r 57.7(1).
[6]   CPR, r 7.4.
[7]   As to which, see **9.14**.
[8]   CPR, PD57, para 2.4.
[9]   At Coronet House, Queen Street, Leeds LS1 2BA: DX 26451 Leeds (Park Square).

PARTIES

9.10 The grant of probate in solemn form is a judicial act which binds all those privy to it, namely all those who are either parties or were aware of the action and had the opportunity to be joined. Generally, therefore, all those persons who would be affected by the making of the order should be joined to the action. If a claim is being brought to propound a will, which will have the effect that those entitled on intestacy will not inherit, then it is best practice to join them.

9.11 However, the persons involved may be too numerous or there may be other reasons why it is inconvenient to join them. In such circumstances, notice should be given to any person who might be affected by the claim, whether under a will in issue or on intestacy.[1] A person on whom notice has been served can then decide whether or not to apply to be joined as a defendant.

9.12 Where there are large numbers of beneficiaries in a particular class, it may be appropriate to seek an order that one of them represent the others. Thus, if under a disputed will there is a class of beneficiaries with the same interest, it may be sensible for one to be joined to the action to represent the others.[2]

9.13 In an action for revocation of a grant any person claiming to be entitled to administer the estate of the deceased under an unrevoked grant must be joined to the action.[3]

TESTAMENTARY SCRIPTS

9.14 Unless the court directs otherwise, the claimant and every defendant who has acknowledged service of the claim must serve an affidavit or witness statement of testamentary scripts.[4] The purpose of this is so that the court and all parties to the probate claim know what wills and drafts of wills are in existence. This may be very important. It is pointless for a claimant seeking a pronouncement against a last will on the grounds of its invalidity to pursue the action on the basis that he would be entitled on intestacy, if in fact there is an earlier will under which he does not benefit and which he cannot attack.

---

[1] See *Young v Holloway* [1895] P 87. See CPR, r 19.8A.
[2] CPR, r 19.6. The court will generally ensure that all persons with any potential interest in the proceedings are joined as parties or served with notice under CPR, r 19. 8A. See Chancery Guide, para 24.1(3).
[3] CPR, r 57.6(1).
[4] CPR, r 57.5(3); CPR, PD57, para 3.2. See the annex to CPR, Part 57 and **Form 37**.

9.15   A testamentary script is defined as:

> 'a will, a draft of a will, written instructions for a will made by or at the request,
> or under the instructions, of the testator and any document purporting to be
> evidence of the contents, or to be a copy, of a will which is alleged to have been
> lost or destroyed.'[1]

9.16   The affidavit or witness statement must describe any testamentary
script of the deceased person whose estate is the subject of the action of
which he has knowledge or, if he does not know of such a script, he must
state that. If any such script of which he has knowledge is not in his
possession or under his control, he must give the name and address of the
person in whose possession or under whose control it is, or if he does not
know the name and address of such person, he must state that.[2]

9.17   Any testamentary script in the possession of the person filing the
affidavit or witness statement must be filed with it.[3]

9.18   Unless the court otherwise directs, the affidavit or witness statement of
testamentary scripts must be filed by the claimant when the claim form is
issued and by the defendant when he acknowledges service.[4] Where there is
no acknowledgement of service, the claimant must file either in accordance
with a direction given by the court (eg at a case management conference) or
before any order is made for the trial of the claim. Even in an uncontested
probate claim, the court is unlikely to dispense with an affidavit or witness
statement of testamentary scripts.

9.19   The penalty for failing to file an affidavit or witness statement is that
the defaulting party will not be able to inspect the affidavit or witness
statement and accompanying testamentary scripts of the other party without
the permission of the court.[5] The claim or defence would not be struck out
for non-compliance with the CPR.

9.20   Any party wishing to have a testamentary script examined by an expert
should apply to the court in accordance with CPR Part 23, explaining the
nature and purpose of the examination and the points to which it should be
directed.[6] The court can make such an order of its own initiative. This
procedure could be important where there are allegations that a will was
forged or not duly executed.

---

[1]   CPR, r 57.1(2)(c). 'Will' includes a codicil: CPR, r 57.1(2)(d).
[2]   CPR, r 57.5(3).
[3]   CPR, r 57.5(1), (2).
[4]   CPR, r 57.5(4). In an emergency the claimant can issue the claim form upon an undertaking to lodge
the requisite documents: CPR, PD57, para 3.3.
[5]   CPR, r 57.5(5).
[6]   For expert evidence, see CPR, Part 35.

LODGMENT OF GRANT IN REVOCATION ACTION

9.21 In an action for revocation of a grant, the grant must be lodged on issue of the claim. If it is in possession or under the control of the defendant, then that defendant must lodge the grant when he acknowledges the service of the claim form on him.[1]

9.22 An application may be made to compel a person to lodge a grant if he fails to comply with the rules and the court can make such an order of its own initiative. The penalty for failure to comply is that the person against whom the order is made cannot take any step in the claim until he has complied.[2]

CONTENTS OF PARTICULARS OF CLAIM AND DEFENCE AND COUNTERCLAIM

9.23 The particulars of claim must contain a concise statement of the facts on which the claimant relies.[3] Particulars must be given of pleas frequently found in probate actions, such as undue influence, lack of mental capacity and fraud.[4] Similarly, a party who wishes to contend that a will was not duly executed must set out the contention specifically and give particulars of the facts and matters relied on.[5]

9.24 Further, where the claimant disputes the interest of a defendant, he must state in his particulars of claim that he denies the interest of that defendant. Thus, for example, if the defendant has filed an appearance to a warning to his caveat on the basis that he is the child of the deceased and therefore entitled on intestacy, the claimant should, if it be the case, state in his particulars of claim that he denies that the defendant is the child.[6] It will then be for the defendant to plead in his defence the facts on which he relies to support his claim that he is the child of the deceased.

9.25 The defence must comply with the requirements of CPR, r 16.5 and set out a positive case, not merely a bare denial of the claimant's case. Full particulars must also be given of any allegations as outlined above, such as want of execution, lack of sound memory and understanding, or fraud or

---

[1] CPR, r 57.6(2)–(4).
[2] CPR, r 57.5(5).
[3] CPR, r 16.4. See Chancery Guide, Appendix 1. See Chapter 2.
[4] CPR, PD16, para 8.2; CPR, r 57.7(4)(b)(c). See *Re Earl of Shrewsbury's Estate* [1922] P 112 (particulars ordered of unsoundness of mind and undue influence). Such allegations should never be put forward unless the party who pleads them has reasonable grounds upon which to support them: *Spiers v English* [1907] P 122.
[5] CPR, r 57.7(4)(a).
[6] CPR, r 57.7(2).

undue influence.[1] Where a claimant or defendant alleges that at the time the will in issue was executed the testator did not know and approve the contents thereof, that party must specify in his statement of case the nature of the case on which he intends to rely.[2]

9.26 Notwithstanding the requirement to set out a positive defence, in a probate claim the defendant may give notice that he will raise no positive case but will insist on the will being proved in solemn form, and for that purpose will cross-examine the witnesses who attested the will.[3] This has important costs ramifications which are dealt with at **9.68**.

COUNTERCLAIMS

9.27 It is common in probate claims for the defendant to counterclaim. For example, if the claimant is seeking to propound the last will of the deceased in solemn form, the defendant might want to defend on the basis that the will is invalid, but seek to propound an earlier will in solemn form by way of counterclaim. It is usually not until the counterclaim is served that the real issues between the parties become apparent. A defendant who claims that he has any claim or is entitled to any remedy relating to the grant of probate of the will or letters of administration of the estate must add a counterclaim to his defence.[4]

9.28 If no particulars of claim are served, the defendant may seek the permission of the court to serve a counterclaim, and the proceedings will then continue as if the defendant were the claimant.[5]

9.29 The defendant may need to join other parties as defendants to the counterclaim, for example if he wishes to propound a will and needs to join the executors. Application should then be made to the court for that person to be added as defendant to the counterclaim.[6]

COMMONLY FOUND CONTENTIONS IN PROBATE CLAIMS

9.30 A full discussion of the substantive law relating to wills and probate is outside the scope of this chapter. However, it is useful to summarise the more

---

[1] CPR, r 57.7(4).
[2] CPR, r 57.7(3). See **9.33**.
[3] CPR, r 57.7(5). See *Spicer v Spicer* [1899] P 38.
[4] CPR, r 57.8(1).
[5] CPR, r 57.8(2).
[6] CPR, r 20.5.

commonly found contentions which can be used to attack the validity of a will.

Want of due execution

9.31 A contention of want of due execution is that the will does not comply with the Wills Act 1837, for example on the basis that the witnesses did not sign in each other's presence, or they did not see the testator sign.

Incapacity

9.32 A contention of incapacity is that at the time the will was executed the testator was not of sound mind, memory or understanding. As was stated in *Banks v Goodfellow*:

> 'It is essential that the testator shall understand the nature of the act and its effects; the extent of the property of which he is disposing; shall be able to comprehend and appreciate the claims to which he ought to give effect, and with a view to the latter object, that no disorder of the mind shall poison his affections, pervert his sense of right, or prevent the exercise of his natural faculties, that no insane delusion shall influence his will in disposing of his property and bring about a disposal of it which, if his mind had been sound, would not have been made.'[1]

Unsoundness of mind can be the result of mental illness, disability, or even drugs or alcohol.

Want of knowledge and approval

9.33 A contention of want of knowledge and approval may take several different forms.[2] Usually, knowledge and approval of the contents of the will can be proved easily by establishing that the will was read to the testator, or he read it himself and understood it. However, if the testator is suffering from a disability such as deafness or blindness[3] it may be more difficult to establish that he knew and approved the contents of the will. This contention might also be used where the circumstances surrounding the preparation of the will excite the suspicion of the court, as where the solicitor who drew up the will is a major beneficiary.[4] A plea of this kind may also be used where an error has crept into the wording of the will enabling the court to omit words from the will on its admission to probate, although this is of much less importance in cases of a testator dying after 1 January 1983, where rectification of the will can be sought. This contention is often put forward where the party attacking

---

[1]   (1870) LR 5 QB 549, at 565.
[2]   See *Tchilingirian v Ouzounian* [2003] WTLR 709, at 722.
[3]   *In the Goods of Owston* (1862) 2 Sw and Tr 461.
[4]   *Wintle v Nye* [1959] 1 WLR 284, [1959] 1 All ER 552, HL. A solicitor who benefits should ensure that the client is separately advised: *Re a Solicitor* [1975] 1 QB 475.

the validity of the will has limited information as to the circumstances in which it was made.

Undue influence

9.34 A contention of undue influence will succeed only if it can be shown that the mind of the testator has been so dominated that the will is not his own 'will' at all but that of the person influencing him.[1] Actual undue influence must be proved and there has to be some independent evidence tending to show the exercise of an improper influence amounting to coercion.[2] There is no doctrine of presumed undue influence in a probate claim.

Fraud and forgery

9.35 A will is obtained by fraud if, for example, someone makes a false representation about a potential beneficiary. A forged will does not in fact comply with the Wills Act 1837, but a contention of forgery should be specifically included in the statement of case.

Revocation

9.36 It may be alleged that a will has been revoked either by marriage, or the annulment or dissolution of marriage[3] by a subsequent will or by destruction.[4]

DEFAULT

9.37 A defendant in a probate claim must file an acknowledgement of service either 28 days after the service of the claim form or the particulars of claim.[5] If a defendant in a probate action fails to acknowledge service or file a defence, a default judgment cannot be obtained in accordance with CPR, r 10.2 and Part 12. Instead, CPR, PD57, para 10, provides a practice which can be followed.

9.38 Where no defendant acknowledges service, there are two options open to the claimant. He can either apply for the claim to be discontinued, or apply to the court for an order for trial of the claim.[6] The first option may not be sufficient. Discontinuance of an action to propound a will, for example, puts

---

1 *Hall v Hall* (1868) LR 1 P&D 481.
2 *Re Gillick deceased* (unreported) 31 March 1999.
3 Wills Act 1837, ss 18 and 18A, the latter of which applies only to deaths after 1 January 1996.
4 Ibid, s 20 provides that a will is revoked by 'the burning, tearing or otherwise destroying the same by the testator or by some person in his presence and by his direction, with the intention of revoking the same'. There must be an intention to revoke the will: *Giles v Warren* (1872) LR 2 P&D 401.
5 CPR, r 57.4. The defendant in such a claim thereby has an additional 14 days.
6 CPR, r 57.10(3).

the claimant back into the position he was before the action started and, if the defendant continues a caveat, he will still not be able to obtain a grant in common form. Both options require the claimant to file an affidavit or witness statement of service on the defendant and, if he has not already done so, to serve particulars of claim.[1]

9.39 Where there are several defendants, and one or more (but not all of them) fail(s) to acknowledge service, then, after the time for filing acknowledgement of service has passed, the claimant can file an affidavit or witness statement proving service of the claim on the defendant who is in default and can then proceed with the claim as if he had acknowledged service.[2]

9.40 The situation where any party fails to serve a pleading on any other party will apply not only in default of defence but also in default of particulars of claim. The court has three options:

(a)　　　it can dismiss the claim if the defaulting party is the claimant;

(b)　　　it can order the claim to be discontinued;[3] or

(c)　　　it can order the trial of the claim.

9.41 If the court orders that the claim be tried under CPR, r 57.10(3), it can also order that the trial take place on written evidence.[4] Such a trial can lead to a grant of probate in solemn form. There would seem to be no reason why the court could not use this procedure in the case of breach of an order that unless the party in default served a pleading within a specified time that party would be debarred from defending, and order that there be a trial on written evidence.

SUMMARY JUDGMENT

9.42 Summary judgment under CPR Part 24 is available against a claimant or defendant in contentious probate proceedings.[5]

9.43 Used wisely, the ability to apply for summary judgment is a great asset to a party in a probate claim. For example, a claim to propound a will by a testator who has been severely mentally ill for many years should be dealt with in a summary fashion rather than a full trial. A claim that a will has not been properly executed should be dealt with summarily where there is good

---

1　　CPR, r 57.10(4).
2　　CPR, r 57.10(2).
3　　But see **9.38** as to the possible disadvantages of this course.
4　　CPR, r 57.10(5). Any written evidence should comply with CPR, Part 32.
5　　CPR, r 24.3.

evidence from two attesting witnesses. There is nothing in the CPR and, in particular, in r 24.3, which prevents either party having recourse to the striking-out procedure[1] if the claim or defence amounts to an abuse.[2]

9.44 If a claimant or defendant in an application for summary judgment seeks a pronouncement for a will in solemn form, the evidence in support must include an affidavit or witness statement proving the execution of the will.[3]

9.45 If a defendant has given notice in his defence that he raises no positive case[4] but insists that the will be proved in solemn form and for that purpose that he will cross-examine the witness who attested the will, then any application by the claimant for summary judgment is subject to the right of the defendant to require those witnesses to attend for cross-examination.[5]

9.46 It should be noted that the procedure for obtaining judgment under CPR Part 24 where a defendant has filed a defence, albeit one with no real prospects of success, appears to be a more straightforward procedure than where a defendant appears to be in default.

DIRECTIONS AND INTERIM APPLICATIONS

9.47 All probate claims are allocated to the multi-track.[6] Notwithstanding the specific procedure relating to probate claims, essentially their progress to trial will follow a similar pattern to other claims.[7] At the case management stage the court will consider who should be given notice of the claim, whether all appropriate parties have been joined and whether a representation order should be made.[8]

9.48 Where the validity of a will is in question in a probate claim, the solicitor who prepared the will should make available to anyone who requests it a statement of his evidence regarding the execution of the will and the circumstances surrounding it,[9] whether or not he acts for the party propounding the will.

---

[1]   CPR, r 3.4.
[2]   *Shephard v Wheeler* (unreported) 15 June 2000, CA.
[3]   CPR, PD57, para 5.1.
[4]   See CPR, r 57.7(5).
[5]   CPR, PD57, para 5.2.
[6]   CPR, r 57.2(4).
[7]   See Chancery Guide, para 24.1.
[8]   CPR, PD57, para 4.
[9]   *Law Society Gazette* (September 1959), at p 619; and see *Larke v Nugus* [2000] WTLR 1033.

9.49 The draft pre-action protocol for the resolution of probate and trust disputes encourages disclosure of all relevant documents at an early stage. Failure by either party to disclose relevant documents or to be co-operative, preferably before proceedings are issued, can result in costs sanctions. Lack of knowledge or disclosure might mean that it is reasonable for a party to make an allegation or pursue a claim even if he is unsuccessful.[1]

9.50 Expert evidence often plays a significant role in a probate claim, whether it is a handwriting expert brought in to support a claim that the testator did not sign the will, or a medical expert deposing to the testator when the will was executed. The rules as to expert evidence are contained in CPR Part 35.

ADMINISTRATORS PENDING SUIT

9.51 One of the difficulties which often occurs when a probate claim is made is that there is nobody to administer the estate. There may be any number of matters which require attention in the time it takes to get the case to trial.

9.52 Section 117 of the SCA 1981 gives the court jurisdiction to appoint an administrator pending suit. Application is made by notice in the claim to a master or district judge.[2] This must be supported by a witness statement setting out why an administrator pending suit is needed, and naming a candidate. A witness statement from the proposed administrator should be included. It is usual practice to have an affidavit of fitness of the proposed administrator sworn by a disinterested party, although there is nothing in the rules requiring this.

9.53 Rules on the giving of security by a receiver, service of the order and the remuneration of the receiver apply to an administrator appointed under SCA 1981, s 117.[3] The court may fix such remuneration as it thinks fit and can order that the remuneration be paid out of the estate of the deceased.[4] It is important that an application for remuneration for a professional administrator is sought as part of any order appointing him.

9.54 Once an order has been made appointing an administrator, he must apply to the Family Division for a grant of letters of administration.[5] The administrator has all the powers of a normal administrator, but cannot

---

[1] See *Smith v Smith* (1866) LR 1 P&D 239; *Carapeto v Good* [2002] WTLR 1305.
[2] CPR, PD57, paras 8.1 and 8.3.
[3] CPR, PD57, para 8.2(1).
[4] SCA 1981, s 117(3).
[5] CPR, PD57, para 8.4.

distribute the estate. The appointment of the administrator pending suit ends automatically when a final order in the probate claim is made, but will continue if there is an appeal.[1] There is no need to include anything about the administrator pending suit in the final order made.

APPLICATION FOR ORDER TO BRING IN WILL AND RELATED APPLICATIONS

9.55 Useful tools are available in probate claims where testamentary documents are in the possession of third parties. Where it appears that there are reasonable grounds for believing that any person has knowledge of a document which is or purports to be a testamentary document, and whether or not any legal proceedings are pending, the court may order that person to attend for the purpose of being examined in open court, and the court may require any person who is before it in compliance with the order to answer any question relating to the document concerned. If appropriate, the court may also order that person to bring in the document in such manner as it may direct.[2]

9.56 Application must be made by way of notice in accordance with CPR Part 23, which must be served on the person against the whom the order is sought.[3] The application must be made to a master or district judge.[4] Any person who, having been required by the court to do so under s 122 of the SCA 1981, fails to attend for examination, answer any question or bring in any document, is guilty of contempt of court.

9.57 Section 123 of the SCA 1981 states that where it appears that any person not party to the proceedings has in his possession, custody or power any document which is or purports to be a testamentary document, whether or not any legal proceedings are pending, the court may issue a witness summons[5] requiring that person to bring in the document in such manner as the court may direct in the witness summons.

9.58 The application may be made without notice to a master or district judge and must be supported by a witness statement setting out the grounds of the application.[6] If the person against whom the witness summons has

---

[1]   CPR, PD49, para 8.5.
[2]   SCA 1981, s 122.
[3]   CPR, PD57, para 7.1.
[4]   CPR, PD57, para 7.3.
[5]   For the procedure, see CPR, Part 34. See also *Khanna v Lovell White Durrant* [1994] 4 All ER 267.
[6]   CPR, PD57, para 7.2.

been directed does not have the testamentary document in his possession or under his control, he can file a witness statement to that effect.[1]

COMPROMISE

9.59 Compromising a probate claim is not entirely straightforward because of the quasi inquisitorial function of the court, the need in many cases to have proof in solemn form and the necessity to make sure that all those affected by the compromise are bound. There are three ways in which a probate claim may be compromised:[2]

(a)   discontinuance or dismissal;
(b)   trial of the claim on written evidence;
(c)   applications under s 49 of the Administration of Justice Act 1985.

Each of these possibilities has its own advantages and disadvantages, and they are dealt with in turn below.

Discontinuance or dismissal

9.60 It is not open to a party to a probate claim simply to decide to discontinue it.[3] The claim can be discontinued only if the court so orders.[4] On a compromise, discontinuance or dismissal of the claim may be sought on the basis that the court will then order that a grant of probate or letters of administration be made to the persons entitled thereto.[5] This means that there will be a grant in common form to the person who can establish a right to such a grant. It will not assist if a grant in solemn form is needed, or if there is no agreement to remove a caveat. Such a consent order will almost always contain an order that any caveat which has been entered be removed, thus enabling the person whom it has determined should apply for a grant to do so. The terms of the order can then be set out in a schedule.

Trial of the action

9.61 In most cases where it is desirable that there be a grant in solemn form, the method most appropriate[6] on a compromise will be to seek an order that the case be tried on written evidence.[7] This may be particularly useful where a minor beneficiary cannot consent to a compromise or where, for whatever reason, not all the beneficiaries affected can provide their consent but the

---

[1]   CPR, PD57, para 7.4.
[2]   CPR, PD57, para 6.1.
[3]   CPR, Part 38 (discontinuance) does not apply to probate claims: CPR, r 57.11(1).
[4]   CPR, r 57.11(2). Application is in accordance with CPR, Part 23. See Chancery Guide, para 24.1(7).
[5]   CPR, r 57.11(2)(b).
[6]   SCA 1981, s 49(2).
[7]   CPR, PD57, para 6.1(1). For a form of order, see Practice Form PF38CH.

parties to the action agree. Evidence will usually be on affidavits or witness statements, and affidavits or witness statements of testamentary scripts will be necessary.

Section 49 of the Administration of Justice Act 1985

9.62 The Administration of Justice Act 1985 (AJA 1985) introduces a very useful method of obtaining a consent order where all the 'relevant beneficiaries' consent. A relevant beneficiary is someone beneficially interested under a will in dispute, or, in case of intestacy, someone entitled as a beneficiary under that intestacy.[1] Applications may be heard by a master or district judge and must be supported by an affidavit or witness statement identifying the relevant beneficiaries and exhibiting their consents. It will still be necessary to ensure that affidavits of scripts or witness statements are before the court.[2]

RECTIFICATION OF WILLS

9.63 Paragraphs 9–11 of CPR PD57 relate to an application for rectification of a will, although it is not a probate claim as such. A claim for rectification of a will is made under s 20 of the Administration of Justice Act 1982 on the basis that the will does not carry out the intentions of the testator by reason of a clerical error[3] or the failure to understand the instructions of the testator. An application must be brought within 6 months from the date of the grant.[4] It will normally be appropriate to use the claim form procedure under CPR Part 7 rather than the alternative procedure in CPR Part 8. Where a claim to rectify a will is non-contentious, these provisions will not apply.[5]

9.64 Every personal representative of the estate must be joined as a party to an action for rectification.[6] If the claimant is the person to whom the grant was made in respect of the relevant will, he must lodge the probate or letters of administration, with the will annexed, with the court when the claim form is issued. If the defendant has the probate or letters of administration in his possession or control he must lodge this in the relevant office within 14 days after the service of the claim form on him.[7] The court can alter these time-limits.

---

[1] AJA 1985, s 49(2).
[2] CPR, PD57, para 6.2.
[3] See *Re Segelman* [1996] Ch 171, at 183; *Re Morris* [1971] P 62; and *Re Munday* [2003] WTLR 1161.
[4] AJA 1982, s 20(2). There is a discretion to extend the period.
[5] Application can be made to the Family Division under the Non-Contentious Probate Rules 1987, SI 1987/2024, r 55.
[6] CPR, r 57.12(2).
[7] CPR, PD57, para 10.

9.65   When an order is made for rectification of a will, a copy is sent to the Family Division and a memorandum of the order is endorsed on grant or permanently annexed to it.[1]

COSTS

9.66   The court has a discretion over how costs should be dealt with, but generally costs follow the event.[2] The court can, however, make other orders, and specifically can take into account the conduct of the parties, whether before or after the proceedings commenced, any lack of disclosure or co-operation in the proceedings, whether pursuing a particular issue was reasonable, the manner in which a party has pursued its claim and whether a successful claimant has exaggerated a claim. These are all likely to influence the court in a probate claim. The court can also make orders which award a party only part of his costs or costs relating to a specific part of the proceedings. Usually the costs of the caveat, warning and appearance are relevant in any contentious probate proceedings.[3]

9.67   Offers under CPR Part 36 are unlikely to play any great part in probate claims where the outcome is all or nothing, notwithstanding the fact that the rules now apply to non-monetary offers. However, parties and their legal representatives are encouraged to enter into discussions and/or negotiations prior to commencing proceedings.[4]

9.68   Where a defendant has simply given notice of his intention to have the will proved in solemn form, the court will not order costs against him unless there were no reasonable grounds to oppose the will.[5]

9.69   A distinction must be drawn between the costs a party may be able to claim out of the estate and those he may be able to recover against another party. In cases where it is difficult to enforce a costs order against a party, or where the losing party is legally aided, the issue of claiming costs out of the estate is very important.

9.70   The general rule is that a personal representative is entitled to be paid the costs of proceedings on an indemnity basis out of the estate in so far as they are not recovered from or paid by any other person.[6] In general, an

---

[1]   CPR, PD57, para 11.

[2]   CPR, r 44.3(2)(a). In trust cases a robust approach has been seen in cases such as *Breadner v Granville Grossman* [2001] Ch 523, whilst the principle of costs following the event have been applied in *D'Abo v Paget* (2000) *The Times*, August 10, ChD. For the general principles, see *Re Fuld* [1968] P 727.

[3]   See *Salter v Salter* [1896] P 291.

[4]   Draft Pre-action Protocol for the Resolution of Probate and Trust Disputes, para 2.9.

[5]   CPR, r 57.7(5).

[6]   CPR, r 48.4.

executor who proves a will in solemn form is entitled to costs out of the estate and has a right to take those costs without any order of the court.[1] Subject to CPR Part 44, an executor who puts forward a will which he must have known he could not prove must pay the costs, although he will not necessarily be condemned if he had reasonable grounds for believing that the will was valid.[2]

9.71 A beneficiary who proves a will in solemn form (because, for example, the executor has chosen to take no action) will usually be entitled to take his costs out of the estate but, unlike an executor, he must obtain an order to do so.

9.72 If a party successfully opposes a grant of probate, and obtains a grant himself, or manages to have a grant in common form revoked and obtain letters of administration, he will be entitled to recoup his costs out of the estate and can then pursue any party against whom he obtains a costs order.

9.73 In general, any party who unsuccessfully opposes probate, or a party who propounds a will which the court holds to be invalid, or who seeks to revoke a grant which is held to be valid, will have to pay the costs subject to the court exercising its discretion in accordance with the criteria set out in CPR Part 44.

9.74 An exception to these general rules in probate claims is that if the action has in fact been caused by the fault of the testator, the costs of all parties should be paid out of the estate.[3] A similar rule applies where for other reasons there were reasonable grounds of suspicion requiring the court to investigate the circumstances surrounding the preparation of the will, but where ultimately it pronounced in its favour.[4]

---

1   See *Wild v Plant* [1926] P 139. An order of the court will require his costs to be taxed and, therefore, no order is probably preferable, see *Re Coles' Estate* (1962) 106 SJ 837.
2   *Boughton v Knight* (1873) LR 1 P&D 456.
3   *Re Hall-Dare* [1916] 1 Ch 272.
4   One principle 'is that if a person who makes a will or persons who are interested in the residue have been really the cause of the litigation a case is made out for costs to come out of the estate. Another principle is that, if the circumstances lead reasonably to an investigation of the matter, then the costs may be left to be borne by those who have incurred them': *Spiers v English* [1907] P 122, at 123.

9.75 As in other claims, it may be that in a probate claim there will have to be a separate bundle of documents (eg the correspondence passing before the claim was commenced) to deal with any application for costs at the end of the trial.

Chapter 10

FAMILY PROVISION

Helene Pines Richman

INTRODUCTION

10.1   The Inheritance (Provisions for Family and Dependants) Act 1975 (I(PFD)A 1975) allows certain persons to claim financial provision out of the estate of a deceased person who at the time of death was domiciled in England and Wales.[1] It will be for the claimant to prove where the deceased was domiciled when he or she died.[2] The ground of the application is that the will or intestacy of the deceased fails to make reasonable financial provision for the claimant. 'Reasonable financial provision' is defined in respect of a spouse of the deceased (except where there has been a judicial separation decree in force and the separation is continuing) as 'such financial provision as it would be reasonable in all the circumstances of the case for a husband or wife to receive, whether or not that provision is required for his or her maintenance'.[3] In the case of other claimants, 'reasonable financial provision' *none spouse* is defined as 'such financial provision as would be reasonable in all the circumstances of the case for the applicant to receive for his or her maintenance'.[4]

10.2   The claim is judged on the facts as at the date of the hearing, and not the date of death.[5] In applications by children who become adults or who are in their teenage years at the time of the hearing, facts concerning financial needs during the period between the application and the hearing appear to be considered since maintenance can be awarded for this period.[6] There is no burden of proof on either party in a claim brought under the I(PFD)A 1975.[7] However, it is clear that the evidential burden is upon the claimant to show that reasonable financial provision has not been made.[8]

---

1   *Bheekhun v Williams* [1997] Fam Law 379, CA (foreign domicile).
2   *Shaffer v Glento and Shaffer* [2004] EWHC 188 (Ch).
3   I(PFD)A 1975, s 1(2)(a).
4   Ibid, s 1(2)(b).
5   Ibid, s 3(5).
6   See *Re J (A Minor)* (unreported) 9 December 1991, CA; *Re Collins* [1990] Fam 56; *Re Tomlinson* (unreported) 3 July 1996; *Coughlan and Coughlan v Coughlan* (unreported) 24 November 2000.
7   *Re Ducksbury, Ducksbury v Ducksbury* [1966] 1 WLR 1226; *Re Coventry* [1980] Ch 461, at 474E–F.
8   *Re Crawford* (1983) 4 FLR 273, at 278D; *Williams v Roberts* [1986] 1 FLR 349, at 354C–D; *Davis v Davis* [1993] 1 FLR 54, at 61E; *Re Abram* [1996] 2 FLR 379, at 390D.

10.3 Section 3 of the I(PFD)A 1975 lays down a number of factors to which the court is directed to have regard. An important factor is the size and nature of the net estate of the deceased (which should be valued as at the date of the order for reasonable financial provision[1]). Section 25(1) sets out what constitutes 'net estate'. The size of the estate will be significant because a small estate may not be able to provide a level of maintenance sufficient to justify an application for financial provision and it may affect the parties' eligibility for state benefits, which in turn affects the need for maintenance from the estate. However, applications can be made when '[t]he smallness of the estate neither excludes jurisdiction nor full consideration'.[2] If the net estate at the date of the hearing is nil, the court may look at the size of the estate at death, and consider what caused it to be dissipated in the interim period.[3] The net estate may include a severable share in property in which the deceased had a joint tenancy,[4] as well as money or property forming the subject-matter of a disposition or contract made by the deceased during his lifetime if the disposition or contract was made by the deceased with the intention of defeating an application under the Act.[5] Dispositions falling within s 10 must have been made less than six years before the date of the deceased's death.

CLAIMANTS

10.4 There are six categories of claimant:

(1)   A spouse,[6] which includes a divorced spouse where the deceased has died within 12 months of the decree absolute subject to any provisions found in the applicable matrimonial proceedings order,[7] or judicially separated spouse, or a spouse whose marriage has been annulled. A spouse whose marriage has been the subject of a separation order under the Family Law Act 1996 is treated in the same way as a judicially separated spouse for the purpose of the Act, ie as a 'husband' or 'wife'. The term also includes a person who in good faith entered into a void marriage with the deceased which was not annulled or dissolved before the death of the deceased in a manner recognised under English law unless that person entered into a later marriage before the deceased

---

1   *Re Gale, Gale v Gale* [1966] Ch 236, CA.
2   *Re Clayton* [1966] 1 WLR 971D–F.
3   *Coughlan and Coughlan v Coughlan* (unreported) 24 November 2000.
4   I(PFD)A 1975, s 9.
5   Ibid, ss 10, 11 and 12.
6   Ibid, s 1(1)(a).
7   Ibid, s 14(1).

died.[1] A party to a polygamous marriage is also treated as a spouse of the deceased.[2]

(2) A former spouse who has not remarried (unless he has obtained final orders in ancillary relief proceedings or a compromise out of court relating to both income and capital, in which case a court would generally be reluctant to make an order for provision under the Act and would do so only in exceptional circumstances).[3]

(3) A person living in the same household as the deceased and as the husband or wife of the deceased during the whole of the period of two years ending with the death of the deceased.[4] ?

(4) A child of the deceased (including an adult child),[5] which includes an illegitimate child[6] and a child *en ventre sa mere*.[7]

(5) Any person (not being a child of the deceased) who in the case of any marriage to which the deceased was at any time a party, was treated by the deceased as a child of the family in relation to that marriage.[8]

(6) Any person (not being a person included in the foregoing sections of this paragraph) who immediately before the death of the deceased was being maintained by the deceased, either wholly or partly.[9] Maintained is defined as when 'the deceased, otherwise than for full valuable consideration, was making a substantial contribution in money or money's worth towards the reasonable needs of that person'.

The Civil Partnership Bill (HL53) makes proposals for the inclusion within s 1(1) of same-sex couples whose partnership has been legally registered and to give them the same rights as those that apply to spouses.

---

1 I(PFD)A 1975, s 25(4).
2 Matrimonial Proceedings (Polygamous Marriages) Act 1972; *Re Sehola Surjit Kaur v Glan Kaur* [1978] 3 All ER 385.
3 Ibid, s 1(1)(b). See *Cameron v Treasury Solicitor* [1996] 2 FLR 716, CA; *Benson v Benson* [1996] 1 FLR 692; *Re Fullard* [1982] Fam 42, CA; *Barrass v Harding and Newman* [2001] 1 FLR 138, CA.
4 I(PFD)A 1975, s 1(1A); see also *Re Watson (Deceased)* [1999] 1 FLR 878.
5 Ibid, s 1(1)(c); *Coventry v Coventry* [1980] Ch 461; *affirmed* [1979] 3 All ER 815; *Re Callaghan (Deceased)* [1985] Fam 1; *Re Debenham (Deceased)* [1986] 1 FLR 404; *In re Jennings Deceased* [1994] Ch 286; *Re Goodchild (Deceased) and another* [1996] 1 FLR 591; *Re Hancock (Deceased)* [1998] 2 FLR 346; *Re Pearce (Deceased)* [1998] 2 FLR 705; *Espinosa v Bourke* [1999] 1 FLR 747.
6 Ibid, s 25(1).
7 Ibid.
8 Ibid, s 1(1)(d).
9 Ibid, s 1(1)(e); *Layton v Martin* [1986] 2 FLR 227; *Kourgky v Lusher* (1983) 4 FLR 65; *Sen v Headley* [1991] Ch 425, CA; *Beaumont, Martin v Midland Bank Trust Co* [1980] 1 All ER 266; *Jelley v Iliffe* [1981] Fam 128 applied in *Graham v Murphy* [1997] 1 FLR 860; *Rees v Newberry and the Institute of Cancer Research* [1998] 1 FLR 1041; *Re Dymott* [1980], CA Transcript 1942 (unreported); *Malone v Harrison* [1979] 1 WLR 1353; *Re Haig* [1979] LS Gaz R 476; *Rhodes v Dean* [1996] CLY 555, CA; *Re P* (unreported) (1996); *Re B (Deceased)* [2000] 2 WLR 929, CA, sub nom *Bouette v Rose* [2000] 1 FLR 363.

DEFENDANTS

10.5 The defendants are the testator's personal representatives and any beneficiaries whose beneficial interests may be affected by an order for financial provision. Generally, minor pecuniary and other legatees need not be joined, which ensures that costs are kept on a reasonable footing. Such parties can always be added by the court. Where the beneficiaries are numerous and have the same interest in the proceedings, an application should be made for a representation order.[1] If the beneficiaries are children or patients within the meaning of CPR, r 21.1, the proceedings may be defended on their behalf through a litigation friend.[2] Where the personal representatives have no beneficial interest in the estate, they may seek a direction from the court either that they have no further active role in the proceedings or that the legal representative of the beneficiaries represent them at trial.[3]

JURISDICTION

10.6 An application under I(PFD)A 1975 is governed by CPR, r 57.14 and can be commenced in either the Family or Chancery Division of the High Court or in the county court.[4] Proceedings in the Chancery Division must be issued either out of Chancery Chambers or a Chancery district registry. The procedure for an application is the same in both the High Court and the county court and both courts have unlimited jurisdiction to grant relief under the Act. If the application involves the taking of complicated accounts or disputes about trusts, the Chancery Division may be preferable. Proceedings should commence in the Family Division if there have been previous matrimonial proceedings in that Division and/or the application involves consideration of family law issues such as the validity of a marriage or divorce decree. An application can be transferred from one Division to another by order of the court made in the Division where the application is pending.[5]

10.7 Uncontested or contested matters may be heard by Chancery masters, Family Division district judges, or county court district judges.[6] Where difficult issues of fact or law arise, or questions of jurisdiction, the application

---

[1] CPR, r 19.7.

[2] CPR, r 21.2. The court may make an order that the child be entitled to bring or to defend any claim without the appointment of a litigation friend: CPR, r 21.2(3).

[3] See CPR, PD57, para 15 (personal representative should state this in Section A of acknowledgement of service).

[4] CPR, r 57.15.

[5] CPR, r 30.5.

[6] CPR, r 2.4.

may be referred to a judge, provided the size of the estate warrants such referral.[1]

10.8 Claims of less than £25,000 are generally tried in the county court; claims of more than £50,000 are tried in the High Court unless, having regard to the relevant criteria, the court considers that the case should be tried in the High Court or the county court, respectively.[2] In all cases, the courts should consider the following in deciding whether to transfer an application from one court to another:

(a)   the financial value of the claim and the amount in dispute, if different;
(b)   whether it would be more convenient or fair for hearings (including the trial) to be held in some other court;
(c)   the availability of a judge specialising in the type of claim in question;
(d)   whether the facts, legal issues, remedies or procedures involved are simple or complex;
(e)   the importance of the outcome of the claim to the public in general;
(f)   whether court facilities are inadequate to deal with the disabilities of any party or potential witness.

Applications to transfer can be made by application notice supported by a witness statement or affidavit and a copy of any draft order which the claimant seeks.[3] The application should be made as soon as it becomes apparent that it is necessary or desirable to make it[4] and must be served as soon as possible after it is filed,[5] together with the evidence to be relied upon and any draft order.[6]

VENUE

10.9 CPR, r 57.14 does not give specific directions concerning where applications should be commenced when they are to be brought in the county court. Accordingly, proceedings can be commenced in any county court subject to the power of transfer under CPR Part 30.

---

1   *Practice Note (Inheritance: Family Provision)* [1976] 1 WLR 418, para 6; *Re Beaumont, Martin v Midland Bank Trust Co* [1980] Ch 444, at 460; but see *Re Abram* [1996] 2 FLR 379, at 388H–389A ('the jurisdiction is now comparatively rarely exercised by a judge in open court, but more usually by masters and district judges in chambers').
2   CPR, PD29, para 2.2; High Court and County Courts Jurisdiction Order 1991, SI 1991/724, Art 7.
3   CPR, r 23.7(2) and (3).
4   CPR, PD23, para 2.7.
5   CPR, r 23.7(1)(a).
6   CPR, r 23.7(3).

THE APPLICATION

10.10 An application under I(PFD)A 1975 is made by issuing a <u>Part 8 claim</u> <u>form.</u>[1] The CPR apply to all proceedings under the Act, including those brought in the Family Division, except that the provisions of the Family Proceedings Rules 1991[2] relating to the drawing-up and service of orders apply instead of the provisions in Part 40 and its Practice Direction. Proceedings follow the procedure in CPR Part 8 except as modified by CPR, r 57.16(3)–(5) relating to the written evidence, which must be filed and served by the claimant with the claim form and the time for the defendant to acknowledge service and file written evidence. A hearing date for directions

may be requested at the time the claim form is issued.[3] The claim form should state specifically <u>every relief sought</u>, including permission to bring the application out of time, if necessary, and any orders under ss 9, 10 and 11 of the I(PFD)A 1975. Although the claimant may intend to apply for interim relief, it is not necessary to include this request in the claim form. It is, however, considered by some to be good practice and, in any event, the application for an interim order will be dealt with faster if made in the claim form. The supporting witness statement or affidavit will, accordingly, have to set out the grounds upon which relief is sought. A witness statement or affidavit by the claimant, exhibiting an official copy of the grant of representation and of every testamentary document admitted to proof, must be filed with the court and served with the claim form on every defendant.[4]

10.11 Every claimant must make his own application, although an application by two or more claimants may be made jointly, in which case one claim form may be issued by one solicitor on behalf of all of the claimants. Thereafter, if their interests are in conflict, claimants may appear by separate solicitors or counsel, or in person. At any stage of the proceedings, if it appears to the court that one or more of the claimants ought to be separately represented, the court can adjourn the proceedings for the applicants to obtain separate legal representation.[5]

10.12 The affidavit or witness statement accompanying the claim form should set out the particulars of any known relevant previous proceedings which may be crucial to the decision of whether the application ought to be in the Family Division or Chancery Division, and may result in the court transferring the application to the appropriate division. The claimant should also set out clearly which category of claimant he is. If the applicant is a widow, she

---

[1]   Form N208.
[2]   SI 1991/1247.
[3]   CPR, PD8, para 4.1.
[4]   CPR, r 57.16; PD57, para 16.
[5]   CPR, PD57, para 17.

should attach a copy of the marriage certificate. A divorcee should attach a copy of the decree absolute and any order for ancillary relief. A child should attach a copy of his birth certificate. In all cases, the death certificate must be exhibited, along with an official copy of the grant of representation to the deceased's estate and every testamentary document admitted to proof.[1] Any other matters which the court is directed by the I(PFD)A 1975 to take into consideration must also be addressed in the affidavit or witness statement, which should set out the facts chronologically and in narrative form. The claimant's financial needs, resources and general circumstances should be particularised, along with the history of his relationship with the deceased. It may be helpful to explain why it is believed that the deceased failed to make reasonable financial provision for the claimant.

Bankruptcy of applicant

10.13 A bankrupt may apply for reasonable financial provision under the Act without joining in the trustee because the right to make an application does not vest in the trustee.[2] This is because a mere possibility of an interest reposing in the bankrupt not coupled with an existing right or interest will not pass to the trustee. However, any award will be considered after-acquired property and may be claimed by the trustee accordingly.[3] It follows that it is unlikely that an application by a bankrupt will win favour with the court.[4]

Death of applicant

10.14 If a claimant dies before the hearing, no claim can be made by the claimant's estate because claims under the I(PFD)A 1975 do not survive the death of the claimant.[5]

Applications by claimant who has unlawfully killed the deceased

10.15 The forfeiture rule applies to family provision, so that a person who unlawfully kills another will not succeed in an application for reasonable financial provision out of the deceased's estate.[6] However, the Forfeiture Act 1982 gives the court a discretion not to apply the rule strictly where the claimant is not morally culpable for the death of the deceased so that it would be unjust to deny him a benefit.[7]

---

[1] CPR, r 57.16.

[2] *Williams and Muir Hunter on Bankruptcy* (Sweet & Maxwell, 2003), at paras 3–624; *Ex parte Dever: Re Suse and Sibeth* (1887) 18 QBD 660, CA.

[3] Under s 307 of the Insolvency Act 1986.

[4] See *Davy-Chiesman v Davy-Chiesman* [1984] Fam 48, at 64 and 69; *Wayling v Jones* [1995] 2 FLR 1029 (discussed at first instance).

[5] See *Whytte v Ticehurst* [1986] Fam 64, at 66 and 70; *Re R (Deceased); R v O* [1986] Fam Law 58; *Re Bramwell* [1988] 2 FLR 263; but compare *Smith v Smith (Smith Intervening)* [1992] Fam 69 (where the court allowed the claimant's estate to retain an award representing the wife's property entitlement).

[6] *Re Royse, Royse v Royse* [1985] Fam 22.

[7] *Re K* [1985] Ch 85.

RESPONSE TO APPLICATION

10.16 Every defendant must file and serve on the claimant and any other party an acknowledgement of service[1] and any written evidence relied upon not more than 21 days after service of the claim form on him.[2] When the evidence is lodged, a copy must be served on the claimant and on every defendant who is not represented by the same solicitor.

10.17 The affidavit or witness statement filed by a personal representative must state:

(a)   full particulars of the value of the net estate as set out in s 25(1) of the I(PFD)A 1975 (shortly before the hearing of the application it is usual for the personal representative to give the current value of the net estate in a supplemental affidavit or witness statement);

(b)   the persons or classes of persons beneficially interested in the estate and the names and (unless they are parties to the claim) addresses of all living beneficiaries and the value of their interests in the estate so far as they are known;

(c)   whether any living beneficiary (and if so, his name) is a child or patient within the meaning of CPR, r 21.1(2); and

(d)   any other facts which might affect the exercise of the court's powers under the Act.[3]

10.18 If the personal representative wishes to remain neutral in relation to the claim and agrees to abide by any decision the court may make, he should state this in Section A of the acknowledgement of service form.[4]

10.19 If the personal representative is also a beneficiary, he cannot be compelled to disclose by affidavit his own personal financial position.[5] However, any beneficiary who fails to disclose his financial circumstances may risk an adverse inference by the court. A defendant beneficiary can be pressured to give evidence by being called as a witness, by obtaining disclosure against him and by being served a witness summons to produce documents.[6] Defendant beneficiaries should particularise the reasons why the deceased made the relevant dispositions and all other material facts which the court should take into account.

---

[1]   Practice Form N210.

[2]   CPR, r 57.16(4).

[3]   CPR, PD57, para 16.

[4]   CPR, PD57, para 15.

[5]   See *Re Clark* [1981] CLY 2884; *Wynne v Wynne* [1980] 1 WLR 69.

[6]   CPR, Part 34. See *Senior v Holdsworth ex parte Independent Television News Limited* [1976] QB 23; *Morgan v Morgan* [1977] Fam 122; *Williams v Williams* [1988] QB 161; *Khanna v Lovell White Durrant* [1995] 1 WLR 121.

10.20 The court shall have regard to the following matters:

(a)   the financial resources and financial needs which the applicant has or is likely to have in the foreseeable future;

(b)   the financial resources and financial needs which any other applicant for an order under s 2 of the I(PFD)A 1975 has or is likely to have in the foreseeable future;

(c)   the financial resources and financial needs which any beneficiary of the estate of the deceased has or is likely to have in the foreseeable future;

(d)   any obligations and responsibilities which the deceased had towards any applicant for an order under s 2 or towards any beneficiary of the estate of the deceased;

(e)   the size and nature of the net estate of the deceased;

(f)   any physical or mental disability of any applicant for an order under s 2 or any beneficiary of the estate of the deceased;

(g)   any other matter, including the conduct of the applicant or any other person, which in the circumstances of the case the court may consider relevant.[1]

10.21 For applications made by the husband or wife, or former husband or wife who has not re-married, the court shall also have regard to:

'(a)   the age of the applicant and the duration of the marriage;

(b)   the contribution made by the applicant to the welfare of the family of the deceased, including any contribution made by looking after the home or caring for the family.'[2]

Where an application is made by a wife or husband of the deceased, the court will look at the provision which the claimant might reasonably have expected to receive if the marriage had been terminated by divorce rather than by death (although in divorce proceedings the court will take into account the financial position of each spouse, so the situation is not wholly analogous).[3]

10.22 Where an application is made by a claimant who had lived for at least 2 years before the death of the deceased as the husband or wife of the deceased, the court shall have regard to:

'(a)   the age of the applicant and the length of the period during which the applicant lived as the husband or wife of the deceased and in the same household as the deceased;

[1]   I(PFD)A 1975, s 3(1).
[2]   Ibid, s 3(2).
[3]   See *McNulty v McNulty and Anor* (unreported) 30 January 2002 (applying *White v White* [2001] 2 All ER 43).

(b)   the contribution made by the applicant to the welfare of the family of the deceased, including any contribution made by looking after the home or the caring of the family.'[1]

10.23 Where applications are made by children of the deceased or by any other person not being a child but who was treated by the deceased as a child of the family, the court shall have regard:

'(a)   to whether the deceased had assumed any responsibility for the applicant's maintenance and, if so, to the extent to which and the basis upon which the deceased assumed that responsibility and to the length of time for which the deceased discharged that responsibility;

(b)   to whether in assuming and discharging that responsibility the deceased did so knowing that the applicant was not his own child;

(c)   to the liability of any other person to maintain the applicant.'[2]

10.24 As to all other claimants, the court will take note of the extent to which and the basis upon which the deceased assumed responsibility for maintenance of the claimant and for what length of time.[3]

TIME-LIMITS

10.25 All applications must be made within 6 months of the date on which a grant of representation is taken out.[4] A claimant will not be able to rely on the timely filing of an application of another claimant as stopping the time-limits from running.[5] However, it is likely that the court will extend the time for filing an application in such circumstances when another claimant has filed his application on time. The 6-month limitation period runs from and includes the day on which the grant of representation was taken out.[6] It is possible to make an application under I(PFD)A 1975 before the grant of representation.[7]

10.26 The time-limit applies to all claimants, including those under a disability. However, in deciding whether to extend the time the courts will give great weight to the fact that a claimant is under a disability.[8]

---

1   I(PFD)A 1975, s 3(2A).
2   Ibid, s 3(3).
3   Ibid, s 3(4).
4   Ibid, s 4.
5   *Re Trott* [1958] 1 WLR 604.
6   *Miller v DeCourcey* [1969] 1 WLR 583.
7   *In re Searle* [1949] Ch 73. See also *Re McBroom* [1992] 2 FLR 49, where Eastham J came to the opposite conclusion, with regret; and *Re Parker's Estate, Parker v Gibson* [1999] NI 315, where *Re McBroom* was considered.
8   *Re C* [1995] 2 FLR 24; *Re Trott* [1958] 2 All ER 296.

10.27 In order to start the 6-month limitation period running, the grant of representation must be a <u>general grant</u> not limited to particular property,[1] although it can be limited in duration but giving the personal representatives full powers to distribute. It is unclear whether grants limited for a particular purpose, such as a grant *ad collingenda bona* or *ad litem*, will be left out of account in determining when representation was first taken out. In as much as such grants do not generally permit distribution of the estate, they will not generally start time running. The position in respect of grants *ad litem* was considered in *Re Johnson*[2] by Latey J, who held that a grant *ad litem* to enable proceedings to be taken in a personal injuries action did not start the time running for a family provision claim. However, it is possible that a grant *ad litem* to defend a family provision claim will start the limitation period running. Grants limited to settled land or trust property are not counted for purposes of s 4 of the I(PFD)A 1975, and a grant limited to the real estate or personal estate does not start time running unless a grant limited to the remainder of the estate is made at the same time or has been made previously.[3] In the case of a grant of probate which is revoked, time starts running from the date of the second grant of probate or letters of administration. If no grant has been taken out, the claimant may apply for an order appointing an administrator under s 116 of the SCA 1981, and time will start running from the date of the order.[4] Alternatively, the claimant can apply to issue a citation to accept a grant if the claimant would himself be entitled to a grant in the event of the person cited renouncing his right to the grant.[5] If there is a will, the claimant can apply to issue a citation to propound the will.[6]

10.28 The court has a discretion under s 4 of the I(PFD)A 1975 to extend the time-limit for making an application under the Act. Guidelines for the court's exercise of its discretion to extend the time were laid down in 1980 by Megarry V-C in *Re Salmon, Coard v National Westminster Bank*.[7]

(1)   The discretion is wide and unfettered and must be exercised judicially and in accordance with what is 'just and proper'.

(2)   'The onus lies on the plaintiff to establish sufficient grounds for taking the case out of the general rule, and depriving those who are protected by it of its benefits ... [t]he applicant must make out a substantial case for it being just and proper for the court to exercise its statutory discretion to extend time.'

---

[1]   By analogy to I(PFD)A 1975, s 23.
[2]   [1987] CLY 3882.
[3]   I(PFD)A 1975, s 23.
[4]   *In the Estate of Simpson; In the Estate of Gunning* [1936] P 40.
[5]   Non-contentious Probate Rules 1987, SI 1987/2024, r 47.
[6]   Ibid, r 48.
[7]   [1981] Ch 167.

(3)   The court must consider how promptly the claimant acted and the circumstances which resulted in the delay.

(4)   Regard must be had to whether the defendant was notified that an application would be made and, if so, when.

(5)   Regard must be had to whether the estate has been distributed. Megarry V-C stated that the court could go behind the distribution and ascertain whether any of the beneficiaries had actually changed their position.

(6)   Regard must be had to whether refusal to extend the time-limit will effect any claim which the claimant may have against a third party, such as his legal representatives.

(7)   The court will consider whether or not negotiations had been taking place within the time-limit and, if not, whether the defendants have not taken the point that any application would be out of time.

10.29 The guidelines in *Re Salmon* are still the starting point in pursuing an application to extend the time-limit. Nevertheless, since *Re Salmon* the courts have become progressively more relaxed about extending time and it is now rare for an extension to be refused merely because it is out of time.[1] More recently, the issues of prejudice to the defendants and whether the claimant has an arguable case have become central in deciding whether to extend the time-limit. It has been held that the weakness of a claimant's case should not be a factor weighing against the applicant.[2] Conversely, it has been held that the likelihood of success is a reason for extending the time-limit.[3] The reason for the delay in filing an application is still important.[4] If there is a good reason for the delay, the court may give permission for an extension regardless of whether the defendants will be prejudiced.[5] Errors and mistakes by legal advisers are sometimes reasons to grant an extension of time, usually when coupled with other factors.[6] Delays in getting public funding are also generally an acceptable excuse, although where there has been delay on the part of the Legal Services Commission, it may be advisable for the applicants to start proceedings with their own resources or via means of an emergency public funding certificate.[7]

Applying for permission to make application out of time

10.30 An application for permission to apply out of time should be included in the Part 8 claim form as a separate head of relief. The supporting witness

---

[1]   See *Stock v Brown* [1994] 1 FLR 840; *Polackova v Sobolewski* (unreported) 28 October 1985, CA; *Re C* [1995] 2 FLR 24; *Re Gonin* [1977] 2 All ER 720, at 735–736; *Re Longley, Longley and Longley v Longley* [1981] CLY 2885; *Re Ruttie* [1970] 1 WLR 89; *Re Denis* [1981] 2 All ER 140.

[2]   See *Polackova v Sobolewski* (unreported) 28 October 1985, CA.

[3]   See *Re C* [1995] 2 FLR 24; *Escritt v Escritt* (1982) 3 FLR 280.

[4]   See *Baker v Fear* (unreported) 12 November 1993, CA; *Re Chittock (Dec'd); Chittock v Stevens* (unreported) 24 February 2000.

[5]   See *Smith v Loosley* (unreported) 18 June 1986, CA; *Stock v Brown* [1994] 1 FLR 840.

[6]   In *Re Chittock (Dec'd); Chittock v Stephens* (unreported) 24 February 2000.

[7]   *Re Salmon, Coard v National Westminster Bank* [1981] Ch 167, at 177G–H.

statement or affidavit should be a wholly complete recitation of why the application should be granted.[1] In addition to filing the application as quickly as possible, the defendants should be informed that proceedings are or will be commenced, and should be invited to undertake not to distribute pending determination of the application for permission to apply out of time. If they refuse, an application for an interlocutory injunction restraining distribution may be made and it may be prudent to register in the Land Registry a pending land action as a land charge.[2]

APPLICATION FOR ORDER UNDER I(PFD)A 1975, SECTION 9

10.31 Section 9 of the I(PFD)A 1975 provides for the making of an order directing that the severable share of a deceased's property held on a joint tenancy forms part of the 'net estate' for purposes of making a reasonable financial provision order. It applies not only to real property but also, inter alia, to joint bank accounts and insurance policies. The time-limit for an application under s 9 is strict: the deceased's severable share cannot be made part of the net estate if an application for reasonable financial provision is made more than 6 months from the date when representation was first taken out. There is no provision for extending the time-limit. An application under s 9 can be made before the application for reasonable financial provision, and it is possible for a court to make an order that the severable share forms part of the net estate without making an order later in respect of financial provision.[3] It is advisable to make an application under s 9 as early as possible to avoid the possibility that the survivor dissipates the formerly jointly held property because s 9 does not establish liability for anything done before an application is made.[4]

10.32 Once an order is made directing that the severable share of a deceased's jointly held property is part of the net estate, the order should be registered as an order affecting the relevant property. Before the order is made, it is possible to register a charge as a pending land action concerning a claim where there is no pre-existing proprietary interest.[5] Whether a claim for an undivided share of the proceeds of sale of land in respect of land beneficially owned is a 'pending land action' is less clear.[6] However, there is an argument that such a

---

[1] *Practice Note (Inheritance: Family Provision)* [1976] 1 WLR 418, para 3.

[2] Land Charges Act 1972, s 5(1)(a); *Whittingham v Whittingham* [1979] Fam 1; *Sowerby v Sowerby* (1982) 44 P&CR 192; *Perez-Adamson v Perez-Rivas* [1987] Fam 89.

[3] I(PFD)A 1975, s 9(1) and (3). See also discussion in *Tyler's Family Provision* (Butterworths, 1997), at p 302.

[4] Ibid, s 9(3).

[5] Land Charges Act 1972, s 5; Land Registration Act 2002, s 87; *Whittingham v Whittingham* [1979] Fam 1.

[6] See discussion in *Tyler's Family Provision* (Butterworths, 1997), at p 303.

claim may be registered in view of the general trend to hold an interest behind a trust for sale of land as an interest in land.[1]

Conduct of estate pending application under I(PFD)A 1975

10.33 There is a general duty not to distribute the estate pending an application under the I(PFD)A 1975. Hence, personal representatives should not ordinarily distribute for the first 6 months after the grant of representation in order to avoid conflict with a claim under the Act. If they do so, they may be held personally liable. In certain cases, however, following the general rule can result in hardship. The case of *Re Ralphs*[2] established guidelines for distribution of part of an estate before the 6-month period has expired:

(a)   a claimant who has also received a benefit under a will or who is entitled on intestacy should ordinarily be paid his entitlement pending his application for supplemental provision;

(b)   a legatee of a small legacy in comparison to the size of the residue or a legatee who has a strong claim on the deceased and is in need should be paid.

The personal representatives should decide what payments ought to be made and then obtain the consent of the claimant and beneficiaries likely to be affected. In the absence of consent, an application to court for permission to make a payment should be made. The court may order the party unreasonably withholding the consent to pay the costs of the application.[3] After the 6-month period has expired without an application being made, the personal representatives are free to distribute without incurring any personal liability.[4] Nevertheless, it is possible that the distributed property may be recovered from the beneficiaries, if needed, by a successful late application.[5]

STRIKING OUT APPLICATIONS

10.34 Applications under the I(PFD)A 1975 which disclose no reasonable basis upon which they may succeed may be struck out by the court either of its own initiative or upon application by a defendant to the claim.[6] A claim will be struck out only in the most obvious of cases and where there is no doubt that the applicant will be unsuccessful.[7]

---

[1]   See discussion in *Tyler's Family Provision* (Butterworths, 1997), at p 303. See also *Williams & Glyn's Bank v Boland* [1981] AC 487.

[2]   [1968] 1 WLR 1522.

[3]   See *Re Ralphs* [1968] 1 WLR 1522, at 1525.

[4]   I(PFD)A 1975, s 20(1).

[5]   Ibid, s 20(1).

[6]   CPR, r 3.4.

[7]   *Jelley v Iliffe* [1981] Fam 128, at 140.

INTERIM AWARDS

10.35 The court has power to make an <u>interim award</u> provided the following three cumulative requirements are met:[1]

(a) 'the applicant is in <u>immediate need of financial assistance</u>, but [that] it is not yet possible to determine what order (if any) should be made';[2]

(b) 'property forming part of the net estate of the deceased is or <u>can be made available</u> to meet the need of the applicant';[3] (in *Barnsley v Ward*[4] the Court of Appeal held that property could be made available if it could <u>be easily sold</u>, regardless of whether it would increase in value if retained in the estate); and

(c) it would be a <u>proper exercise of the court's discretion</u> to order an interim order for provision.[5]

The application should be made on a CPR application notice, supported by an affidavit or witness statement and the procedure set out in CPR Part 25 should be followed. In considering an order, the court must have regard to the matters specified in s 3 of the I(PFD)A 1975, 'so far as the urgency of the case admits'.[6] The court has the power to order the payment of a lump sum as well as periodical payments,[7] but does not have the power to order that an applicant may live in a particular residence or that personal representatives may purchase property for the applicant's use.[8] The court can order that the payments continue up until the substantive hearing.[9] The court also has power to vary the order.[10] The interim order is almost invariably made 'subject to such conditions and restrictions, if any, as the court may impose,'[11] which will invariably include the condition that any sum paid is to be regarded as paid on account of any provision made under s 2.[12] The usual order for an interim award will provide that the applicant will not have to repay the estate if no order under s 2 of the I(PFD)A 1975 is ultimately made. In *Barnsley v Ward*,[13] it was said that the interim order holds 'the situation as reasonably and fairly as possible pending final determination'.

---

[1] I(PFD)A 1975, s 5(1).
[2] Ibid, s 5(1)(a).
[3] Ibid, s 5(1)(b).
[4] (Unreported) 18 January 1980.
[5] I(PFD)A 1975, s 5(1).
[6] Ibid, s 5(3).
[7] Ibid, s 5(1); *Barnsley v Ward* (unreported) 18 January 1980, CA; *Re Besterman* [1984] Ch 458, at 463A–C.
[8] *Tyler's Family Provision* (Butterworths, 1997), at p 373.
[9] I(PFD)A 1975, s 5(1), although in *Re Besterman* the interim order carried forth until the final judgment.
[10] *Barnsley v Ward* (unreported) 18 January 1980, CA.
[11] I(PFD)A 1975, s 5(1).
[12] Ibid, s 5(4).
[13] (Unreported) 18 January 1980, CA.

PRESERVING PROPERTY PENDING HEARING OF APPLICATION

10.36 The court can exercise its discretion to preserve specific assets pending determination of an application for reasonable financial provision.[1] The claimant must show that he has an arguable case for being awarded financial provision which consists of the particular item of property and that it would be proper for the court to exercise its discretion to make the order. Consideration must be had to the position of the beneficiaries, the creditors of the estate and the personal representatives' duties in administering the estate.[2] Pursuant to s 2, the court can order the purchase of a home for the occupation of the claimant pending the hearing of the main application.[3] Conditions may be imposed by the court in exercising its jurisdiction to make such an order. For example, the claimant may be ordered to pay the outgoings on the property or to give an undertaking in damages which may be secured.[4]

OFFERS TO COMPROMISE

10.37 An offer to settle may be made in accordance with CPR Part 36. The offer must be made in writing, relate to the whole or part of the claim, state whether it takes into account any counterclaim, and state whether it includes interest and, if it does not, give the details relating to interest.[5] Part 36 offers made more than 21 days before the hearing should remain capable of being accepted for 21 days.[6] After the 21-day period has expired, the parties are still entitled to agree, but the liability to costs must also be agreed; if they are not, the court must give permission for the offer to be accepted.[7] If the offer is made less than 21 days before the trial, the same provisions in regard to acceptance apply.[8] Any offer may be withdrawn with no consequential cost implications, provided it has not been accepted or more than 21 days have passed since the offer was made.[9] An offer is accepted when notice of its acceptance is received by the offeror.[10]

10.38 The costs implications of CPR Part 36 payments are as follows:

---

[1]   I(PFD)A 1975, s 2(1)(c); *Sobesto v Farren* [1981] Conv 224, CA.
[2]   *Sobesto v Farren* [1981] Conv 224, CA.
[3]   *Barry v Barry* [1992] Fam 140.
[4]   See discussion in *Tyler's Family Provision* (Butterworths, 1997), at p 376.
[5]   CPR, r 36.6(2).
[6]   CPR, r 36.11.
[7]   CPR, r 36.11(2)(b).
[8]   CPR, r 36.11(2)(a).
[9]   CPR, r 36.5.
[10] CPR, r 36.8.

(1) When a defendant's offer is accepted without the necessity for sanction by the court, the claimant will get his costs up to the date of service of the notice of acceptance, payable on the standard basis if not agreed,[1] out of the estate.

(2) Where a claimant's offer is accepted, the claimant gets costs up to the date of service of the defendant's notice of acceptance[2] out of the estate.

(3) If the claimant proceeds to hearing and fails to better the offer, he will be ordered to pay the costs incurred by the defendant after the latest date on which the offer could have been accepted without permission of the court.[3]

(4) If the claimant betters his own offer, he gets costs plus interest on the whole or part of the award at the rate of up to 10% above base rate for some or all of the period starting with the latest date on which the defendant could have accepted.[4]

10.39 Personal representatives have no power to compromise claims under the Act unless the beneficiaries affected give them actual authority or unless the court makes an order.[5]

10.40 If an offer is accepted, the agreement can be contained in a simple deed of family arrangement provided all parties are known and *sui juris*, and a child or patient is not involved. If a court order is made, it can either be in a consent order or an order staying further proceedings on agreed terms in the Tomlin form. If the interests of a child and/or patient are affected, approval of the court will be necessary and the procedure as outlined in CPR Part 21 and Part 8 must be followed. If charities are involved, the charitable trustees or the corporate charity (if its memorandum or articles permit) have power to compromise a claim.[6] The Charity Commissioners and Attorney-General, if party to the proceedings, can authorise a compromise.[7] Every final order embodying the terms of a compromise made in proceedings in the Chancery Division must contain a direction that a memorandum of the order will be endorsed on or permanently annexed to the probate or letters of administration, and a copy of the order will be sent to the Principal Registry of the Family Division with the relevant grant of probate or letters of administration for endorsement even if the order is not, strictly speaking, an order under I(PFD)A 1975.

---

[1]   CPR, r 36.13.
[2]   CPR, r 36.14.
[3]   CPR, r 36.20.
[4]   CPR, r 36.21.
[5]   CPR, r 19.7A.
[6]   Trustee Act 1925, s 15; *Re Earl of Strafford* [1980] Ch 28.
[7]   Tudor *Charities* (Sweet & Maxwell, 9th edn, 2003), at p 400.

ORDERS

10.41 The court can make the following orders.

(1)   An order for the claimant to receive periodical payments out of the net estate of the deceased for such term as may be specified in the order.[1] If the order is for payment of a fixed sum, this is paid out of income, with a power to resort to capital if the income is insufficient[2] and any excess should go to the beneficiaries. Necessary details regarding the fund and the periodical payments should be in consequential directions given by the court.

(2)   An order for the payment to the claimant out of the estate of a lump sum of such amount as may be so specified. This will come out of income, with a power to resort to capital if the income is not enough. The court can order the lump sum to be paid by instalments and this can be varied later. The court should give directions as to apply interest.[3]

(3)   An order for the transfer to the claimant of such property comprised in the estate as may be so specified. Property transfer orders cannot thereafter be varied.[4]

(4)   An order for the settlement for the benefit of the claimant of such property comprised in the estate as may be specified.[5]

(5)   An order for the acquisition out of property comprised in the estate of such property as may be specified and for the transfer of the property so acquired to the claimant or for the settlement thereof for his benefit.[6]

(6)   An order varying an ante-nuptial or post-nuptial settlement (including such a settlement made by will) made on the parties to a marriage to which the deceased was one of the parties, the variation being for the benefit of the surviving party to that marriage, or any child of the marriage, or any person who was treated by the deceased as a child of the family in relation to that marriage.[7]

It should be noted that courts do not usually make awards of periodical payments, and generally make awards of lump sum payments when making orders for reasonable financial provision. Lump sums are particularly suitable where the claimant is a spouse seeking a 'just share', where a claimant seeks

---

[1]   I(PFD)A 1975, s 2(1)(a).
[2]   *Re Gale* [1966] Ch 236, at 242B–C.
[3]   I(PFD)A 1975, s 2(1)(b).
[4]   Ibid, s 2(1)(c).
[5]   Ibid, s 2(1)(d).
[6]   Ibid, s 2(1)(e).
[7]   Ibid, s 2(1)(f); see also *Brooks v Brooks* [1996] AC 375; *T v T* [1998] 1 FLR 1072; and *Burrow v Burrow* [1999] 1 FLR 508.

provision for a specific purpose (eg the purchase of a home or to go abroad permanently), where maintenance will include an element of capital for future contingencies, where the estate cannot satisfy all claims upon it, or where the claimant's claim is restitutionary and based on a specific sum incurred in detrimental reliance upon the request of the deceased.

10.42 When the needs of the claimant and the beneficiaries are unclear at the time of the hearing, although it is obvious that financial provision for the claimant is necessary, it is possible to argue for the application to be stood over until a specified date or event.[1] Alternatively, the court can make an order for financial provision, but impose conditions which might take effect upon subsequent events.[2] The use of trusts can be an effective tool to respond to future events.

10.43 After any order other than an order under s 15 of the I(PFD)A 1975 or an order dismissing an application has been drawn up and sealed, the court will retain the grant of probate or letters of administration and send it, with an office copy of the order, to the Principal Registry of the Family Division, where a memorandum of the order is endorsed on, or permanently annexed to, the grant.

COSTS

10.44 Generally, the costs of the personal representatives are paid out of the estate and assessed on an indemnity basis.[3] Defendant beneficiaries are not allowed costs out of the estate automatically.[4] The usual rule is that costs follow the event, but there are numerous cases where costs do not strictly follow the event – usually because the application and opposition had some merit or an arguable point of law was involved,[5] or one or more of the parties has a disability.[6] If the claimant succeeds but is awarded less than the whole of the estate, the usual order is that all parties' costs come out of the estate on a standard basis, except for the personal representatives who have their costs assessed on an indemnity basis. It appears that if the claimant gets the entire estate, the beneficiaries will have to pay the costs personally.[7]

---

[1]   *Re Bateman* (1941) 85 SJ 454; *Re Franks* [1948] Ch 62; *Re Rodwell* [1970] Ch 726.
[2]   *Re Doring* [1955] 1 WLR 1217; *Re Blanch* [1967] 1 WLR 987; *Re Mason* (1975) Fam Law 124; *Re Debenham* [1986] 1 FLR 404.
[3]   *Alsop Wilkinson v Neary* [1995] 1 All ER 431.
[4]   Ibid.
[5]   *Re Dorgan* [1948] Ch 366; *Cameron v Treasury Solicitor* [1996] 2 FLR 716.
[6]   *Re Watkins* [1949] 1 All ER 695.
[7]   *Millward v Shenton* [1972] 1 WLR 711; *Re Bayliss* (unreported) 9 December 1977.

VARYING THE ORDER

10.45 An application to vary an order for periodical payments may be made by the claimant[1] or any person who could have made an application for financial provision.[2] Additionally, the personal representatives, trustees of any relevant property or any beneficiary of the estate can make an application to vary or discharge the order or suspend or revive any provision of the order.[3] No form of order other than for periodical payments may be varied.[4] In considering the application, the court will look at all the circumstances of the case, including any change of circumstances and any turn of events since the hearing of the original application.

---

[1]   I(PFD)A 1975, s 6(1); *Fricker v Personal Representatives of Fricker* (1982) 3 FLR 228.
[2]   Ibid, s 6(5)(a).
[3]   Ibid, s 6(5)(b), (c) and (d).
[4]   Ibid, s 6(1); *Fricker v Personal Representatives of Fricker* (1982) 3 FLR 228.

Chapter 11

CHARITIES

Richard Wilson

INTRODUCTION

11.1 Charities are involved in and affected by a wide range of legal proceedings. When dealing with litigation involving charities, the first step is to ascertain whether the proceedings in question are 'charity proceedings' or whether they are simply other proceedings which happen to involve a charity, since specific procedural rules apply in relation to 'charity proceedings'.[1]

CHARITY PROCEEDINGS

Definition of 'charity proceedings'

11.2 'Charity proceedings' are proceedings in any court in England or Wales brought under the court's jurisdiction with respect to charities, or brought under the court's jurisdiction with respect to trusts in relation to the administration of a trust for charitable purposes'.[2] This includes all proceedings seeking relief in the administration of a charitable trust.[3] The following are examples of 'charity proceedings':

(a)   an application by charity trustees for directions as to their duties in the administration of a charity;

(b)   an application for the appointment, removal or replacement of charity trustees;

(c)   an application for a scheme;

(d)   an application for administration of a charitable trust by the court;

(e)   a *Beddoe* order authorising the trustees of a charitable trust to bring or defend proceedings.[4]

---

[1]   Charities Act 1993 (CA 1993), s 33; CPR, Part 64 and CPR, PD64.

[2]   CA 1993, s 33(8).

[3]   *Holme v Guy* (1877) 5 ChD 901.

[4]   *Re Beddoe* [1893] Ch 547, CA; see Chapter 8 for a discussion of the procedure for obtaining a *Beddoe* order.

11.3 The following types of proceedings have been held *not* to be 'charity proceedings':

(a) proceedings to determine whether a gift or legacy creates a charitable trust;[1]

(b) proceedings in relation to an institution established under the laws of a foreign legal system, as such an institution is not a 'charity' even where all its activities are carried out in the United Kingdom;[2]

(c) proceedings brought by or against a charity in relation to common law rights with third parties, eg actions to recover possession of land, for breach of contract or in tort;[3]

(d) matters relating to the administration of an exempt charity.

Procedural matters relating to other proceedings concerning charities are dealt with below.[4]

Jurisdiction

11.4 The High Court is the usual forum for charity proceedings, and the appropriate division of the High Court for such proceedings is the Chancery Division. Whilst CPR Part 64 contains no specific replacement for RSC Ord 108, r 2 (which expressly assigned charity proceedings to the Chancery Division), the Chancery Division is clearly the appropriate division of the High Court for such matters. Furthermore, an application to the court for leave to commence charity proceedings must be made to a judge of the Chancery Division.[5]

11.5 Where proceedings involve a trust for charitable purposes, it is theoretically possible for charity proceedings in relation to it to be commenced in the county court, provided the value of the trust fund does not exceed the current county court limit[6] of £30,000.[7] However, it is extremely rare for such proceedings to be brought in the county court, and the High Court will almost invariably be a far more appropriate forum.

Claimants in charity proceedings

11.6 Charity proceedings may only be commenced by the following persons:

---

1 *Hauxwell v Barton-upon-Humber Urban District Council* [1974] Ch 432; *Re Shum's Trusts* (1904) 91 LT 192.
2 *Gaudiya Mission v Brahmachary* [1998] Ch 341; *Camille and Henry Dreyfus Foundation Inc v IRC* [1954] Ch 672, CA.
3 *British Diabetic Association v Diabetic Society of Great Britain* [1995] 4 All ER 812, ChD.
4 At **11.25–11.45**.
5 CA 1993, s 33(5).
6 County Courts Act 1984, s 23(b)(i).
7 County Courts Jurisdiction Order 1981, SI 1981/1123.

(a)   the Charity Commissioners;[1]
(b)   the Attorney-General;[2]
(c)   the charity itself[3] (provided it is a charitable company and therefore has legal personality);
(d)   any of the charity trustees[4] (being the persons(s) having the general control and management of the administration of a charity);[5]
(e)   any person interested in the charity;[6]
(f)   in the case of a local charity, any two or more inhabitants of the area of the charity.[7]

11.7   The Charity Commissioners may commence charity proceedings of their own motion, but their powers are exercisable only with the agreement of the Attorney-General on each occasion.[8]

11.8   A 'person interested in the charity' generally means a person with some good reason for commencing proceedings concerning the due administration of a charity in which he has an interest which is materially greater than, or different from, that possessed by an ordinary member of the public.[9] In *Re Hampton Fuel Allotment Charity*[10] the Court of Appeal held that the Richmond Borough Council was a 'person interested' in a charity, which had been established for the purposes of relieving hardship or distress in the 'ancient town of Hampton' (which was entirely within the borough of Richmond), as the council was also concerned with the relief of the need, hardship or distress of the people living within its area of administration, and consequently its interests and those of the charity were closely linked. Accordingly, the council had a greater interest than an ordinary member of the public. In *Scott v The National Trust*[11] the plaintiffs were tenant farmers and members of hunts aggrieved by the defendant charity's decision to ban stag hunting on its land. The court held that as the plaintiffs could be considered partners of the charity in the management of the land in question, they had an interest materially greater than or different from that of ordinary members of the public, and therefore a sufficient interest to entitle them to commence charity proceedings.

11.9   A 'local charity' is defined as:

---

[1]   CA 1993, s 32.
[2]   Ibid, s 33(6).
[3]   CA 1993, s 33(1).
[4]   Ibid, s 33(1).
[5]   Ibid, s 97(1).
[6]   Ibid, s 33(1).
[7]   Ibid, s 33(1).
[8]   Ibid, s 32(5).
[9]   *Re Hampton Fuel Allotment Charity* [1989] Ch 484 CA.
[10]   Ibid.
[11]   [1997] 2 All ER 705, ChD.

'… in relation to any area, a charity established for purposes which are by their nature or by the trusts of the charity directed wholly or mainly to the benefit of that area or of part of it.'[1]

Defendants to charity proceedings

11.10 It is a specific requirement of the Practice Direction to CPR Part 64 that the Attorney-General be joined as a party to all charity proceedings save for those commenced by the Charity Commissioners.[2] Any document required or authorised to be served on the Charity Commissioners or the Attorney-General must be served on the Treasury Solicitor in accordance with CPR, Sch 1 RSC Ord 77, r 4(1).[3]

Other specific rules in relation to joinder of parties

11.11 Many of the claims which are within the definition of 'charity proceedings' are also claims for the determination of questions arising in the execution of a trust, and therefore claims to which Section I of CPR 64 applies.[4] In such cases, CPR, r 64.4 contains specific procedural rules in relation to the inclusion of parties to the claim, which apply in addition to the rules on charity proceedings. All trustees must be parties to the claim.[5] If the claim is brought by the trustees, any of them who does not consent to being a claimant must be joined as a defendant.[6] The claimant(s) may also make parties to the claim any persons with an interest under the trust, whom it is appropriate to make parties having regard to the nature of the order sought.[7] In the case of a charitable trust this provision should not be taken as a suggestion that the claimant should join a vast number of persons who benefit from the charitable trust: their interests are normally represented by the Attorney-General, who, as explained previously, must be joined as a party to charity proceedings.[8]

Requirement for authorisation or leave to commence charity proceedings

11.12 Subject to two specific exceptions (see **11.13** and **11.14**), the authorisation of the Charity Commissioners is required before any charity

proceedings relating to a charity (other than an exempt charity) may be

---

1   CA 1993, s 96(1).
2   CPR, PD64, para 7. Section 32(4) of the CA 1993 prohibits any rule of law or practice from requiring the Attorney-General to be a party to proceedings commenced by the Charity Commissioners in exercise of their powers under s 32.
3   CPR, PD64, para 8.
4   CPR, r 64.2(a)(ii).
5   CPR, r 64.4(a).
6   CPR, r 64.4(b).
7   CPR, r 64.4(c).
8   See **11.10**.

'entertained or proceeded with in any court'.[1] However, authorisation is not required for the taking of proceedings in a pending claim, or the bringing of an appeal.[2] Therefore, if funds have been paid into court under a statutory provision, there is no need for consent to be sought before making an application to the court asking it to deal with the fund.[3]

11.13 The first exception is where the proceedings in question are commenced by either the Charity Commissioners or the Attorney-General.[4]

11.14 The second exception is where a judge of the Chancery Division has made an order giving leave to bring proceedings.[5] Such an application may be made only if the authorisation of the Charity Commissioners has been sought and refused. Therefore, it is not open to an applicant simply to apply to the court in the first instance, rather than asking the Charity Commissioners. If an application is made before any application to the Charity Commissioners it will either be stayed whilst the applicant seeks the authorisation of the Charity Commissioners, or struck out.[6] The procedure concerning applications to the court for leave is dealt with at **11.17–11.23**.

11.15 If charity proceedings are commenced without the requisite authorisation from the Charity Commissioners or the leave of the court, they are liable to be stayed pending the obtaining of such authorisation or leave, or struck out.

Application for authorisation from Charity Commissioners

11.16 There is no formal procedure for an application under s 33(2) of the Charities Act 1993 (CA 1993) for the Charity Commissioners' authorisation for the commencement of charity proceedings. An application usually takes the form of a letter setting out the details of the charity in question, the proposed claimant's position in relation to the charity (in particular the basis on which the proposed claimant asserts that he has the requisite standing to bring charity proceedings in accordance with s 33(1) of the CA 1993), and the basis of the proposed proceedings (including the facts and circumstances that have led the proposed claimant to conclude that it is necessary to bring charity proceedings). The application should be sent to the following address: The Secretary, The Charity Commission, Harmsworth House, 13–15 Bouverie Street, London EC4Y 8DP, and should be accompanied by a proposed notice of appeal. In the absence of special reasons for doing so, the Commissioners are prohibited by statute from giving their authorisation for the taking of

---

[1]   CA 1993, s 33(2).
[2]   Ibid, s 33(4).
[3]   *Re Lister's Hospital* (1855) 6 De GM&G 184.
[4]   CA 1993, s 33(6).
[5]   Ibid, s 33(5).
[6]   Under CPR, r 3.4.

charity proceedings if they consider that the case may be dealt with under the powers conferred on them by the CA 1993 (save for the powers under s 32).[1] If, on an application for authorisation for the commencement of charity proceedings under s 33, the Charity Commissioners consider that it is desirable for legal proceedings to be taken in respect of a charity (other than an exempt charity) or its property or affairs, and that those proceedings should be brought by the Attorney-General, they are required to inform the Attorney-General and send him such statements and particulars as they think necessary to explain the matter.[2] Therefore, the Charity Commissioners may refuse to give their authorisation to the party who has applied for it, but proceedings on the same issues will be brought by the Attorney-General after the Charity Commissioners have referred the matter to him.

Application to court for permission

11.17 Within 21 days after the refusal by the Charity Commissioners to authorise the bringing of charity proceedings under s 33(2) of the CA 1993, the proposed claimant may make an application to the Chancery Division of the High Court for leave to commence charity proceedings.[3]

11.18 The application must be made using the CPR Part 8 procedure[4] (therefore Form N208 must be used), and contain the following information specified in the Practice Direction to CPR Part 64:[5]

(a)   the name, address and description of the applicant;

(b)   the details of the proceedings he wishes to take;

(c)   the date of the Charity Commissioners' refusal to grant an order authorising the taking of proceedings;

(d)   the grounds on which the applicant alleges that it is a proper case for taking proceedings; and

(e)   if the application is made with the consent of any other party to the proposed proceedings, that fact.

It is also common practice for the applicant to file a draft of the order sought with the claim form.

11.19 Where the Charity Commissioners have given reasons for their refusal to grant authorisation for the commencement of proceedings, a copy of those reasons must be filed with the claim form. Under the CPR Part 8 procedure it is normal for the claim form to be accompanied by a witness statement in

---

[1]   CA 1993, s 3(3).
[2]   Ibid, s 33(7).
[3]   CPR, r 64.6(1).
[4]   CPR, r 64.6(2).
[5]   CPR, PD64, para 9.

support.[1] However, in the case of applications for the court's leave, it is unnecessary to file a witness statement in most cases. The requirements set out above (at **11.18**) ensure that the claim form (which must be verified by a statement of truth) contains all the requisite information for the court to make its decision,[2] and therefore unless the facts of the application are especially complicated or there is some other additional information which the applicant considers would be of assistance to the court, the filing of a witness statement is unlikely to be either necessary or helpful. Where the Charity Commissioners (or any other defendant) enter a substantive response to the application (in the form of a witness statement), the applicant may, within 14 days of receipt of the defendant's evidence, deal with any matters raised by filing and serving a witness statement in reply.[3]

11.20 The Charity Commissioners must be named as a party to the application for leave, but the applicant is not required to serve the claim form on them or any other party.[4] As the application is a precursor to the commencement of charity proceedings, the application itself cannot be charity proceedings and therefore it is not necessary to name the Attorney-General as a party to it. The judge may require the Charity Commissioners to file a written statement of the reasons for their decision.[5] If the Commissioners have already provided such a statement to the applicant (when refusing the original request for authorisation) that statement should have been filed by the applicant with the claim form, in accordance with CPR PD64, para 9.2. If the judge requires the filing of the statement by the Charity Commissioners, the court will serve it on the applicant.[6]

11.21 Having considered the application on paper, the judge may either give permission to the applicant without a hearing,[7] or order that there be a hearing of the application.[8] CPR Part 64 contains no provision for the judge to dismiss the application without a hearing. However, there is nothing in CPR Part 64 which purports to restrict the court's case management power to strike out a claim on the grounds set out in CPR, r 3.4, for example if the application is made before any request for authorisation has been made to the Charity Commissioners. In practice, however, in cases where the judge decides not to grant permission without a hearing (on whatever basis), it is normal for there to be a hearing so that the applicant may make representations to the court.

---

1   CPR, r 8.5.
2   CPR, r 8.5(7).
3   CPR, r 8.5(5) and (6).
4   CPR, r 64.6(3).
5   CPR, r 64.6(4).
6   CPR, r 64.6(5).
7   CPR, r 64.6(6)(a).
8   CPR, r 64.6(6)(b).

11.22 On an application for leave, the court is not exercising an appellate jurisdiction in respect of the decision of the Charity Commissioners to refuse to authorise proceedings. Thus, the court is entitled to make its own decision on whether leave should be given, rather than simply deciding whether the decision of the Charity Commissioners was in some way wrong in law. However, the reasons given by the Charity Commissioners for their refusal will be considered by the court.

11.23 A party who is dissatisfied with the decision of the court on an application under s 33(5) of the CA 1993 may appeal against the decision of the court in the normal way under CPR Part 52.

Form of charity proceedings

11.24 Whilst there is a specific requirement that an application for leave to commence charity proceedings be made by way of a Part 8 claim, there is no specific requirement in the CPR that charity proceedings should be commenced using either a Part 7 or Part 8 claim form, and therefore the normal rules apply. Charity proceedings usually involve seeking the determination by the court of a question which does not involve a substantial dispute of fact, and as a consequence the Part 8 claims procedure is often appropriate. In respect of certain claims, however, the use of the Part 8 procedure is compulsory. Section I of CPR Part 64 applies in relation to claims for the court to determine any question arising in the administration of the estate of a deceased person or the execution of a trust.[1] Since many charities are trusts, numerous claims brought in relation to them will be within the scope of Section I of CPR Part 64, for example: applications by the trustees for directions as to how they should exercise their powers; applications for construction of the trust instrument; and claims for the removal or replacement of charity trustees. Any claim within Section I of Part 64 must be made by issuing a Part 8 claim form,[2] and therefore Form N208 is the appropriate form to use for the commencement of such claims.

APPEALS AGAINST ORDERS OF CHARITY COMMISSIONERS

Orders under CA 1993, s 16

11.25 Section 16(1) of the CA 1993 confers on the Charity Commissioners concurrent jurisdiction with the High Court in relation to certain matters pertaining to charities. Those matters are:

---

[1]   CPR, r 64.2(a).
[2]   CPR, r 64.3.

(a) establishing a scheme for the administration of a charity;

(b) appointing, discharging or removing a charity trustee or trustee for a charity, or removing an officer or employee;

(c) vesting or transferring property or requiring or entitling any person to call for or make any transfer of property or any payment.

11.26 The Charity Commissioners do not have jurisdiction under s 16 to:

(a) try or determine the title at law or in equity to any property as between a charity or trustee for a charity and a person holding or claiming the property, or an interest in it adversely to the charity; or

(b) determine any question as to the existence or extent of any charge or trust.[1]

Orders under CA 1993, s 18

11.27 Section 18 of the CA 1993 empowers the Charity Commissioners to make a wide range of orders for the protection of charities. The Commissioners must have instituted an inquiry into the affairs of a charity under s 8, and be satisfied that:

(a) there is or has been misconduct or mismanagement in the administration of the charity; or

(b) it is necessary or desirable to act for the purpose of protecting the property of the charity or securing a proper application for the purposes of the charity of that property or of property, coming to the charity.

If the Charity Commissioners are so satisfied they may make any one or more of the following orders under s 18(1):

(a) an order suspending any trustee, charity trustee, officer, agent or employee of the charity from the exercise of his office or employment pending consideration being given to his removal;

(b) an order appointing such number of additional charity trustees as they consider necessary for the proper administration of the charity;

(c) an order vesting any property held by or on trust for the charity in the official custodian for charities, or requiring the persons in whom any such property is vested to transfer it to him or appointing any person to transfer any such property to him;

(d) an order requiring any person who holds any property on behalf of the charity, or of any trustee for it, not to part with the property without the consent of the Charity Commissioners;

---

[1] CA 1993, s 16(3).

(e)   an order preventing the debtor of any charity from making any payments in or towards the discharge of his liability to the charity without the approval of the Charity Commissioners;

(f)   an order restricting (notwithstanding anything in the trusts of the charity) the transactions which may be entered into, or the nature or amount of the payments which may be made, in the administration of the charity without the approval of the Charity Commissioners;

(g)   an order appointing a receiver and manager in respect of the property and affairs of the charity.

11.28 Power is also given in similar circumstances to make an order under s 18(2):

(a)   removing any trustee, charity trustee, officer, agent or employee of the charity who has been responsible for or privy to the misconduct or mismanagement, or has by his conduct contributed to it or facilitated it; and/or

(b)   establishing a scheme for the administration of the charity.

11.29 The Charity Commissioners may (under s 18(4)) also order the removal of a charity trustee of their own motion where:

(a)   within the previous 5 years the trustee, having previously been adjudged bankrupt or had his estate sequestrated, has been discharged, or having previously made a composition or arrangement with, or granted a trust deed for, his creditors, has been discharged in respect of it;

(b)   the trustee is a corporation in liquidation;

(c)   the trustee is incapable of acting by reason of mental disorder within the meaning of the Mental Health Act 1983;

(d)   the trustee has not acted and will not declare his willingness or unwillingness to act;

(e)   the trustee is outside England and Wales or cannot be found or does not act, and his absence or failure to act impedes the proper administration of the charity.

11.30 The Charity Commissioners may also of their own motion make an order appointing a person to be a charity trustee:

(a)   in place of a charity trustee removed by them;

(b)   where there are no charity trustees, or where by reason of vacancies or the absence or incapacity of any of their number the charity cannot apply for the appointment;

(c)   where there is a single charity trustee, not being a corporation aggregate, and the Charity Commissioners are of the opinion that it is necessary to increase the number of trustees for the proper administration of the charity;

(d)   where they are of the opinion that it is necessary for the proper administration of the charity to have an additional charity trustee because one of the existing trustees who ought nevertheless to remain a charity trustee either cannot be found, or does not act, or is outside England and Wales.

Right of appeal

11.31 Where the Charity Commissioners have made an order in exercise of their jurisdiction under s 16 of the CA 1993, an appeal may be brought in the High Court against the order by the Attorney-General[1] or within the period of 3 months beginning on the day after the order is published by:

(a)   the charity or any of the charity trustees;

(b)   any person removed from any office or employment by the order, unless he is removed with the concurrence of the charity trustees or with the approval of the special visitor (if any) of the charity.[2]

11.32 The same right of appeal exists in relation to orders made under s 18 of the CA 1993. Section 18(8) provides that subss (11)–(13) of s 16 apply to orders made under s 18, subject only to the exception contained in s 18(9) in relation to the necessity for certification of suitability for, or leave to, appeal, (see **11.39**). Accordingly, references in this chapter to s 16 in the context of the procedure for appeals to the High Court should (unless expressly stated to the contrary) be read as including s 18.

Appeals procedure

11.33 Appeals under s 16 of the CA 1993 must be brought in accordance with CPR Part 52 by way of an appellant's notice (Form N161). Special rules governing appeals against orders of the Charity Commissioners are contained in the Practice Direction to CPR Part 52.[3]

11.34 Unless he is an appellant, the Attorney-General must be made a respondent to any appeal.[4] The appellant's notice must state all the grounds on which he appeals, and the appellant may not rely on any additional grounds unless the court gives permission for him to do so.[5] If the Charity Commissioners have certified that the case is a proper one for an appeal, a

---

[1]   CA 1993, s 16(11).
[2]   Ibid, s 16(12).
[3]   CPR, PD52, para 23.8A.
[4]   CPR, PD52, para 23.8A(2).
[5]   CPR, PD52, para 23.8A(3).

copy of their certificate to that effect must be filed with the appellant's notice.[1] If no such certificate has been given by the Charity Commissioners, the appellant must obtain leave to appeal from a judge of the Chancery Division.[2]

Certificate or leave to appeal

11.35 An appeal pursuant to s 16(12) of the CA 1993 may only be brought if the Charity Commissioners have certified that it is a proper case for an appeal, or leave to appeal has been obtained from a judge of the Chancery.[3]

11.36 The application for leave to appeal may (and usually will) be made in the appellant's notice.[4] Where the appellant makes the application in his appellant's notice, it must state the following:

(a)   that the appellant has requested that the Charity Commissioners certify that the case is a proper one for an appeal, and that they have refused to do so;

(b)   the date of such refusal;

(c)   the grounds on which the appellant alleges that it is a proper case for an appeal; and

(d)   where the appeal is made with the consent of any other party to the proposed appeal, the fact of such consent.[5]

11.37 Where the Charity Commissioners have given reasons for their refusal to certify that the case is a proper one for an appeal, a copy of the reasons must be attached to the appellant's notice.[6] Where the Charity Commissioners have not provided reasons for their refusal, the court has power to direct them to provide reasons before it determines the application for leave to appeal.[7] A copy of any reasons provided by the Charity Commissioners to the court in compliance with such a direction will be served by the court on the appellant.[8]

11.38 Other than under the foregoing specific rules, an application for leave proceeds in accordance with the general procedure for applications for permission to appeal set out in CPR Part 52. An application for permission to appeal will therefore be considered first by a judge 'on paper', ie without an oral hearing. If leave is not granted, the appellant may request (within

---

[1]   CPR, PD52, para 13.8A(5).
[2]   CA 1993, s 16(13).
[3]   Ibid.
[4]   CPR, PD52, para 23.8A(6).
[5]   CPR, PD52, para 23.8A(6)(a).
[6]   CPR, PD52, para 23.8A(6)(b).
[7]   CPR, PD52, para 23.8A(6)(c).
[8]   CPR, PD52, para 23.8A(6)(d).

7 days of the refusal) reconsideration of the decision at a hearing.[1] Under the general rules in CPR Part 52, permission to appeal is granted only if the court considers that the appellant has a real prospect of succeeding, or that there is some other compelling reason why the appeal should be heard.[2]

11.39 Under s 18(9) of the CA 1993 no certificate or leave to appeal is required for an appeal against an order made by the Charity Commissioners under s 18 if the appeal is:

(a)   brought by a charity or any of the charity trustees of a charity against an order under s 18(1)(vii) appointing a receiver and manager in respect of the charity's property and affairs; or

(b)   brought by a person against whom an order has been made under s 18(2)(i) or (4)(a) removing him from his office or employment.

The appeal

11.40 If a certificate of suitability or leave for appeal is given (or if the appeal is one for which no such certificate or leave is required) the appeal will proceed in accordance with the general rules in CPR Part 52. There are no specific modifications of these rules pertaining to charity matters.

Decisions concerning registration

11.41 Under s 3 of the CA 1993, the Charity Commissioners are required to keep and maintain a register of charities, onto which all charities (except those specified in s 3(5)) are required to be entered. Section 4 of the Act confers upon certain persons the right to appeal against such decision to the High Court.[3] The persons entitled to appeal are:

(a)   the Attorney-General;

(b)   the charity trustees of the institution; or

(c)   any person whose objection or application (pursuant to s 4(2) of the CA 1993) is disallowed by the decision.

11.42 No certificate of suitability or leave to appeal is required: the relevant persons are entitled to appeal as of right. If the Attorney-General is not the appellant, he must be made a party to the appeal,[4] and the appellant's notice (Form N161) must contain the grounds on which the appeal is brought. No other grounds may be relied upon without the permission of the court.[5]

---

[1]   CPR, r 52.3(4) and (5).
[2]   CPR, r 52.3(6).
[3]   CA 1993, s 4(3).
[4]   CPR, PD52, para 23.8A(2).
[5]   CPR, PD52, para 23.8A(3).

11.43 No further procedural rules apply specifically to appeals under s 4 of the CA 1993, and therefore the appeal proceeds in accordance with the general rules under CPR Part 52.

OTHER PROCEEDINGS INVOLVING CHARITIES

11.44 In any litigation not involving charity proceedings or appeals against orders of the Charity Commissioners, a charity (or the trustees thereof) is in the same position as an ordinary litigant. Where the charity is a body corporate it is capable of suing (and being sued) in its own name. Where the charity is a trust, the appropriate parties are the trustees. It will usually be appropriate for the Attorney-General to be named as a party for the purpose of representing the interests of charities generally (as opposed to specific charities able to instruct legal representatives themselves). A common situation where the Attorney-General must be joined as a party to proceedings is where a will creates a discretionary trust for the benefit of charities generally, or for the benefit of particular types of charity such as 'animal charities' or 'children's charities'. If a claim is brought concerning the will or the estate (such as a claim concerning the validity of the will, or a claim under the Inheritance (Provision for Family and Dependants) Act 1975) before the trustees have made any appointments in favour of any particular charities, the Attorney-General is the appropriate party to represent the interests of the charity in the litigation.

11.45 As noted above (at **11.3**) proceedings to determine whether a charitable trust has been created are not charity proceedings. Only the Attorney-General[1] and the Charity Commissioners[2] are entitled to bring proceedings to determine the existence of a charitable trust.

COSTS

11.46 Costs of litigation are a matter for the discretion of the court,[3] and it is therefore impossible to set out any firm rules. In general, the costs of charity trustees are treated in a similar way to those of the trustees of private trusts.

11.47 In non-hostile litigation (for example, where assistance of the court is sought in relation to trustees' powers or duties), trustees are normally entitled to their costs out of the trust fund, assessed on an indemnity basis.[4] Other

---

[1] *Hauxwell v Barton-upon-Humber Urban District Council* [1974] Ch 432.
[2] CA 1993, s 32(1).
[3] Supreme Court Act 1981, s 51(1).
[4] CPR, r 48.4, see Chapter 8.

parties to such litigation will usually recover their costs from the trust fund, albeit on a standard basis.[1]

11.48 The general rule in hostile litigation is that costs follow the event, ie the unsuccessful party pays the costs of the successful party.[2] It is usually appropriate for trustees to seek protection in relation to the costs of the action by obtaining a direction from the Charity Commissioners[3] or a *Beddoe* order[4] which gives the trustees directions as to whether they should pursue (or defend) the claim in question, and entitles them to recover the costs from the trust fund provided they act in accordance with the court's direction. It should be noted, however, that where an application for a *Beddoe* order is made by the trustees of a charitable trust, the application constitutes charity proceedings, and therefore the authorisation of the Charity Commissioners (or the leave of the court) is required before the application may be made.[5]

---

[1]   CPR, r 44.4.
[2]   *D'Abo v Paget* [2000] WTLR 863.
[3]   Under CA 1993, s 26.
[4]   *Re Beddoe* [1893] 1 Ch 547.
[5]   CA 1993, s 33(2).

Chapter 12

PARTNERSHIPS

Timothy Sisley

PRELIMINARY INSTRUCTIONS

12.1   Before proceeding it is important to establish that what a claimant thinks is a partnership is in fact a partnership, and not (for example) a joint venture or a loose association before incorporation of a company.[1] If no written partnership agreement exists, the terms may be found in instructions to accountants that never resulted in agreement, minutes of meetings, or accounts. The original terms even in a written agreement may have been varied by agreement or conduct.[2]

12.2   A partnership for a single venture or a fixed term will dissolve when the venture is completed or the is term over. A partnership is automatically dissolved by death, bankruptcy or supervening illegality.[3] Generally, an agreement will require a notice period, but a partnership at will can be dissolved by notice with immediate effect.[4]

12.3   When the single venture or the fixed term is continuing, or when a notice period has not expired, the disgruntled partner will need to seek dissolution by the court. In unclear cases, he may be forced into the uncomfortable argument that there has been a repudiatory breach.[5]

12.4   The following is an outline checklist of issues commonly encountered in partnership cases:

(a)   a claim against one partner for losses attributable to his misconduct or negligence;

(b)   analogous but conceptually distinct, whether there should be a claim for accounting on the footing of wilful default, ie whether another partner

---

[1]   Partnership Act 1890 (PA 1890), s 2.
[2]   Ibid, s 19.
[3]   Ibid, ss 33 and 34.
[4]   Ibid, s 32(c).
[5]   *Hurst v Bryk* [2002] 1 AC 185.

should be charged with what the business would have earned but for his deliberate default;

(c)   whether there was an agreement for additional payments for management;[1]

(d)   whether one partner is vulnerable under an obligation to devote his whole time and attention to the partnership business;

(e)   interest on unequal capital contributions;[2]

(f)   whether the assets used in the partnership (i) are properly partnership property or (ii) still belong to a partner individually;[3]

(g)   whether one partner has charged his house to secure the partnership borrowing;

(h)   who is liable to the landlord for the covenants in a lease of the partnership premises;

(i)   restrictive covenants;

(j)   whether the past partnership accounts need to be re-examined;

(k)   public notification of dissolution;[4]

(l)   whether other partners are carrying on the partnership business, and whether the claimant wishes to do so.

12.5 Excessive drawings can be dealt with on accounting, but single large withdrawals in anticipation of the proceedings may require an urgent injunction. The risk of dissipation must be considered.

12.6 If the partnership assets are in peril or the partnership continues in business until sale but the partners cannot come to terms on management, it may be necessary to appoint a receiver to manage the business until sale. Since this can be expensive, the cost of appointing a receiver must be weighed against the benefit of selling the business as a going concern. Despite the expense, it is probably best to appoint an accountant since accountants are insured, and it is less likely that security will need to be provided by the business.

12.7 It is important that a claimant understands that he is in a relationship of equality with his partners or former partners. The business does not belong to one partner any more than to the others. If the claimant continues to trade in the partnership business after the other partners have abandoned it, including after formal dissolution, he will be under a duty to account to those partners for a share of the profits, or to pay interest on capital.[5] However, he will recover an allowance for his efforts.

---

1   PA 1890, s 24(6).
2   Ibid, s 24(3).
3   Ibid, s 20(1).
4   Ibid, s 37.
5   Ibid, s 42(1).

12.8   If the claimant wishes to establish a separate successor business he may be in breach of fiduciary duty to his former partners if, before sale, he supplants the goodwill of the old business or siphons off exclusive supply contracts. Until winding-up he may hold personal appointments (solicitor trusteeships, appointments as liquidator, etc) on trust for the partnership.[1]

12.9   The costs of an action can be vastly disproportionate to the value of the partnership, and particularly the costs of an account. It is therefore important that before proceeding to trial, mediation is considered as an alternative. In addition, the firm's accountant can be requested to prepare closing accounts.[2]

PROCEEDINGS

12.10 Actions in the High Court relating to dissolution and partnership accounts are assigned to the Chancery Division.[3] For practical purposes, this means that any action between partners must be heard in the county court or in the Chancery Division. The Queen's Bench Division has no jursidiction to hear partnership disputes. The county court jurisdiction is limited to actions where partnership assets do not exceed £30,000, unless the partners consent *in writing* to jurisdiction.[4]

12.11 There are no traps for the unwary in the CPR which apply especially to actions between partners. No relevant pre-action protocol has been issued. The Chancery Guide contains a useful chapter on partnerships, which may be referred to as a *vade mecum* also in the county court.

12.12 It is usually best practice to avoid the county court, to forestall disputes over the value of the partnership and to reduce the risk of unreliable judgments.

12.13 The claimant will usually request standard remedies, chiefly winding-up, which embraces sale of the partnership property, and an account. All partners must be joined, so that they are bound by the judgment. Any partner who is not a claimant must be cited as a defendant.

12.14 Partnership actions are not among those specified in the CPR as being appropriate for the Part 8 procedure.[5] It is the alternative to a contentious approach, but there is little to recommend it. Proper pleadings should be obtained with a Part 7 claim.

---

[1]   *Don King Productions Inc v Warren* [2000] Ch 291.
[2]   Chancery Guide, para 22.4.
[3]   Supreme Court Act 1981 (SCA 1981), s 61(1) and Sch 1.
[4]   County Courts Act 1984, ss 23(f) and 24(2)(g); County Courts Jurisdiction Order 1981, SI 1981/1123.
[5]   CPR, r 8.1 and PD8, para 1.4.

12.15 There may be no purpose in defending. A defendant does not need to make a CPR Part 20 claim for the range of winding-up relief. Once the question of concluding the partnership affairs is before the court, those orders will follow no matter who sought them in the first place; and if the claimant discontinues, a defendant can always add that claim.[1] It is only necessary to claim a contribution or indemnity from other defendants when the claimant makes some unusual allegation, not for ordinary accounting.

INTERIM RELIEF

12.16 It will usually be the balance of convenience to claim interim relief to keep the partnership property safe and to preserve its value pending winding-up. Examples of applications for interim relief are:

(a) to require a defaulting partner to account for or deliver up any money or property he has misappropriated;[2]

(b) to require sale of any partnership asset which it is desirable to sell quickly, including perishable stock;[3]

(c) the appointment of a receiver.[4]

SUMMARY APPLICATIONS

12.17 Resolution of the affairs of the partnership is usually a matter of urgency. The claimant will need to realise his capital or equalise the deficit he has borne. More importantly, the Inland Revenue will not wait for extended litigation to establish the closing accounts before issuing an assessment. It may be important that an application for summary judgment is made as soon as possible.

12.18 Summary orders can be obtained for dissolution of the partnership,[5] for a declaration as to the date of dissolution[6] and for accounting purposes.[7] The account can deal with all issues or leave some outstanding for later adjudication. Most importantly, sale of the partnership property can be ordered summarily. Unless there is serious dispute about the existence or terms of a partnership, the court will make a summary order for an account immediately.[8]

---

[1] CPR, Part 38.

[2] CPR, r 25.1(1)(c)(i).

[3] CPR, r 25.1(1)(c)(v).

[4] SCA 1981, s 37(1).

[5] CPR, r 24.3(2).

[6] CPR, r 24.3(2) and/or r 25.1(1)(b).

[7] CPR, PD24, para 6.

[8] Chancery Guide, para 22.1.

12.19 Disputed issues should be left simultaneously with the account in the hands of the master or district judge, for expediency.[1] It will be no impediment to summary judgment that not all the matters in issue are dealt with. In fact, it is advisable to achieve the resolution of as many issues as possible as early as possible, not just on costs grounds. A trial on the seriously disputed issues will rarely settle everything in contention, and the lesser questions of accounting may be referred back to the master or district judge, which questions could have been resolved a long time beforehand.

ACCOUNTING

12.20 The purpose of accounting is to establish the amount of assets available for distribution on final winding-up. The areas to be addressed will usually be (i) the respective capital contributions, (ii) receipts, (iii) payments and (iv) the respective drawings. The account can be carried out together with an inquiry into what exactly constitutes the partnership property, and where any missing assets have gone.

12.21 Unless fraud, misrepresentation or error is alleged, the partners will be bound by settled accounts, ie the annual accounts approved by the partners and submitted to the Inland Revenue. The usual starting point will consequently be the date to which the last approved accounts were drawn.

12.22 At this stage issues of wilful default[2] and any just allowance for managing the partnership business[3] may be introduced. If those or any other issues remain in contention as to principle, the account can be completed subject to a later adjustment, when it should be straightforward to insert a few lines to the figures for the final result.

12.23 The master or district judge will take the account.[4] He can direct a hearing to resolve any issue that arises during the process.[5] One party to the litigation begins by producing an account verified by affidavit or witness statement.[6] Although the Practice Direction supplementing Part 40 of the CPR states that the opposite side to the party applying should begin with the account (the accounting party), there is no reason why this should be so, and the sensible reality is that the party applying is more likely to be able to open the process by producing figures.

---

[1] Chancery Guide, paras 22.1–22.3.
[2] CPR, PD40, para 3.1(b).
[3] Ibid, para 4.
[4] Ibid, para 9.2.
[5] Ibid, para 5.
[6] Ibid, para 2.

12.24 The other party then gives written notice of the items to which he objects, with detailed counter-figures of how the account is alleged to be inaccurate and what should be added or taken away.[1]

12.25 This exchange of figures constitutes the framework for adjudication, and is followed by disclosure. Expert evidence on wilful default or just allowances should be considered. There are potential penalties for delay.[2]

SALE OF THE PARTNERSHIP PROPERTY

12.26 The court has complete discretion on the manner of sale of partnership property, bearing in mind the interest of all the partners.

12.27 An interim order for sale of any asset is made under CPR, r 25.1(1)(c)(v). A final order for the sale of land is made under CPR Sch 1, and RSC Ord 31, and a final order for the sale of any other asset is made under the inherent jurisdiction of the court.[3]

12.28 It is important to consider what manner of sale is most advantageous, for example sale by consensus to one or more partners, private auction, public auction, or instructions to one or more business transfer agents to find a private buyer. The business could be offered as one lot, or broken up into components. It is usual for there to be two orders, one for sale in principle and the second to fix the detail of reserve and remuneration.

12.29 If possible, a comprehensive scheme should be put before the court which ties up all loose ends and minimises the possibility of having to come back for a second order or more directions. A sensible package will avoid complications.

COSTS

12.30 The usual order is that costs be paid out of the partnership assets. This is subject to the overriding discretion of the court, and a party who loses on

---

[1] CPR, PD40, paras 3.1 and 3.2.

[2] Ibid, para 6.1.

[3] In the county court, which is without inherent jurisdiction, the jurisdiction to order sale of assets other than land in a partnership action is conferred by s 23 of the County Courts Act 1984.

clear issues or who has been guilty of wasteful misconduct cannot expect to spread the expense among his former partners.

Chapter 13

CHANCERY PROCEDURE – BANKRUPTCY[1]

Peter Shaw

INTRODUCTION

13.1 The primary sources of practice and procedure in bankruptcy are:

(a)   the Insolvency Act 1986 (the Act);[2]
(b)   the Insolvency Rules 1986 (the Rules);[3] and
(c)   the *Practice Direction: Insolvency Proceedings*[4] ('the Practice Direction').

The CPR, the practice and procedure of the High Court and of the county court (including any Practice Direction), apply to insolvency proceedings any necessary modifications, except so far as inconsistent with the Rules.[5] All insolvency proceedings are allocated to the multi-track (provision for which is made in CPR Part 29) and all provisions of the CPR which provide for allocation questionnaires and track allocation will not apply.[6]

FORM OF PROCEEDINGS – GENERAL

13.2 Applications and petitions governed by the Act and the Rules shall be issued in the forms prescribed under the Rules, and not by the CPR. Save for

---

[1]   This chapter covers the procedural matters relating to statutory demands and bankruptcy petitions, and general insolvency procedural rules. It is not concerned with specific applications arising in the course of bankruptcy which are beyond the scope of this work. Unfortunately, owing to confines of space, the procedure relating to individual voluntary arrangements which appeared in the first edition has had to be removed.

[2]   As amended by the Insolvency Act 2000 and the Enterprise Act 2002. The bankruptcy and personal insolvency provisions of the Enterprise Act 2002 came into force on 1 April 2004.

[3]   SI 1986/1925. The Rules have been amended on numerous occasions, most significantly for present purposes by the Insolvency (Amendment) (No 2) Rules 2002, SI 2002/2712, which implemented important changes to the individual voluntary arrangement (IVA) regime with effect from 1 January 2003; and the Insolvency (Amendment) Rules 2003, SI 2003/1730, which made further amendments to IVAs consequent upon the coming into force of the personal insolvency provisions of the Enterprise Act 2002 on 1 April 2004.

[4]   [2000] BCC 92.

[5]   Insolvency Rules 1986 (IR 1986), r 7.51 (as amended).

[6]   IR 1986, r 7.51(2) (as amended).

specific applications[1] and petitions for bankruptcy orders, all applications made to the court under the Act or the Rules are made in the form either of (a) an originating application, ie an application to the court which is not an application in pending proceedings before the court,[2] or (b) an ordinary application. An originating application is in the form prescribed in Form 7.1 to the Rules and not in the form of a Part 7 or Part 8 claim form under the CPR. An ordinary application is in Form 7.2.

13.3   An originating application must set out the grounds on which the applicant claims to be entitled to the relief sought.[3] There is no requirement for an originating or ordinary application to be verified by a statement of truth in the manner prescribed by CPR Part 22.

FILING AND SERVICE OF PROCEEDINGS

13.4   Unless the court otherwise directs, the applicant must serve a sealed copy of the application endorsed with a venue for the hearing on the respondent(s).[4] Except where the Rules otherwise provide, service of documents in insolvency proceedings in the High Court will be the responsibility of the parties and will not be undertaken by the court.[5] The practice in the county court remains less clear. However, r 7.4(3) places the obligation on the applicant to serve his application. The High Court practice ought to be followed in the county court.

13.5   Unless the provisions of the Act or the Rules provide otherwise, an application must be served at least 14 days before the date fixed for the hearing.[6] The court may (without prejudice to its general power to extend or abridge time-limits)[7] hear the application immediately without notice to or the attendance of the other parties, or authorise a shorter period of service. CPR, r 2.8 (time) applies as regards the computation of time to do anything required or authorised by the Rules,[8] and CPR, r 3.1(2)(a) (court's management powers) enables the court to extend or shorten the time for compliance with anything required or authorised to be done by the Rules.[9]

---

[1]   In which there are prescribed forms set out in Sch 4 to the Rules, eg an application to set aside a statutory demand (Form 6.4).

[2]   IR 1986, r 7.2(1).

[3]   Ibid, r 7.3(2).

[4]   Ibid, r 7.4(3).

[5]   Practice Direction, para 1.3.

[6]   IR 1986, r 7.4(5).

[7]   See s 376 of the Insolvency Act 1986 (IA 1986) for the power to extend time-limits.

[8]   IR 1986, r 12.9 (as amended).

[9]   Note that this provision does not permit the court to vary a time prescribed by the Act; although s 376 permits the court to extend time in relation to bankruptcy and personal insolvency time-limits set out in the Act.

RULES AS TO SERVICE – ORIGINATING AND ORDINARY APPLICATIONS[1]

13.6 A document served by post must be in a pre-paid envelope for either first- or second-class post and may be sent to the recipient's last known address.[2] When sent by first-class post the document is treated as served on the second business day after posting. When sent by second-class post, the document is treated as served on the fourth business day after posting.[3] CPR Part 6 applies to any matter relating to the service of documents and the giving of notice in insolvency proceedings.[4]

13.7 The application of CPR Part 6 applies only to the giving of notice in 'insolvency proceedings'. These are defined[5] as any proceedings under the Act or the Rules and do not include the service of a statutory demand,[6] which are governed by separate provisions in the Rules and the Practice Direction. Save for documents for which specific provision is made, all of the methods available for service prescribed by CPR, r 6.2 will apply.

EVIDENCE

13.8 Evidence may be given by affidavit unless the Rules otherwise provide or the court otherwise directs.[7] The court may order the attendance for cross-examination of the deponent.[8] Where a deponent has been ordered to attend for cross-examination and does not do so the affidavit cannot be used in evidence without leave.[9]

13.9 A witness statement verified by a statement of truth may be used as an alternative to an affidavit[10] (subject to certain exceptions in which an affidavit is mandatory[11]). There is no provision in the Rules for evidence to be given by way of an application notice under CPR, r 32.6.

---

[1]   Special rules apply to service out of the jurisdiction – cf r 12.12. Due to confines of space the discussion of service out of the jurisdiction is not included here.
[2]   IR 1986, r 12.10(1A).
[3]   Ibid, r 12.10(2) and (3).
[4]   Ibid, r 12.11 (as amended) and subject to r 12.10.
[5]   Ibid, r 13.7.
[6]   *Re A Debtor (No 1 of 1987, Lancaster)* [1989] 1 WLR 271, CA.
[7]   IR 1986, r 7.7(1).
[8]   Ibid, r 7.7(1).
[9]   Ibid, r 7.7(2).
[10] Ibid, r 7.57(5).
[11] Ibid, rr 7.57(6); r 6.60 (statement of affairs); rr 6.66 and 6.72 (further disclosure by a Bankrupt at the request of the Official Receiver), rr 6.65 and 6.70 (provision of accounts by a Bankrupt), r 6.99 (verification of proof of debt) and rr 9.3 and 9.4 (examinations).

13.10 Any party to insolvency proceedings may apply to the court for an order in accordance with CPR Part 18 (further information) or CPR Part 31 (disclosure and inspection of documents)[1]. An application under CPR, r 7.60 may be made without notice being served on any other party.[2]

STATUTORY DEMANDS

13.11 The most common route to bankruptcy is by a creditor's petition presented pursuant to s 267 of the Act which satisfies the following conditions:[3]

(a)   the amount of the debt or debts is equal to or exceeds the bankruptcy level, presently £750;[4]

(b)   the debt, or each of the debts, is for a liquidated sum payable to the petitioning creditor or one or more of the petitioning creditors, either immediately or at some time certain, future time and is unsecured;

(c)   the debt, or each of the debts, is a debt which the debtor appears either unable to pay or to have no reasonable prospect of being able to pay; and

(d)   there is no outstanding application to set aside a statutory demand served in respect of the debt or debts.

13.12 'Inability to pay' is defined[5] as being either (a) a statutory demand served by the petitioning creditor requiring the debtor to pay the debt or secure or compound it to the creditor's satisfaction, which statutory demand has neither been complied with nor set aside in accordance with the Rules;[6] or (b) execution or other process on a judgment or order of the court has been returned unsatisfied in whole or part. In most cases the failure of the debtor to pay, secure or compound to the creditor's satisfaction within 3 weeks of the service of the statutory demand forms the basis of the bankruptcy petition. In large part, the practice and procedure relating to the form and content of statutory demands, their service and applications to set aside are self-contained within Chapter 1 of Part 6 to the Rules and in the Practice Direction. Written evidence in support of an application to set aside a

---

[1]   IR 1986, r 7.60 (as amended). It may be considered that the express inclusion within the Rules of a power to order disclosure against *any other party* in accordance with CPR, Part 31 operates to exclude the power to order disclosure against non parties which exists in CPR, r 31.17.

[2]   Ibid, r 7.60(2).

[3]   IA 1986, s 267(2).

[4]   Ibid, s 267(4).

[5]   Ibid, s 268.

[6]   Or in the case of a debt payable in the future, that there is a reasonable prospect that the debtor will be able to pay the debt when it falls due.

statutory demand[1] and to prove service of a statutory demand[2] may be in the form of either an affidavit or a witness statement.[3]

FORM OF STATUTORY DEMAND

13.13 The Act requires[4] the service of a statutory demand 'in the prescribed form'. Three forms are prescribed in Sch 4 to the Rules: Form 6.1 (debt for a liquidated demand payable immediately); Form 6.2 (debt for a liquidated demand following a judgment of the court); and Form 6.3 (debt payable at a future date). A creditor cannot petition or serve a statutory demand in respect of any element of his debt which is secured. If a creditor holds security in respect of the debt, the full amount of the debt must be specified, but the creditor must identify the security in the demand and place a value upon it at the date of the demand, and the amount claimed in the statutory demand must be limited to the balance due after giving credit for the value of the security.[5] 'Security in respect of the debt' refers to security over any property of the debtor and not security provided by a third party.[6]

SERVICE OF STATUTORY DEMAND[7]

13.14 The creditor is under an overriding obligation to do all that is reasonable for the purpose of bringing the statutory demand to the attention of the debtor, and if practicable to effect personal service.[8]

The following must be noted.

(1)   Service by advertisement is permissible where the creditor has a judgment and believes with reasonable cause that the debtor is avoiding service and there is no real prospect of the judgment being recovered by execution or other legal process.[9] The Practice Direction sets out a form of service which the court will accept;[10]

(2)   A statutory demand may be served by insertion through the letter box or by first-class post.[11] As a statutory demand is an extrajudicial

---

[1]   Practice Direction, para 12.1.
[2]   Practice Direction, para 13.1.
[3]   Ibid, para 13.4.
[4]   IA 1986, s 268(1) and (2).
[5]   IR 1986, r 6.1(5).
[6]   IA 1986, s 383(2); and *Re A Debtor (No 310 of 1988)* [1989] 1 WLR 452, Knox J.
[7]   The practice and procedure as to service of a statutory demand are set out in IR 1986, rr 6.3 and 6.11, and Practice Direction, paras 11 and 13.
[8]   IR 1986, r 6.3(2).
[9]   Ibid, r 6.3(3).
[10] Practice Direction, para 11.
[11] Ibid, para 11.1.

document,[1] it is not possible to obtain an order for substituted service. In all cases where substituted service (which will, of course, be without an order) is effected, the creditor must have taken all those steps which would justify the court making an order for substituted service of a petition.[2] Upon issuing a bankruptcy petition the creditor must file an affidavit of service of the statutory demand. Failure to comply with the requirements may mean that the court declines to issue the petition.[3]

(3)   The following steps will usually suffice to justify an order for substituted service of a petition and the service of a statutory demand.[4]

(a)   A personal call is made at the place of residence and business of the debtor (or either of such places as are known).

(b)   A letter of appointment is sent at least 2 business days before the proposed further appointment.

(c)   The letter should state (i) that if the appointment time is inconvenient, the debtor should name some other time and place; (ii) that in the case of a statutory demand, if the debtor fails to keep the appointment, the creditor will serve either by advertisement, post or letter box and the court will subsequently be asked to treat such as service; (iii) that in the case of a petition, if the debtor fails to keep the appointment, the creditor will apply to the court for an order for substituted service.

(d)   In attending any appointment made by letter, inquiry should be made whether the debtor has received the previous letters, or, if the debtor is away, whether letters are being forwarded.

(e)   If the debtor is represented by a solicitor, an attempt should be made to arrange personal service through the solicitor. A statutory demand may be served on a solicitor (or any other person) who is duly authorised to accept service.[5]

Where the court makes an order for substituted service of a petition by first-class post, the order will normally provide that service is deemed to be effected on the seventh day after posting.[6] The same method of calculating service may be applied to service of a statutory demand.[7]

---

[1]   *Re A Debtor (No 190 of 1987)* (1988) *The Times*, 26 April, Vinelott J.
[2]   Practice Direction, para 11.3.
[3]   IR 1986, r 6.11(9); Practice Direction, para 11.3.
[4]   Practice Direction, para 11.4.
[5]   IR 1986, r 6.11(4).
[6]   Practice Direction, para 11.5.
[7]   Ibid.

APPLICATION TO SET ASIDE STATUTORY DEMAND

13.15 The debtor may apply to set aside the statutory demand within 18 days of service.[1] The form of application is prescribed Form 6.4. CPR r 2.8 applies to the computation of time.[2] The date of service of the demand itself does not count for the purposes of calculating the 18-day period. Written evidence is required in support of the application to set aside in Form 6.5.[3] This must state the date upon which the statutory demand came into the debtor's hands, the grounds for setting aside, and must exhibit a copy of the statutory demand.[4] The requirement for 'written evidence' allows the evidence to be either in the form of an affidavit or a witness statement.[5]

13.16 Where a statutory demand is served by a minister of the Crown or a government department which is based upon a judgment and which states that the creditor intends to petition in the High Court, an application to set aside must be issued by the High Court. In all other cases an application to set aside must be issued by the court in which the debtor would have been entitled to present his own bankruptcy petition.[6] A petition must be presented to the High Court in cases in which:[7] (a) the debtor has resided or worked in the London insolvency district for the greater part of 6 months prior to presentation of the petition (application to set aside) or for a longer period in those 6 months than in any other district; or (b) the debtor is not resident in England and Wales.

13.17 In any other case the application to set aside the statutory demand must be issued:[8]

(a) in the county court for the insolvency district in which the debtor has resided or carried on business for the 6-month period; or

(b) if he has resided in one insolvency district and carried on business in another, in the county court for the district in which he has carried on business; or

(c) if, during the 6-month period, he has carried on business in more than one insolvency district, in the county court for the district which has been his principal place of business for the longest.

---

[1] IR 1986, r 6.4(1).
[2] Ibid, r 12.9 (as amended).
[3] Practice Direction, para 12.1.
[4] IR 1986, r 6.4(4).
[5] Practice Direction, para 13.4.
[6] IR 1986, rr 6.4(2), 6.40(1) and (2).
[7] Ibid, r 6.40(1).
[8] Ibid, r 6.40(2).

13.18 The court may extend time for the hearing of an application to set aside a statutory demand which is issued after expiry of the 18-day period.[1] A debtor who wishes to apply to set aside a statutory demand after the expiry of 18 days must apply for an extension of time within which to apply.[2] Ordinarily a combined application will need to be issued which seeks (a) an order for an extension of time, and (b) an order setting aside the statutory demand. The following additional paragraphs will need to be added to the affidavit or witness statement in support:[3]

> '3. That to the best of my knowledge and belief the creditor(s) named in the demand has/have not presented a petition against me.
>
> That the reasons for my failure to apply to set aside the demand within 18 days after service are as follows ...'

The application both for the extension of time and the substantive application to set aside will be heard by a bankruptcy registrar (in the High Court), or by a district judge (in the county court).[4] Where the period of 18 days from service of the demand has expired and the debtor wishes to apply for an extension of time to apply to set aside the demand, he must apply to the judge for an order restraining presentation of the petition. In such circumstances the affidavit or witness statement in support of the application to set aside must contain the following paragraph:[5]

> '5. Unless restrained by injunction the creditor(s) may present a bankruptcy petition against me.'

In most cases, an application for an injunction to restrain presentation of a petition will be unnecessary since the filing in court of an application to set aside will prevent the issue of a petition. The conditions for the presentation of a bankruptcy petition include that there is no outstanding application to set aside a statutory demand.[6]

HEARING OF APPLICATION TO SET ASIDE

13.19 If it is satisfied that no sufficient cause is shown, the court may dismiss the application to set aside without giving notice to the creditor. Time for compliance with the demand begins to run again from the date the application to set aside is dismissed.[7] If the application is not dismissed, the court will give

---

[1]   IA 1986, s 376.
[2]   Practice Direction, para 12.5.
[3]   Ibid, para 12.5.
[4]   Ibid, para 9 and Practice Statement set out in *Muir Hunter*, para 9-27.
[5]   Ibid, para 12.5.
[6]   IA 1986, s 267(2).
[7]   IR 1986, r 6.5(1).

at least 7 days' notice of a hearing to the debtor, the creditor and the person named in the demand as being the person to whom the debtor may communicate concerning the demand.[1] The first hearing of the application is a summary hearing (usually listed for no more than 15 minutes) in which the court will either summarily determine the application or adjourn it and give directions. If the creditor wishes to oppose the application and put in evidence, the directions will usually provide for a time to serve such evidence, with a further period for the debtor/applicant to put in evidence in reply. The applicant usually has the final opportunity to put in evidence. The High Court will usually fix a date and time for the hearing of the adjourned application.

13.20 Where the statutory demand is based upon a judgment or order, the court will not at this stage go behind the judgment and inquire into the validity of the debt; nor, as a general rule, will it adjourn the application to await the result of an application to set aside the judgment.[2]

13.21 Where the debtor claims to have a counterclaim, set-off or cross-demand, *whether or not he could have raised it in the action in which the judgment or order was given*, which equals or exceeds the amount of the debt or debts specified in the statutory demand, the court will set aside the statutory demand if, in its opinion on the evidence, there is a genuine triable issue.[3]

13.22 Where the debt, not being the subject of a judgment or order, is disputed the court will normally set aside the demand on being satisfied that there is a genuine triable issue.[4] The debtor does not need to show that its defence offers a reasonable prospect of success. If the genuine dispute is not to the whole debt, but merely part, the debtor cannot have the demand set aside unless the undisputed element is less than the statutory minimum.[5] Where the undisputed element is greater than the statutory minimum, the debtor will need to pay, compound or secure the undisputed element to the creditor's satisfaction.

13.23 Whilst there is a conflict of authority on the point it is generally considered that a statutory demand cannot be set aside conditionally, eg on payment of money into court or a joint account.[6]

13.24 If the court dismisses the application to set aside it must make an order authorising the creditor to present a bankruptcy petition forthwith or on or

---

[1]   IR 1986, r 6.5(2).
[2]   Practice Direction, para 12.3.
[3]   Ibid, para 12.4.
[4]   Ibid, para 12.4.
[5]   *Re A Debtor (Nos 49 and 50 of 1992)* [1995] Ch 66.
[6]   In *Re A Debtor (No 517 of 1991)* (1991) *The Times*, November 25, Ferris J considered that a statutory demand could be conditionally set aside. That has been doubted in *Re A Debtor (No 90 of 1992)* (1993) *The Times*, 12 July, Knox J; and *Re A Debtor (32-SD-91)* [1994] BCC 524, Vinelott J.

after a date to be specified.[1] In appropriate cases the court may be invited to order a date for the authorising of a petition which allows time for the debtor to secure the debt.

13.25 Rule 7.55 of the Rules, which provides that no insolvency proceedings will be invalidated by reason of any formal defect or irregularity, does not apply to applications to set aside statutory demands since they are not insolvency proceedings.[2] A demand for a wrongly overstated amount will not be set aside solely as a consequence of the overstatement; it may, however, be set aside where it is perplexing.[3] Further, the use of the wrong form will not necessarily lead to the statutory demand being set aside.[4]

13.26 It is a ground for setting aside the statutory demand if the creditor either (a) omits to value its security in the statutory demand, or (b) the court is satisfied that the value of the security is equal to or greater than the debt claimed.[5] Rule 6.5(5) provides that where the court is satisfied that the security is undervalued, the creditor may be required to amend its demand accordingly. 'Security' means security over the property of the debtor, and not that of a third party.[6]

13.27 An appeal against a decision on an application to set aside a statutory demand is not a trial on the merits. Accordingly, fresh evidence may be adduced and is not subject to the principles restricting the introduction of such evidence on appeal set out in *Ladd v Marshall.*[7]

COSTS

13.28 The use of statutory demands in both personal and corporate insolvency has been described as a high-risk strategy.[8] Where the debt is subject to a bona fide dispute the demand may constitute an abuse of process and its setting-aside may be on terms that the creditor pay the debtor's costs on an indemnity basis.[9] Where a solicitor or director swears an affidavit in support of a statutory demand or a bankruptcy petition without adequate

---

[1] IR 1986, r 6.5(5).

[2] *Re A Debtor (No 190 of 1987)* (1988) *The Times*, May 21, Vinelott J; *Re A Debtor (No 1 of 1987, Lancaster)* [1989] 1 WLR 271, CA.

[3] *Re A Debtor (No 1 of 1987, Lancaster)* [1989] 1 WLR 271, CA; and *Re A Debtor (490-SD-1991)* [1992] 1 WLR 507, Hoffmann J; not following his previous decision in *Re A Debtor (No 10 of 1988)* [1989] 1 WLR 405.

[4] *Cartwright v Staffordshire and Moorlands District Council* [1998] BPIR 328.

[5] IR 1986, r 6.5(4)(c).

[6] IA 1986, s 383(2); and *Re A Debtor (No 310 of 1988)* [1989] 1 WLR 452, Knox J.

[7] [1954] 1 WLR 1489; see *Royal Bank of Scotland v Binnell* [1996] BPIR 352; *Laurier v United Overseas Bank* [1996] BPIR 635; *Salvridge v Hussein* [1999] BPIR 410; *Purvis v HM Customs and Excise* [1999] BPIR 396.

[8] *In Re A Company (No 0012209 of 1991)* [1992] 1 WLR 351, per Hoffmann J.

[9] Ibid.

grounds for his belief, he may be ordered to pay the costs personally.[1] Rule 7.33 incorporates the costs provisions of CPR Parts 43–48 (save for the provisions relating to fast track costs in Part 46). The summary assessment procedure applies to applications to set aside statutory demands.

CREDITOR'S BANKRUPTCY PETITIONS

13.29 Pursuant to s 264 of the Act, a bankruptcy petition may be presented by any of the following:[2]

(a) one of the debtor's creditors, or jointly by more than one of them;
(b) the debtor;
(c) the supervisor of, or any person (other than the debtor) who is bound by, an IVA;
(d) where a criminal bankruptcy order has been made, the official petitioner or any person specified in the order in pursuance of s 39(3)(b) of the Powers of the Criminal Courts Act 1973.

13.30 A bankruptcy petition cannot be presented unless the debtor:[3]

(a) is domiciled in England and Wales; or
(b) is personally present in England and Wales on the day of presentation of the petition; or
(c) at any time within 3 years ending on the day of presentation has been ordinarily resident or had a place of residence in England and Wales, or has carried on business in England and Wales.

Carrying on business includes being a member of a firm or partnership and conducting business through an agent or manager for the debtor or the partnership.[4]

13.31 These jurisdiction provisions are subject to Art 3 of the EC Regulation on Insolvency Proceedings 2000 which requires that bankruptcy proceedings be commenced where the debtor has his centre of main interests.[5] Where those interests are in another EC Member State, the English court will not have jurisdiction.

---

[1] *Re A Company (No 006798 of 1995)* [1996] 1 WLR 491; *Re A Company (No 003689 of 1998)* (1998) *The Times*, October 7.
[2] A bankruptcy petition may also be presented by a temporary administrator or a liquidator appointed under the EC Regulation on Insolvency Proceedings 2000.
[3] IA 1986, s 265(1). This is subject to Art 3 of the EC Regulation where the debtor has his centre of main interests in another EC Member State.
[4] Ibid, s 265(2).
[5] Ibid, s 265(3).

13.32 The grounds for the presentation of a bankruptcy petition[1] have been noted above.[2] There are four prescribed statutory forms of creditor's petition set out in Sch 4 to the Rules:

Form 6.7   failure to comply with a statutory demand for a liquidated sum payable immediately;

Form 6.8   failure to comply with a statutory demand for a liquidated sum payable at a future date;

Form 6.9   where execution or other legal process on a judgment has been returned in whole or in part;

Form 6.10   default in connection with a voluntary arrangement.

A petition presented on the basis of an unsatisfied execution is limited to a return by the High Court sheriff or county court bailiff. It does not cover other forms of judgment enforcement such as garnishee or charging orders. The usual practice (at least in the High Court) is that the sheriff's or bailiff's return must be produced to the court. It must be shown that there was a serious attempt to levy execution. A return which simply states that the sheriff or bailiff was unable to gain access will be insufficient.[3]

FORMALITIES

13.33 The contents of the petition are prescribed in the relevant form, rr 6.7 and 6.8 of the Rules and para 15 of the Practice Direction. The petition does not require dating, signing or witnessing.[4] Where the petition is based on a statutory demand, only the debt claimed in the demand may be included.[5] A creditor cannot claim in the petition a greater sum than that included in the demand, eg by including interest accrued from the date of the demand.[6] However, r 7.55 may save a petition from being dismissed where it irregularly includes post-statutory demand interest.[7]

13.34 The petition must set out the date of service of the statutory demand.[8] In the case of personal service, the date of service as set out in the affidavit of service should be recited and whether service is effected before or after 5 pm on Monday to Friday or at any time on a Saturday or a Sunday.[9] In the case of substituted service (other than by advertisement) the date alleged in the

---

[1]   Set out in IA 1986, ss 267 and 268.
[2]   See **13.12** and **13.13**.
[3]   *Re A Debtor (No 340 of 1992)* [1994] 2 BCLC 171, Aldous J; [1996] 2 All ER 211, CA.
[4]   Practice Direction, para 15.1.
[5]   Practice Direction, para 15.3.
[6]   IR 1986, r 6.8(1)(c).
[7]   See *Re A Debtor (No 510 of 1997)* (1998) *The Times*, June 18.
[8]   Practice Direction, para 15.5.
[9]   See CPR, r 6.7(2) and (3).

affidavit of service should be recited. This will usually be 7 days after posting or letter box insertion. In the case of substituted service by advertisement[1] it will be the date of the advertisement or, as the case may be, the first advertisement.

13.35 Where the petition is based on a statutory demand following a county court judgment a certificate must be endorsed on the petition stating:[2]

> 'I/We certify that on the   day of   20   I/We attended on the county court and was/were informed by an officer of the court that no money had been paid into court in the action or matter [*name*] v [*name*] [*Claim no*] pursuant to the statutory demand.'

The endorsement is not required if the petition is additionally based on a debt over £750 which is not the subject of a county court judgment.

ISSUE OF PETITION

13.36 The petition will be issued in the High Court in the following cases:[3]

(a)   if the petition is presented by a minister of the Crown or a government department and either (i) it is based on a statutory demand which has specified an intention to petition in that court, or (ii) the petition is based upon an unsatisfied execution;

(b)   if the debtor has resided or carried on business within the London insolvency district for the greater part of the 6 months immediately preceding the presentation of the petition, or for a longer period in those 6 months than any other insolvency district;

(c)   the debtor is not resident in England and Wales;

(d)   the petitioner is unable to ascertain the residence or place of business of the debtor.

In any other case the petition will be presented in the county court for the insolvency district in which the debtor has resided or carried on business for the longest period during those 6 months.[4] If he has carried on business in one district and resided in another, the petition will be presented to the court in the insolvency district in which he has resided.[5] If he has carried on business in more than one district in the 6-month period, the petition will be presented to the court in the insolvency district which is or has been his

---

1   IR 1986, r 6.3.
2   Practice Direction, para 15.7(2).
3   IR 1986, r 6.9(1).
4   Ibid, r 6.9(2).
5   Ibid, r 6.9(2).

principal place of business for the longest period.[1] Where an IVA is in force it will be presented in the court in which the nominees report was submitted.[2] If the petition is presented in the wrong court, the court has power[3] to transfer it, or order that the proceedings continue in the court in which they have been commenced.

13.37 In order to issue a petition there must be presented to the court:[4]

(a)   an affidavit or witness statement verified by a statement of truth;[5]

(b)   where the petition is based upon a statutory demand, an affidavit (or witness statement verified by a statement of truth) of service of the demand exhibiting a copy of the petition;

(c)   the court issue fee plus the deposit for the Official Receiver's fees – if a bankruptcy order is not made, the deposit will be returned.

Sufficient copies of the petition must be filed for service on the debtor and on the supervisor of any IVA in force.[6]

Prescribed forms are available for affidavit of service of the demand. Form 6.11 sets out the form for personal service; Form 6.12 sets out the form for substituted service. Where the demand has been acknowledged (however served) the acknowledgement must be exhibited to the affidavit.[7] If the demand has been neither personally served nor acknowledged, the affidavit of service must set out the steps taken to serve the debtor personally and state the means whereby it was sought to bring the demand to the debtor's attention. It must also specify a date by which, to the best of the knowledge, information and belief of the deponent, the demand was brought to the debtor's attention.[8] The date specified will be deemed to be the date of service unless the court otherwise orders.[9] The court, however, may decline to file a petition if it is not satisfied that the creditor has discharged the obligation to do all that is reasonable to bring the demand to the debtor's attention.[10] If there is a delay of greater than 4 months between the service of the statutory demand and the presentation of the petition, the reasons for the delay must be explained in the affidavit verifying the petition.[11]

---

[1]   IR 1986, r 6.9(4).

[2]   Ibid, r 6.9(4A).

[3]   Under ibid, r 7.12.

[4]   Ibid, r 6.10.

[5]   In accordance with ibid, rr 6.12(1) and 7.57(5).

[6]   Ibid, r 6.10(3).

[7]   Ibid, r 6.11(4).

[8]   Ibid, r 6.11(5).

[9]   Ibid, r 6.11(7).

[10]   Ibid, r 6.11(9).

[11]   Ibid, r 6.12(7).

EXPEDITED PETITION

13.38 A petition based on a statutory demand should not ordinarily be issued until 3 weeks have elapsed from the service of the demand until any application to set aside the demand has been disposed of by the court.[1] However, under s 270 of the Act the court may permit a petition to be expedited if there is a serious possibility that the debtor's property will be diminished during that period and the petition contains a statement to that effect. An expedited petition may even be issued where there is an outstanding application to set aside the demand.[2] In cases where there is strong evidence of potential dissipation of assets prior to the making of a bankruptcy order, the court may appoint the Official Receiver as interim manager of the debtor's property.[3]

13.39 The court will not usually hear a petition until at least 14 days have elapsed since it was served on the debtor.[4] This time-limit may be abridged if it appears that the debtor has absconded, it is a proper case for an expedited hearing, or the debtor consents.[5] However, a bankruptcy order will not be made on an expedited petition until at least 3 weeks have elapsed from the service of the statutory demand.[6]

SERVICE OF PETITION

13.40 As with statutory demands, the overriding requirement is to effect personal service on the debtor.[7] If the court is satisfied that the debtor is keeping out of the way to avoid service, or for any other cause, it may order substituted service of the petition.[8] Paragraph 11.4 of the Practice Direction sets out the attempts to serve which will usually be required to justify an order for substituted service. Service of the petition will need to be proved by an affidavit or witness statement verified by a statement of truth exhibiting a copy of the petition and, in cases where substituted service of the petition has been ordered, a copy of the order.[9]

---

[1]   IA 1986, s 268(1)(a); IR 1986, and r 6.4(3).
[2]   *Focus Insurance v A Debtor* [1994] 1 WLR 46.
[3]   IA 1986, s 286.
[4]   IR 1986, r 6.18(1).
[5]   Ibid, r 6.18(2).
[6]   Ibid, r 6.18(2).
[7]   Ibid, r 6.14(1).
[8]   Ibid, r 6.14(2).
[9]   Ibid, r 6.15.

MATTERS BEFORE HEARING OF PETITION

13.41 The court has jurisdiction over various matters before the hearing of the petition. The most important are as follows.

Consensual dismissal or withdrawal of petition with leave

13.42 A petition cannot be withdrawn save with leave of the court,[1] eg where the petition debt has been paid or terms of settlement have been agreed.

13.43 Where the petitioner applies to the court for the petition to be dismissed or withdrawn, he must (unless the court otherwise requires) file an affidavit setting out the grounds of the application and the circumstances in which it is made.[2] If, following presentation of the petition, payment has been made, the affidavit must set out (a) what dispositions have been made for the purposes of the settlement, (b) whether any dispositions were of the debtor, and (c) whether any disposition of the debtor's property was made with leave of the court.

13.44 The court cannot give leave to withdraw the petition before it is heard.[3] In practice, the High Court will permit withdrawal of the petition before service and will order it to be dismissed after service. The court will usually dispense with the detailed affidavit where no creditors have given notice supporting the petition. Such orders may be made without attendance.[4] Where a petition is withdrawn or dismissed after payment of the petitioning debt, the petitioning creditor will usually be entitled to an order for costs.[5]

Non-consensual dismissal

13.45 The court may dismiss a petition,[6] eg for want of prosecution.

Disclosure and further information

13.46 Any party to insolvency proceedings may apply to the court for orders for clarification and further information in accordance with CPR Part 18, and for disclosure in accordance with CPR Part 31.[7]

Security for costs

13.47 Rule 7.51 of the Rules incorporates the provisions of the CPR into insolvency proceedings, save in so far as they are inconsistent with the Rules.

---

[1]　IA 1986, s 266(2).
[2]　IR 1986, r 6.32.
[3]　Ibid, r 6.32(3).
[4]　Practice Direction, para 16.3(2).
[5]　*Re A Debtor (No 510 of 1997)* (1998) *The Times*, June 18.
[6]　IA 1986, s 266.
[7]　IR 1986, r 7.60 (as amended).

Accordingly, the principles upon which the court will order a claimant to proceedings to provide security will apply to petitions. In addition to these provisions, in relation to petitions presented in respect of debts payable in the future the petitioner may be required to give security for the debtor's costs.[1]

HEARING OF PETITION

13.48 The petition will not be heard until at least 14 days after service on the debtor (subject to expedition or where the debtor has absconded).[2] The persons who may appear are the petitioner, the debtor, the supervisor of any IVA in force and any creditor who has given notice of intention to appear.[3] A creditor who has not given notice may appear with leave of the court.[4]

13.49 A debtor opposing the petition must, not later than 7 days before the day fixed for the hearing, file and serve a notice specifying the grounds of opposition.[5] The Rules provide no penal sanction for non-compliance with this rule. Failure to serve a notice probably amounts to an irregularity under r 7.55, which may be waived. Whilst there is a conflict of first instance authority on the point, the Court of Appeal has held that on the hearing of the petition the debtor cannot go back and re-argue the grounds on which he unsuccessfully sought to have the statutory demand set aside.[6]

13.50 The court will not make a bankruptcy order unless it is satisfied that the debt or one of the debts in respect of which the petition was presented is either:[7] (a) a debt, having been payable at the date of presentation or having become payable, which has neither been paid nor secured or compounded for; or (b) a debt which the debtor has no reasonable prospect of being able to pay when it falls due. The court may dismiss the petition if it is satisfied that the debtor is able to pay all his debts (including contingent and prospective liabilities), or is satisfied that the debtor has made an offer to secure or compound the petition debt, that the acceptance of the offer would have required the dismissal of the petition, and that the creditor has unreasonably refused.[8]

13.51 The court may make a bankruptcy order if satisfied that the statements in the petition are true and the petition debt has not been paid, secured or

---

[1]   IR 1986, r 6.17.
[2]   Ibid, r 6.18.
[3]   Ibid, r 6.23.
[4]   Ibid, r 6.23(4).
[5]   Ibid, r 6.21.
[6]   *Turner v Royal Bank of Scotland* [2000] BPIR 683.
[7]   IA 1986, s 271(1).
[8]   Ibid, s 271(3).

compounded for.[1] The court must investigate the statements in the petition, including the underlying debt. Where the debt is disputed the court may give directions for service of evidence, disclosure, and for deponents to attend for cross-examination. If the petition is brought in respect of a judgment, the court may stay or dismiss the petition on the ground that an appeal is pending or that execution has been stayed.[2] A petition will not be dismissed solely on the grounds that the debt is overstated. [3]

13.52 Where an appeal is pending from the judgment on which the petition is based the court may stay or dismiss the petition where the appeal is genuine.[4] If the petitioning creditor fails to appear at the hearing of the petition he will not be entitled to present another petition in respect of the same debt without leave.[5] If the petition has not been served by the hearing date the petitioner may apply for an extension stating the reasons why the petition has not been served.[6]

ADJOURNMENT AND SUBSTITUTION

13.53 The court has power to adjourn the hearing of the petition,[7] but repeated adjournments to allow the debtor to make payments by instalments are improper.

13.54 Two separate provisions in the Rules[8] allow supporting creditors to take over a petition in circumstances where the original petitioning creditor is found not to be entitled to continue with its petition, or for a variety of reasons does not proceed with it. Where a petitioner is found not to be entitled to petition, consents to withdraw the petition, allows it to be dismissed, consents to adjournment, fails to appear or does not seek a bankruptcy order, a supporting creditor may apply for substitution provided it satisfies three conditions:[9]

(a)   it has given notice of intention to appear pursuant to r 6.23;
(b)   it is desirous of prosecuting the petition;
(c)   it was in a position to present its own petition on the date when the petition was presented.

---

[1]   IR 1986, r 6.25(1).
[2]   Ibid, r 6.25(2).
[3]   Ibid, r 6.25(3).
[4]   *Re A Debtor (No 799 of 1994) ex parte Cobbs Property Services* [1995] 1 WLR 467.
[5]   IR 1986, r 6.26.
[6]   Ibid, r 6.28.
[7]   Ibid, r 6.29.
[8]   Ibid, rr 6.30 and 6.31.
[9]   Ibid, r 6.30.

13.55 A substituting creditor must therefore have either served a statutory demand more than 21 days before the petition in respect of which there was no outstanding application to set aside, or had an unsatisfied sheriff's return. If an order for substitution is made, the petition must be amended to include the details of the substituted debt, re-verified and re-served.

13.56 As an alternative to substitution, the court may authorise a supporting creditor to have the carriage of the petition in place of the original petitioner.[1] If an application is successful, the petition is not amended but is proceeded with in its original form by the 'new' petitioner. The petition is prosecuted on its original basis. The applicant must have served notice of support[2] and must be an unpaid and unsecured creditor.[3] The court may order change in carriage of the petition where the petitioner intends to secure the postponement, adjournment or withdrawal of the petition, or does not intend to prosecute it diligently, or at all.[4] Whilst r 6.31 contains none of the restrictions on the ability of the new petitioner to present its own petition, it provides[5] that no order can be made if the petitioner's debt has been paid, secured or compounded by either a disposition by a third party or a disposition by the debtor which has been ratified by the court.[6]

MAKING A BANKRUPTCY ORDER

13.57 A bankruptcy order will be settled by the court and state the date of presentation of the petition and the time and date of the order.[7] The usual order as to costs is that the petitioning creditor's costs are paid as an expense of the bankruptcy. If the debt is paid before the hearing of the petition the petitioner will generally be entitled to its costs.[8] Copies of the order are sent by the court to the Official Receiver, who sends a copy to the debtor and a copy to the Chief Land Registrar.[9]

---

[1]   IR 1986, r 6.31.
[2]   Ibid, r 6.23.
[3]   Ibid, r 6.31(2)(a).
[4]   Ibid, r 6.31(2)(b).
[5]   Ibid, r 6.31(3).
[6]   IA 1986, s 284.
[7]   IR 1986, r 6.33.
[8]   *Re A Debtor (No 510 of 1997)* (1998) *The Times*, June 18.
[9]   IR 1986, r 6.34.

BANKRUPTCY PETITION IN CONNECTION WITH IVAs

13.58 A supervisor or person bound by an IVA may petition for the bankruptcy of the debtor.[1] The court will not make a bankruptcy order unless it is satisfied:

(a)   that the debtor has failed to comply with his obligations under the IVA; or

(b)   that materially false or misleading information was provided by the debtor to the creditors in relation to the approval of the IVA; or

(c)   the debtor failed to do anything reasonably required of him by the supervisor for the purposes of the IVA.[2]

13.59 There is no requirement for a bankruptcy petition to be preceded in these circumstances by a statutory demand. The petition is made using Form 6.10. The rules in Chapter 6 relating to a creditor's petition also apply to a petition under s 264(1)(c) of the Act with any necessary modifications.[3]

13.60 The petition may contain a request for the appointment as trustee in bankruptcy of a person who was the former supervisor of an IVA.[4] In such case the proposed appointee must, not less than 2 days before the hearing of the petition, file in court a report giving particulars of the date on which he gave written notice to those creditors bound by the arrangement of his intention to seek appointment, such date to be at least 10 days before the day on which the report is filed, and detail any responses.[5]

APPEALS IN BANKRUPTCY

13.61 Any order made by a county court or registrar of the High Court in bankruptcy proceedings may be appealed to a single judge of the High Court ('a first appeal').[6] The procedure and practice for a first appeal are governed by r 7.49, applying CPR Part 52, subject to modifications made in Part 4 of the Practice Direction. A first appeal does not require the permission of any court.[7] An appeal from a single judge of the High Court which is not a decision on a first appeal lies, with permission of the judge or the Court of Appeal, to the Court of Appeal.[8] An appeal from a decision of a judge of the High Court made on a first appeal lies, with the permission of the Court of

---

[1]   IA 1986, s 264(1)(c).
[2]   Ibid, s 276(1).
[3]   IR 1986, r 6.6.
[4]   IA 1986, s 297(5).
[5]   IR 1986, r 6.10(6).
[6]   IA 1986, s 375(2); IR 1986, r 7.48(2); Practice Direction, para 17.2(1).
[7]   Practice Direction, para 17.6.
[8]   Ibid, para 17.3(2).

Appeal, to the Court of Appeal.[1] An appellant's notice is in Form PDIP1; a respondent's notice is in Form PDIP2.

13.62 Appeals in bankruptcy are filed as follows:[2]

(1)   An appeal from a bankruptcy registrar must, or any decision made in the county court may, be filed at the Royal Courts of Justice in London.

(2)   An appeal from a decision in a county court exercising jurisdiction over an area within the Birmingham, Bristol, Cardiff, Leeds, Liverpool, Manchester, Preston or Newcastle upon Tyne Chancery District Registries may be filed in the Chancery District Registry of the High Court appropriate to the area in which the decision was made.

13.63 An appellant's notice must be filed within such period as may be directed by the lower court, or 14 days after the date of decision appealed against.[3] An application for extension of time must be requested in the appeal notice stating the reason for the delay. The court will fix a date for the hearing of the application for an extension.[4]

13.64 Unless the court otherwise orders, an appeal notice must be served by the appellant as soon as is practicable, and in any event not more than 7 days after it is filed.[5] A respondent who wishes to ask the court to uphold the order of the lower court for additional or different reasons must file a respondent's notice within such period as may be directed by the lower court, or 14 days after the date of the appellant's notice.[6] The notice must be served as soon as is practicable, and in any event not more than 7 days after it is filed. A party may not rely on matters not contained in his appeal notice unless the court gives permission.[7]

13.65 An application to vary the time-limits must be made to the appeal court. It may not be agreed by the parties.[8] Unless the appeal court or the lower court orders, an appeal does not operate as a stay. An appeal notice may not be amended without permission of the appeal court. A judge of the appeal court may strike out the whole or part of an appeal notice.

13.66 The appeal court has all the powers of the lower court, plus additional powers to:

---

1   Practice Direction, para 17.3(1).
2   Ibid, para 17.10.
3   Ibid, para 17.11(2).
4   Ibid, para 17.11(1).
5   Ibid, para 17.11(3).
6   Ibid, para 17.12.
7   Ibid, para 17.18(5).
8   Ibid, para 17.13.

(a)   affirm, set aside or vary any order or judgment given by the lower court;

(b)   refer any claim or issue for determination to the lower court;

(c)   order a new trial or hearing;

(d)   make a costs order.[1]

13.67 Every appeal is limited to a review of the decision of the lower court. The appeal court will allow an appeal where the decision of the lower court was wrong or unjust because of a serious procedural or other irregularity in proceedings.[2] The appeal court will not receive oral evidence or evidence that was not before the lower court.[3]

13.68 The following applications may be made to a judge of the appeal court:[4]

(a)   an injunction pending a substantive hearing of the appeal;

(b)   an application for expedition or vacation of the date of an appeal;

(c)   an application for an order striking out the whole or part of an appeal notice;

(d)   an application for a final order on paper pursuant to para 17.22(8) of the Practice Direction.

13.69 All other interim applications must be made to the registrar of appeals in the first instance. An appeal from a registrar of appeals lies to the judge of the appeal court. Permission is not required.[5]

13.70 The Practice Direction sets out various procedural matters for a first appeal to a judge of the High Court, as follows.[6]

(1)   The appellant must file two copies of the appeal notice, plus additional copies for service, a copy of the order under appeal, and a time estimate for the appeal.

(2)   If the documents are correct and in order the court will fix a hearing date. It will send a letter to the appellant setting out the requirements concerning bundles, which must be lodged not less than 7 days before the appeal and should include an approved transcript of the judgment of the lower court.[7]

---

[1]   Practice Direction, para 17.17.
[2]   Ibid, para 17.18(3).
[3]   Ibid, para 17.18(2).
[4]   Ibid, para 17.19.
[5]   Ibid, para 17.20.
[6]   Ibid, para 17.22.
[7]   Or an approved note of the judgment.

(3) The appeal notice must be served on all parties to the proceedings in the lower court who are directly affected. This may include the Official Receiver, or the trustee in bankruptcy. Service of an appeal notice must be proved by a certificate of service.

(4) Skeleton arguments and a chronology must be lodged 2 clear days before the date fixed for hearing. Failure to do so may result in an adverse order for costs.

(5) An appeal may be discontinued or dismissed by consent on paper. The appeal court will not allow an appeal unless it is satisfied that the order of the lower court was wrong. A consent order signed by both parties, or letters of consent, must be lodged in court within 24 hours of the date fixed for the hearing of the appeal.

13.71 Where a judge of the High Court has made a bankruptcy order or dismissed an appeal against such order, and an application is made for a stay pending appeal, the judge will not normally grant a stay of all proceedings, but will confine himself to a stay of advertisement. Where a judge has granted permission to appeal, any stay of advertisement will normally be until the hearing of the appeal, but on terms that it will determine automatically if an appellant's notice is not filed in time. Where the judge has refused permission to appeal, any stay will normally be for a period not exceeding 28 days.[1]

REVIEW, RESCISSION AND VARIATION

13.72 Every court exercising bankruptcy jurisdiction may review, rescind or vary any order made by it in the exercise of that jurisdiction.[2] An application to review, rescind or vary is made to the same court and the same level of tribunal, and not to a judge or court acting on appeal. The court will be invited to review its own decision where there has been some material change in circumstance since the decision was made. In *Re A Debtor (32-SD-1991)*[3] Millett J held that the jurisdiction to review should be exercised rarely and not used as a gateway for late appeals. The restrictions on introducing evidence in appeals set out in *Ladd v Marshall*[4] do not apply to applications to review. The court is not considering what order should have been made on the evidence then available, but rather whether it should review or vary its previous decision on the evidence now available.

---

[1] Practice Direction, para 17.25.
[2] IA 1986, s 375(1).
[3] [1993] 1 WLR 314.
[4] [1954] 1 WLR 1489.

COSTS

13.73 Subject to any inconsistent provisions, Parts 43–45 and 47–48 of the CPR apply to insolvency proceedings.[1] Where the costs, charges or expenses of a person are payable out of the insolvent estate, the amount of those costs, charges or expenses must be decided by detailed assessment unless agreed between the insolvency practitioner and the person entitled to payment. In the absence of agreement the insolvency practitioner must serve notice in writing requiring detailed assessment in accordance with CPR Part 47 in the court to which the insolvency proceedings are allocated.[2]

13.74 In any proceedings, including proceedings on a petition, the court may order costs to be decided by detailed assessment.[3] The practice of the High Court registrars is to summarily assess costs of petitions and other applications in accordance with the procedures set out in the Practice Direction to CPR Part 44. Unless otherwise directed the costs of a trustee in bankruptcy will be allowed on a standard basis pursuant to CPR, rr 44.4 and 44.5.[4] Where costs are awarded against the official receiver or a trustee in bankruptcy, he is personally liable unless the court otherwise directs.[5]

DISTRIBUTION OF BUSINESS BETWEEN JUDGES AND REGISTRARS/DISTRICT JUDGES

13.75 The following applications may be made to the judge and, unless ordered otherwise, heard in public:[6]

---

[1] IR 1986, r 7.33.

[2] Ibid, r 7.34(1). This provision applies to any circumstance in which costs of a third party are payable out of the insolvent estate, eg the costs of any person, including the debtor appearing on a bankruptcy petition: IR 1986, r 6.224(1)(h).

[3] Ibid, r 7.34(4).

[4] In this respect the rule is less generous than costs awarded to an ordinary trustee or personal representative, which are awarded on an indemnity basis: CPR, r 48.4(2).

[5] IR 1986, r 7.39.

[6] Practice Direction, para 9.1.

(a)   applications for committal for contempt;
(b)   applications for injunctions or variations of injunctions;
(c)   applications for directions or interim relief after a matter has been referred to the judge.

13.76   All other applications may be made to the registrar or district judge in the first instance, who may either hear and determine the matter himself or refer it to the judge.

Chapter 14

CORPORATE INSOLVENCY

Sheila M Foley

INTRODUCTION

14.1 The CPR, the practice and procedure of the High Court and of the county court (including any Practice Direction), apply to insolvency proceedings in the High Court and county court, as the case may be, in either case with any necessary modifications, except in so far as inconsistent with the Insolvency Rules 1986 (the Rules). All insolvency proceedings are allocated to the multi-track.

14.2 The courts having jurisdiction to make orders under the Insolvency Act 1986 (the Act) and the Rules in respect of companies are courts which would have jurisdiction to wind up the companies in respect of which the applications relate. The High Court has jurisdiction to wind up all companies registered in England and Wales.[1] All matters involving the exercise of the High Court's jurisdiction under enactments relating to companies are assigned to the Chancery Division, but only certain district registries have a winding-up jurisdiction.[2]

14.3 A county court only has jurisdiction to wind up a company where the amount of the company's share capital paid up or credited as paid up does not exceed £120,000, and where the company has a registered office in the district of the county court.[3]

14.4 In all company insolvency proceedings in the High Court, 'the registrar' means a registrar in bankruptcy of the High Court or, where the proceedings are in a district registry or the county court having winding-up jurisdiction, a district judge.[4] The distribution of business between the judge, the registrar and the court manager is provided for in r 7.6(2) of the Rules and para 5 of the Practice Direction.[5]

---

[1]   IA 1986, s 117(1).
[2]   IR 1986, r 13.2(4); the District Registries are Birmingham, Bristol, Cardiff, Leeds, Liverpool, Manchester, Newcastle-upon-Tyne and Preston.
[3]   IA 1986, s 117(2).
[4]   IR 1986, r 13.2(4) and (5).
[5]   *Practice Direction: Insolvency Proceedings* [2000] BCC 92.

Form of applications

14.5 Part 7 of the Rules deals with the practice and procedure on all applications to the court, whether in corporate or personal insolvency, except for three categories of petition which are listed in r 7.1 as (a) an administration order under Part II, (b) a petition for a winding-up under Part IV, or (c) a petition for a bankruptcy order under Part IX.

14.6 Save for the exceptions listed above, all applications made to the court under the Act or the Rules are made in the form[1] either of:

(a)   an originating application (an application to the court which is not an application in pending proceedings before the court); or[2]
(b)   an ordinary application.[3]

The forms contained in Sch 4 to the Rules are used in insolvency proceedings whether in the High Court or the county court.[4]

14.7 The question whether an application should be originating or ordinary can be determined by ascertaining whether or not the application is to be made in proceedings presently before the court. An error often made by practitioners is based on a belief that once a winding-up order has been made all applications thereafter should be ordinary applications within the winding-up proceedings. This is incorrect. Once a final order has been made on a petition then, unless a general liberty to apply has been ordered, those proceedings are no longer pending proceedings. This applies both to a final order on a petition for winding-up and to an administration.

14.8 An application must be in writing and state the name of the parties, the nature of the relief or order applied for or the directions sought, the names and addresses of the persons (if any) on whom it is intended to serve the application (or that no person is intended to be served), the names and addresses of those persons to whom notice of the application is to be given, and the applicant's address for service.[5] An originating application must set out the grounds on which the applicant claims to be entitled to the relief sought.[6] In practice, reference is often made to a witness statement signed by or on behalf of the applicant in which the grounds are set out. There is no requirement to set out the grounds relied upon for the relief sought in an ordinary application. Either type of application must be signed by the

---

[1]   IR 1986, r 7.2(1).
[2]   Form 7.1.
[3]   Form 7.2.
[4]   IR 1986, r 12.7.
[5]   Ibid, r 7.3(1).
[6]   Ibid, r 7.3(2).

applicant if he is acting in person or, where he is not acting in person, by or on behalf of his solicitor.[1]

14.9 Subject to certain exceptions,[2] where the Rules provide for the use of an affidavit, a witness statement[3] verified by a statement of truth may be used as an alternative.[4]

14.10 On the face of the application, underneath the name of the court and/or district registry in which the application is to be issued, the application must state that it is 'In the Matter of [*name of company to which the proceedings relate*]' and 'And in the Matter of the Insolvency Act 1986'.[5] The parties are described as the applicant and the respondent. Where a liquidator is a party to an application he should be described not by his individual name but as the liquidator. Where the Official Receiver is liquidator, he should be described as 'the Official Receiver as Liquidator' of the particular company. Where an application is brought by a liquidator in the name of a company, the name of the applicant should appear as 'The AB Company Limited'. Although there is no requirement to include the words 'in liquidation' after the name of the company, this practice is often adopted.

Filing and service of applications

14.11 The application must be filed in court, together with sufficient copies for service on each of the respondents, and with one additional copy.[6] Service of documents in the High Court is the responsibility of the party issuing the application.[7] Practitioners are advised to check with the county court in which the application is issued to ascertain the local practice with regard to service.

14.12 Personal service of an application on a respondent is not expressly required. Subject to r 12.10, CPR Part 6 (service of documents) applies as regards any matter relating to the service of documents and the giving of notice in insolvency proceedings.[8] For a document to be properly served by post, it must be contained in an envelope addressed to the person on whom it is to be effected, and pre-paid for either first- or second-class post.[9] A document served by post may be sent to the last-known address of the person

---

1   IR 1986, r 7.3(3).
2   Ibid, r 7.57(6).
3   Ibid, r 7.57(5).
4   Ibid, r 7.57(5) does not apply to rr 3.4, 4.33, 6.60 (statement of affairs), 4.42, 6.66, 6.72
     (further disclosure), 4.39, 4.40, 6.65, 6.70 (accounts) 4.73, 4.77, 6.96, 6.99 (claims) and 9.3 and 9.4
     (examinations).
5   Ibid, r 7.26(1).
6   Ibid, r 7.4(1).
7   Practice Direction, para 1.3.
8   IR 1986, r 12.11.
9   Ibid, r 12.10(1).

to be served.[1] Where first-class post is used, the document is treated as served on the second business day after the date of posting, unless the contrary is shown.[2] Where second-class post is used, the document is treated as served on the fourth business day after the date of posting, unless the contrary is shown.[3] The date of posting is presumed, unless the contrary is shown, to be the date shown on the post mark on the envelope.[4]

14.13 An application must be served at least 14 days before the date fixed for the hearing unless the provisions of the Act or the Rules provide otherwise.[5] Where the case is urgent, the court may (a) hear the application immediately, either with or without notice to, or the attendance of, other parties, or (b) authorise a shorter period of service than the prescribed 14 days.[6] If the court does hear an urgent application it will give directions as to the filing or service of documents as it thinks appropriate in the circumstances.

Hearing applications

14.14 At the first hearing the court will give the directions it considers appropriate to the further conduct of the application. If the application involves substantial disputes of fact, and is a case in which it is likely that the court will direct that particulars of claim and defence be filed and served, it is unnecessary to file evidence in support of the application. However, if a party intends to rely on evidence at the first hearing, the evidence must be served at least 14 days before the hearing.[7]

14.15 The court may at any time give such directions as it thinks fit as to:

(a)   service or notice of the application on or to any person, whether in connection with the venue of a resumed hearing or for any other purpose;

(b)   whether particulars of claim and defence are to be delivered, and generally as to the procedure on the application;

(c)   the manner in which any evidence is to be adduced at a resumed hearing and in particular as to:

    (i)   the taking of evidence wholly or in part by affidavit or orally;

    (ii)   the cross-examination either before the judge or registrar in court or in chambers, of any deponents to affidavits; and

    (iii)   any report to be given by the official receiver or any person mentioned in r 7.9(1)(b);

---

[1]   IR 1986, r 12.10(1A).
[2]   Ibid, r 12.10(2).
[3]   Ibid, r 12.10(3).
[4]   Ibid, r 12.10(4).
[5]   Ibid, r 7.4(5).
[6]   Ibid, r 7.4(6).
[7]   Ibid, r 7.8(1).

(d)   the matters to be dealt with in evidence.[1]

14.16 Any party to insolvency proceedings may apply to the court for an order (a) that any other party clarify any matter which is in dispute in the proceedings, or give additional information in relation to any such matter in accordance with CPR Part 18; or (b) to obtain disclosure from any other party in accordance with CPR Part 31.[2] It should be noted that unless a party applies for disclosure in insolvency proceedings, there is no automatic provision for disclosure.

CREDITORS' WINDING-UP PETITIONS

14.17 Winding-up proceedings are commenced by the presentation of a petition to a court. It is essential that any threat of presentation of a winding-up petition against a company is dealt with without delay. The presentation of a petition and its subsequent advertisement can cause considerable damage to a company's business, even if the petition is subsequently withdrawn, struck out or dismissed.

14.18 This section of the chapter deals with a statutory-defined procedure which enables a person to apply to the court for an order that the affairs of a company be wound up. Section 124 of the Act sets out the range of persons who are permitted to initiate compulsory winding-up proceedings. Section 122(1) sets out the circumstances in which a company may be wound up by the court. The most common ground relied on by creditors is that the company is unable to pay its debts, ie it is insolvent.[3] The following discussion deals with applications of creditors for winding-up orders, and the steps that can be taken by the company to prevent a winding-up order being made.

Provisional liquidator

14.19 The court has power to appoint a provisional liquidator.[4] The effect of the appointment is to grant interim control of the company to a liquidator until the final determination of the liquidation proceedings. Effective winding-up proceedings must be in existence which disclose a good ground for winding-up. Where the appointment of a provisional liquidator is extremely urgent, the application for the appointment may be lodged contemporaneously with the winding-up petition. Applications for a provisional liquidator must be made direct to the judge.[5]

---

[1]   IR 1986, r 7.10(2).
[2]   Ibid, r 7.60(1).
[3]   Ibid, s 122(1)(f).
[4]   Ibid, s 135(1).
[5]   Practice Direction, para 5.1(4).

14.20   Section 135 of the Act does not set out the grounds on which an order may be made, and a review of the authorities is outside the scope of this chapter. The basis for the application is, in most instances, a belief that the assets and affairs of the company are in jeopardy and that the directors and/or shareholders may dissipate the assets while the liquidation proceedings are pending, thereby resulting in creditors being disadvantaged.

14.21   An application can be made by:

(a)   the petitioner;
(b)   a creditor of the company;
(c)   a contributory;
(d)   the company;
(e)   the Secretary of State;
(f)   a temporary administrator;
(g)   a Member State liquidator appointed in main proceedings; or
(h)   any person who, under any enactment, would be entitled to present a petition for the winding-up of the company.[1]

The application must be supported by an affidavit which includes the following matters:

(a)   the grounds on which it is proposed that a provisional liquidator should be appointed;
(b)   if a person other than the official receiver is proposed to be appointed, that the person has consented to act and, to the best of the applicant's belief, is qualified to act as an insolvency practitioner in relation to the company;
(c)   whether or not the official receiver has been informed of the application and, if so, has been furnished with a copy of it;
(d)   whether, to the applicant's knowledge:
　　(i)   there has been proposed or is in force a voluntary arrangement under Part I of the Act; or
　　(ii)   an administrator or administrative receiver is acting in relation to the company; or
　　(iii)   a liquidator has been appointed for its voluntary winding-up; and
(e)   the applicant's estimate of the value of the assets in respect of which the provisional liquidator is to be appointed.[2]

A copy of the application and affidavit in support must be sent to the Official Receiver, who may attend the hearing and make any representations he considers appropriate. If the court is satisfied that sufficient grounds for the

---

[1]   IR 1986, r 4.25(1).
[2]   Ibid, r 4.25(2).

appointment are shown, it may make the order on such terms as it thinks fit. The form of the order appointing the provisional liquidator must specify the functions to be carried out by him in relation to the company's affairs.[1]

14.22 A provisional liquidator may be removed by order of the court.[2] Termination of the appointment can be ordered by the court on its own motion or on the application of the appointee, the petitioner, a creditor or contributory.[3]

Formal demand for payment of debt

14.23 A company is presumed to be insolvent where it neglects to comply with a statutory demand.[4] The demand requires the company to pay the sum due within 3 weeks, and if the company neglects to pay the sum due, or to secure or compound for it, to the reasonable satisfaction of the creditor, it will be presumed to be unable to pay its debts.[5]

14.24 The statutory demand must be in the prescribed form[6] and must satisfy the requirements set out in rr 4.4–4.6 of the Rules. It must be left at the registered office of the debtor company. Personal service of the statutory demand at the registered office is recommended to avoid any dispute over the validity of its service.

14.25 It is not necessary to serve a statutory demand. A failure to pay an undisputed debt which is due and for which a demand has been made is evidence of the company's inability to pay its debts.[7] The failure to pay can be the basis for a petition, notwithstanding the fact that a statutory demand has not been served. This demand should be made in writing and specify a date by which payment should be made. It is advisable that specific reference is made to winding-up proceedings being commenced in the event of non-payment.

14.26 When a statutory demand (or a formal letter of demand threatening to present a petition) is served in respect of a debt, which debt is disputed in good faith on substantial grounds, a petition based on that debt, it is liable to be struck out or dismissed with costs, and the abuse of process may result in an order for indemnity costs.[8] If the alleged debt is genuinely disputed on substantial grounds, or where the petition debt is equalled or exceeded by a true set-off available to the company, or where the company has an unrelated

---

[1]   Form 4.15.
[2]   IA 1986, s 172(1).
[3]   IR 1986, rr 4.25(1) and 4.31(1).
[4]   IA 1986, s 123(1)(a).
[5]   Ibid, s 123(1)(a).
[6]   IR 1986, r 4.5. Form 4.1.
[7]   IA 1986, s 123(1)(e).
[8]   *Re A Company (No 0012209 of 1991)* [1992] BCLC 865.

counterclaim which equals or exceeds the creditor's claim, the company should write to the creditor or its legal representative immediately in terms which include:

(a)   details of why the debt is disputed, with reference to any previous correspondence from the company in which the debt had previously been disputed, details of any set-off or cross-claim;

(b)   reference to the threat of winding-up proceedings being an abuse of process; and

(c)   a request for an undertaking to be given within a stated period of time that a winding-up petition will not be presented, or a request that a particular period of notice be given prior to presentation of the petition to enable the company to make an application to restrain its presentation.

14.27 An application to restrain presentation of a winding-up petition is made by an originating application returnable before the judge in open court.[1] A supporting witness statement must be filed, setting out the facts relied on, including:

(a)   the relationship between the company and the alleged creditor;

(b)   full and detailed particulars of the dispute relating to the claim, including any particulars of set-off and/or cross-claim;

(c)   the attempts made by the company to persuade the creditor that the debt is disputed and that a petition is inappropriate, including details of correspondence in which the dispute was first raised by the company; and

(d)   evidence of the solvency of the company.

The creditor is named as the respondent. The application must be addressed to the creditor who made the demand and should be served (together with the supporting evidence) immediately upon its being issued. The evidence (i) in support of an application to restrain presentation of a petition, (ii) in support of an application to restrain advertisement of the petition, and (iii) contesting the petition may contain hearsay evidence, although direct evidence is preferred where possible.

14.28 If there is insufficient time to issue and await the hearing date of the originating application to restrain presentation of the petition, the company should make an immediate application to the companies court judge for an order restraining presentation of the petition pending the hearing of the originating application. It is not necessary to issue an originating application before making the without notice application. The court may grant an interim

---

[1]   Practice Direction, para 8.1. Form 7.1.

order restraining the presentation until the *inter partes* hearing, on the company's undertaking to issue an originating application forthwith. If there is insufficient time to prepare a witness statement, a draft should be put before the judge, with an undertaking to have the same sworn forthwith. All relevant facts must be placed before the court, including details of the company's financial position. If full and frank disclosure of all relevant facts is not made by the company, the injunction may be set aside irrespective of the merits.[1] If the court restrains presentation of the petition at the without notice hearing, it will usually give directions for the service of the company's evidence and of the order and service of further evidence, and will fix a return day for the *inter partes* hearing. At the final hearing of the application, if the injunction is refused or a without notice injunction is set aside, the creditor may present his petition against the company.

Presentation of petition

14.29 Where:

(a)   no application to restrain presentation of the petition is made during the 3-week period following service of a statutory demand;

(b)   a creditor chooses to proceed on the basis of s 123(1)(e) of the Act (thereby avoiding the 3-week period delay required by the statutory demand method); or

(c)   an application to restrain presentation of the petition has been heard by the judge and dismissed;

a creditor can present a petition to wind up the company. The petition must be in the prescribed form[2] and state the nature of the relief sought and the grounds upon which the petition relies. The petition is presented at the registry of the appropriate court[3] together with an affidavit verifying the matters stated in the petition.[4] The petition is sealed at the court office and the court will fix a date, time and venue for the hearing, which is indorsed on each copy of the petition issued.[5] The petition must be served on the company at its registered office in the prescribed manner.[6]

14.30 The petitioner must advertise the presentation of the petition once in the *London Gazette*, unless the court directs otherwise,[7] no less than 7 business days after the date of service of the petition on the company, and not less than

---

1   *Brink's MAT Ltd v Elcombe* [1988] 1 WLR 1350, at 1356.
2   Form 4.2.
3   IR 1986, r 4.7(1).
4   Ibid, rr 4.7 and 4.12(1).
5   Ibid, r 4.7(6).
6   Ibid, r 4.8(3).
7   Ibid, r 4.11.

7 days before the hearing date.[1] The content of the advertisement must comply with r 4.11(4) of the Rules. Advertising the petition is intended to give other creditors an opportunity to support or oppose the winding-up, and to put on notice those who might trade with the company during the time from the presentation of the petition until it is determined.

14.31 If a company is served with a petition based on a debt which is genuinely disputed on substantial grounds, or the company has a genuine set-off equal to or exceeding the petition debt, an application to restrain advertisement of the petition and the removal of the petition from the file should be issued and heard within the 7-day period (if no undertaking to refrain from advertising has been given) in order to prevent the petition being advertised.[2] The application is made by originating application to the judge and, given the time constraints, will usually be heard immediately with or without notice to the petitioner, with a return day ordered by the court of 7 days. The application must be supported by a witness statement setting out the grounds of opposition. The court will usually give directions as to the filing of evidence, and the matter will be listed to be heard before a judge.

14.32 If the company has previously made an unsuccessful application to the judge for an order restraining presentation of the petition because the debt was not bona fide disputed on substantial grounds, the company may not apply to restrain advertisement on the same ground based on evidence which was, or with reasonable diligence could have been, available to the court on the earlier application.[3] The witness statement in support should include the information set out in **14.27** in addition to an explanation as to why no application to restrain presentation of the petition was issued. If the court grants an injunction restraining advertisement or continues indefinitely an injunction that was ordered at a without notice hearing, it will dismiss or strike out the petition. If the court refuses to grant an injunction restraining advertisement or discharges an earlier injunction, the petitioner will be entitled to advertise the petition.

Hearing of petition

14.33 By 4.30 pm on the Friday preceding the day on which the petition is to be heard, the petitioner must file in court a certificate of compliance with the Rules relating to service and advertisement.[4] On the hearing date, the petitioner must (a) prove service of the petition by affidavit specifying the manner of service[5] with requisite exhibits, and (b) provide an affidavit

---

[1]   IR 1986, r 4.11(2).
[2]   Ibid, r 4.11(2)(b); in calculating the 7-day period, weekends and bank holidays are excluded.
[3]   *Re Portedge Ltd* [1997] BCC 23.
[4]   Practice Direction, para 3.1.
[5]   IR 1986, r 4.9.

verifying the content of the petition.[1] The petitioner must also draw up a list of the persons (if any) who have notified the petitioner that they intend to appear at the hearing, indicating whether they intend to oppose or support the petition. The list is handed to the court before the commencement of the hearing.[2]

14.34 If the company intends to oppose the petition, its affidavit in opposition must be filed in court not less than 7 days before the date fixed for the hearing, and sent to the petitioner forthwith after filing.[3] If the company files an affidavit in opposition, the registrar will (in most instances) give directions for the petitioner to file evidence in answer and for the company to file evidence in reply. When the evidence is complete, the registrar will adjourn the petition to the judge for determination. If the hearing before the judge is estimated to take more than 2 hours, the petition will be adjourned to a date to be fixed.

14.35 In an application requesting a court to exercise its discretion to dismiss a petition (as opposed to an application to restrain presentation of the petition or advertisement), a company may rely on a counterclaim which is not related to the petition debt and is therefore not a true set-off.[4] It is essential that the evidence in opposition to the petition includes the matters noted at **14.27**, together with full particulars of the counterclaim. At the final hearing, the court will either dismiss the petition or order that the company be wound up.

Section 127 – validating transactions pending hearing of winding-up petition

14.36 Where a winding-up order is made, all dispositions of the property of the company since the date of presentation of the petition are void, unless the court orders otherwise.[5] Following a winding-up order, a person who received property from the company after the date of presentation of the petition can be required to restore that property to the company if it would be for the benefit of creditors generally. When a bank becomes aware that a petition has been presented against a customer, it will often freeze the company's account to ensure that it will not have to account for drawings made during the period between the date of presentation of the petition and the date when the winding-up order is made.

14.37 An application to restrain advertisement of the petition is usually coupled with an application under s 127 of the Act to validate the operation of

---

[1]   IR 1986, r 4.12.

[2]   Ibid, r 4.17; Form 4.10.

[3]   Ibid, r 4.18.

[4]   *Re A Company (No 006273 of 1992)* [1993] BCLC 131.

[5]   IA 1986, s 127(2).

the company's bank accounts and dispositions of the company's property in the ordinary course of business, pending the determination of the application to restrain advertisement. An application may be made to the court under s 127 for the prospective validation of a particular transaction before a winding-up order has been made.

14.38 Where an application to restrain advertisement of the petition is necessary, the application can seek additional relief for validation under s 127. The witness statement in support of the application must include evidence supporting the relief sought under s 127. The application may be made on its own, supported by a witness statement. In either instance, the application is made to the Companies Court judge[1] sitting in open court.

14.39 In the majority of cases, the company is the applicant. A shareholder, or the person to whom the property is to be or has been transferred, or a person claiming a proprietary right in the asset disposed of, may be the applicant. If the company is the applicant, the petitioner should be joined as the respondent. If the applicant is a shareholder or the person to whom the property is to be or has been transferred, the petitioner and the company are named as respondents.

14.40 The usual relief sought in a s 127 application is for an order:

(a)   that payments out of the company's bank account to satisfy debts incurred in the ordinary course of the company's business are not avoided pursuant to s 127; and/or

(b)   that the disposition of a specific property of the company is not avoided pursuant to s 127 in the event of the company being wound up.

14.41 Where the validation order is sought to continue to satisfy debts incurred in the ordinary course of business, ie day-to-day trading expenses, the application should be made immediately after service of the petition, and as a matter of urgency if the petition has been advertised. If a disposition of property has occurred after presentation of the petition and validation is required the court will consider whether it would have validated the proposed transfer had a prior application been made; and whether the transaction has had the effect of reducing the assets available in a winding-up for unsecured creditors.[2]

---

[1]   If the application is made prior to any winding-up order, the application should be made to the Companies Court judge, not the registrar; if the application is made after the winding-up order, it may be made to the registrar in the first instance: Practice Direction, para 5.1(2).

[2]   *Re Tramway Building & Construction Co Ltd* [1988] Ch 293.

14.42 An examination of the way in which the courts have exercised their discretion in the past on s 127 applications is outside the scope of this book. The overriding requirement for the court is to 'do its best to ensure that the interests of the unsecured creditors will not be prejudiced'.[1] The court may make a validation order where the company is solvent, has net assets, and is able to pay its debts as they fall due. Where the order is sought to enable the company to continue trading and to operate its bank accounts, the court must be satisfied by credible evidence that the trading is likely to be profitable and therefore for the benefit of all creditors.[2]

Leave for petitioner to withdraw petition

14.43 If, at least 5 days before the hearing of the petition the petitioner, on a without notice application, satisfies the court that (a) the petition has not been advertised, (b) no notices (whether in support or in opposition) have been received by him with reference to the petition, and (c) the company consents to an order being made under r 4.15 of the Rules, the court may grant the petitioner leave to withdraw the petition on such terms as to costs as the parties may agree.[3]

14.44 The application for permission to withdraw is made without notice by ordinary application to the court manager of the companies court.[4] A petitioner wishing to withdraw the petition should telephone the general office of the companies court at least one day before the day on which the application is to be made to ensure that the relevant file is available to the court manager at the hearing of the application. The application should be issued (at the latest) on the morning before the hearing before the court manager. The court manager hears applications at 11.00 am every weekday. The petitioner should ensure that a letter of consent from the company, a signed consent order, and any evidence as to an agreement on costs, are available to the court manager at the hearing.

Rescission of winding-up order

14.45 An application for the rescission of a winding-up order must be made within 7 days after the date on which the order was made.[5] Notice of the application must be given to the Official Receiver,[6] and it is considered good practice to give notice to the petitioning creditor and any supporting or opposing creditors of whom the applicant is aware. Applications will be entertained only if made by (a) a creditor, (b) a contributory, or (c) the

---

[1] *Re Gray's Inn Construction Co Ltd* [1980] 1 WLR 711.
[2] *Hollicourt (Contracts) Ltd (in liquidation) v Bank of Ireland* [2001] 1 BCLC 233.
[3] Form 4.8.
[4] IR 1986, r 13.2(2).
[5] Ibid, r 7.47(4).
[6] Practice Direction, para 7.1.

company jointly with a creditor or contributory. The application must be supported by written evidence of assets and liabilities.[1] Cases in which the making of the winding-up order has not been opposed may (if the application is made promptly) be dealt with on a statement by the applicant's legal representative of the circumstances. However, apart from such cases, the court will usually require any application to be supported by written evidence.[2]

14.46 The court has power to extend time for applying for rescission of a winding-up order[3] in appropriate circumstances. The circumstances in which an application to rescind the winding-up order is likely to succeed are outside the scope of this book.

ADMINISTRATION

14.47 Administration is a temporary measure which contemplates the rescue of a company, or its winding-up on a more favourable basis than would be achieved by an immediate winding-up. There are now two concurrent administration regimes. For most administrations begun from 15 September 2003 onwards, the new Part II of the Act, introduced by the Enterprise Act 2002, s 248, applies. For administrations begun before that date, Part II as originally enacted will continue to apply. The two regimes now have separate rules, each referred to as IR 1986, Part 2. Great care must be taken to ensure that the correct rules are applied. Schedule B1 was inserted into the 1986 Act by the Enterprise Act 2002, s 248. References in the text below to paragraph numbers correspond with paragraph numbering in Sch B1 to the 1986 Act. References to the new Insolvency Rules are indicated by the words 'new IR'.

14.48 An administrator may be appointed in three ways:

(a)   by court order;[4]
(b)   by the holder of a qualifying floating charge;[5]
(c)   by the company or its directors.[6]

The company enters into administration when an administrator is appointed. The administrator must be a licensed insolvency practitioner.

---

1   Practice Direction, para 7.2.
2   Ibid, para 7.4.
3   IR 1986, r 12.9(2).
4   IA 1986, Sch B1, para 10.
5   Ibid, Sch B1, para 14.
6   Ibid, Sch B1, para 22.

Court-appointed administrator

14.49 An application for an administration order may be made by one or more of the following:

(a)   the company;[1]
(b)   its directors;[2]
(c)   one or more of its creditors; or
(d)   the chief executive of the magistrates' court where the court has imposed a fine on the company.[3]

The administration application must be in Form 2.1B and an affidavit complying with the new IR, r 2.4 must be prepared, and sworn and filed with the court in support of the application.[4] A written statement in Form 2.2B, made by each of the proposed administrators, and which includes the matters set out in the new IR, r 2.3(5), must be attached to the application. The application and supporting documents must be filed with the court, with a sufficient number of copies for service and use.[5] An administration application may not be withdrawn without the permission of the court.[6]

14.50   The application, affidavit and supporting documentation must be served on the persons set out in the new IR, r 2.6 not less than 5 days before the date fixed for the hearing[7] in the manner set out in the new IR, r 2.8. Service of the application must be verified by affidavit of service in Form 2.3B, specifying the date on which, and the manner in which, service was effected. The affidavit of service must be filed in court not less than one day before the hearing of the application. After the application is filed, it is the duty of the applicant to notify the court in writing of the existence of any insolvency proceedings, and any insolvency proceedings under the EC Regulation, in relation to the company, as soon as he becomes aware of them.

14.51 Where there is an administrative receiver of a company the court must dismiss an administration application in respect of the company unless:

(1)   the person by or on behalf of whom the receiver was appointed consents to the making of the administration order;
(2)   the court considers that the security by virtue of which the receiver was appointed would be liable to be released or discharged under

---

1   An application by the supervisor of a CVA is treated as if it were an application by the company: new IR 1986, r 2.2(4).
2   This includes a majority of the directors under IR 1986, Sch B1, para 105.
3   Ibid, Sch B1, para 12.
4   New IR, r 2.2.
5   New IR, r 2.6.
6   IR 1986, Sch B1, para 12(3).
7   New IR, r 2.8(1).

ss 238–240 of the Act (transactions at undervalue and preference) if an administration order were made;

(3)   the court considers that the security by virtue of which the receiver was appointed would be avoided under s 245 of the Act (avoidance of floating charge) if an administration order were made; or

(4)   the court considers that the security by virtue of which the receiver was appointed would be challengeable under s 242 (gratuitous alienations) or 243 of the Act (unfair preferences), or under the rule of law in Scotland.

14.52 At the hearing of the application the court may: (a) make the administration order; (b) dismiss it; (c) adjourn it unconditionally or conditionally; (d) make an interim order; (e) wind up the company; or (f) make any other order which the court thinks appropriate.

14.53 The present practice of the companies court is to limit the time of the order to 3 or 6 months and require the administrator either to report back to the court and/or to apply for an extension of the administration order. If it is anticipated that a longer period is necessary, the affidavit in support of the application should provide an estimate of the time required and an explanation sufficient to satisfy the court that the period should be extended. The appointment of the administrator takes effect at a time appointed by the order or, where no time is specified, when the order is made.

APPEALS IN INSOLVENCY PROCEEDINGS

14.54 Every court having jurisdiction to wind up companies under the 1986 Act may review, rescind or vary any order made by it in the exercise of that jurisdiction.[1] An appeal from a decision of a county court or registrar of the High Court lies to a single judge of the High Court; and an appeal from a decision of that judge lies, with the leave of that judge or the Court of Appeal, to the Court of Appeal.[2] Appeals under r 7.47(2) of the Rules are true appeals and do not require a hearing *de novo*. Thus, a decision of a registrar will be overturned only if it was based on an error of law or wrongful exercise of discretion.

14.55 Subject to the provisions of r 7.49(2) and (3) of the Rules, the procedure and practice of the Supreme Court relating to appeals to the Court of Appeal apply to appeals in insolvency proceedings. In relation to any appeal to a single judge of the High Court under r 7.47(2), any reference in the CPR to the Court of Appeal is replaced by a reference to that judge, and any

---

[1]   IR 1986, r 7.47(1).
[2]   Ibid, r 7.47(2).

reference to the registrar of civil appeals is replaced by a reference to the registrar of the High Court who deals with insolvency proceedings of any kind.[1] In insolvency proceedings, the procedure under RSC Ord 59 (appeals to the Court of Appeal) is by ordinary application and not by application notice.[2]

---

[1]   IR 1986, r 7.49(3).
[2]   Ibid, r 7.49(3).

Chapter 17

MORTGAGES

James Hanham & Lana Wood

POSSESSION PROCEEDINGS: GENERAL

15.1 Almost all mortgages expressly give the lender a power of sale.[1] Consequently, most lenders simply require an order for possession to enable them to sell with vacant possession.

15.2 The right to obtain possession arises as soon as the mortgage is executed. A legal mortgagee has a common law right to take possession even without a court order.[2] If the premises are unoccupied, the lender may be entitled to take possession without an order.[3] However, given that the majority of mortgaged properties are occupied, most instances will require an order of the court.

STARTING POSSESSION PROCEEDINGS

15.3 Part 55 of the CPR[4] now makes provision for the bringing of possession claims, including those brought by lenders. It is mandatory for a lender to follow this procedure.[5] Failure to draft, for example, particulars of claim in the correct form (ie in Form 120), is likely to lead to the proceedings being struck out, or at least permission being given for amendment on penalty of costs.

---

[1] Even if there is no express power, LPA 1925, s 101 provides for a power of sale in most circumstances (para **15.59**).

[2] An equitable chargee requires an order of the court.

[3] *Ropaigelach v Barclays Bank Plc* [2000] QB 263.

[4] Introduced by the Civil Procedure (Amendment) Rules 2001, SI 2001/256; in force from 15 October 2001.

[5] CPR, r 55.2.

Which court?

15.4   Mortgage possession proceedings are usually issued in the county court for the district where the property is located. The High Court will be the appropriate court only in exceptional circumstances.[1] Practice Direction PD55[2] gives examples of such circumstances as being (i) complicated disputes of fact, (ii) points of law of general importance, or (iii) the value of the property or the amount of the financial claim made. If the court decides that a claim has erroneously begun in the High Court, it has the power to strike out or transfer the proceedings to the county court (the more usual form of order). Where proceedings are transferred, the court may disallow costs in so far as they relate to that part of the proceedings in the High Court.[3]

Claim form/particulars of claim

15.5   All mortgage possession actions should be brought on a claim form N5. The standard form of particulars of claim (N120) prompts the draftsman to include all the information required by CPR PD55, paras 2.1 and 2.5. The use of the form itself is not compulsory. However, the following particulars are required:

(a)   the identity of the land to which the claim relates;

(b)   whether or not the claim relates to residential property;

(c)   full details of the mortgage and any tenancy (including the identity of the tenant) to which the property is subject;[4] and

(d)   if related to a claim for residential property, whether or not any person has registered an interest pursuant to s 31(10) of the Family Law Act 1996, ss 2(8) or 8(3) of the Matrimonial Homes Act 1983, or s 2(7) of the Matrimonial Homes Act 1967,[5] and, if so, that a notice of the proceedings has been served on them;[6]

(e)   details of the state of the mortgage account showing the amount of the:

    (i)   advance;

    (ii)   current instalments of interest;

    (iii)   sum required to redeem the mortgage (taking into account any penalties for early redemption) at a stated date no more than 14 days after the claim was started, specifying the amount of the solicitor's costs and administration charges;

(f)   the rate of interest payable:

    (i)   at the commencement of the mortgage;

    (ii)   immediately before any arrears arose;

---

1   CPR, PD55, para 1.2.
2   CPR, PD55, para 1.3.
3   CPR, PD55, para 1.3.
4   CPR, PD55, para 2.1.
5   Providing for a spouse's right to occupy in circumstances where this is not vested with the legal estate.
6   CPR, PD55, para 2.5.

(iii)   at the commencement of proceedings;[1]

(g)   where the claim is brought in respect of non-payment of instalments, a schedule detailing:

    (i)   the dates when arrears arose, all amounts due, the dates and amounts of all payments made and a running total of arrears;

    (ii)   any other payments required at the term of the mortgage;[2]

    (iii)   any other sums claimed and an explanation of the nature of the charges;

    (iv)   whether these payments are in arrears and whether or not they have been included in the above figures;

(h)   details of the borrower's circumstances, in particular whether or not the defendant is:

    (i)   in receipt of social security benefits (including credits);

    (ii)   paying contributions pursuant to the provisions of the Social Security (Recovery of Benefits) Act 1997;

(i)   whether any previous attempts have been made to recover the money secured by the mortgage or the mortgaged property itself, when such attempts were started and concluded, and the dates and terms of any orders made.

15.6   Failure to comply with these provisions does not necessarily invalidate the proceedings. The court has power to give directions allowing the claimant to remedy the defects (for instance by adjourning the proceedings to allow the claimant to produce the required information).[3] If there is a technical defect (for instance the address of the mortgaged property is misstated) the court has the discretion to waive the defect.

Notification of hearing

15.7   If possession is sought of residential property (or of premises which includes residential property), the lender is required, not less than 14 days before the date set for the hearing, to send a notice addressed to the 'occupiers' of the property. The notice must:

(a)   state that a claim for possession of the property has been started;

(b)   show the name and address of the claimant, and the address of the court that issued the claim form;

(c)   give details of the hearing.[4]

---

[1]   The best practice is to provide a schedule detailing the interest rates (and any changes thereafter) from the date when arrears arose.

[2]   For example insurance premiums, legal costs, default interest, penalties, administrative costs.

[3]   CPR, r 3.10.

[4]   CPR, r 55.10.

15.8 The notice must be given 14 clear days prior to the hearing, ie the 14 days does not include the day it was served and the day of the hearing.[1] The deemed date of service if served by first-class post is the second day after it was posted, and, if left at the property, the day after it was so left.[2]

DEFENCES AND COUNTERCLAIMS

Undue influence and misrepresentation

15.9 A borrower may have the right to have a mortgage set aside if it can be demonstrated that the mortgage was induced by undue influence or misrepresentation. The issue most commonly arises in circumstances where the matrimonial home is jointly owned and the husband seeks to mortgage it as security for his debts (or the debts of a company through which he carries on business), and induces his wife to agree to the imposition of the charge.[3]

Defences other than misrepresentation or undue influence

15.10 Other defences which may be pleaded, but which are unlikely to arise in cases involving a commercial lender, include forgery of the signature to the mortgage deed, and failure to obtain the consent of beneficiaries who have overriding interests in the mortgage.

Counterclaims

15.11 In the absence of a provision in the mortgage contract to the contrary, the existence of a counterclaim will not defeat the lender's right to possession. The only possible exception to this general rule is a case where the counterclaim is for a liquidated sum by way of set-off, and the amount claimed exceeds the mortgage debt.

15.12 The existence of a counterclaim is a factor which the court may take into account in exercising its discretion under the Administration of Justice Acts 1970 and 1973.[4]

FIRST HEARING

15.13 The court fixes the hearing date when it issues the claim form (the date and time will be entered on the claim form[1]). The first hearing will take place in the '5 minute' possession list.

---

[1] CPR, r 2.8.

[2] CPR, r 6.7(1).

[3] *Royal Bank of Scotland v Etridge (No 2)* [2001] UKHL 44, [2002] 2 AC 773.

[4] *National Westminister Bank Plc v Skelton* [1993] 1 WLR 72n, [1993] 1 All ER 242; *Ashley Guarantee Plc v Zacaria* [1993] 1 WLR 62, [1993] 1 All ER 254; see **15.18**.

15.14 If the borrower attends and raises a defence (or challenges the evidence of the lender), the judge will adjourn the matter and give directions, including directions as to the provision of witness statements and possibly a trial window.

15.15 If the borrower pays the arrears after commencement of the claim, the lender should not withdraw the proceedings, but instead request that the claim be adjourned generally. If further arrears accrue, the claim can be restored, so that the expense and trouble of starting fresh proceedings is avoided.[2]

15.16 If the borrower raises no defence, the court will proceed to hear the matter.

POWERS OF COURT TO ADJOURN, SUSPEND OR OTHERWISE DELAY EFFECT OF ORDER FOR POSSESSION WHERE NO DEFENCE RAISED

Non-residential land

15.17 If the borrower puts forward no defence and the lender proves the arrears, the lender will be entitled to possession. The court has no inherent power to refuse to make an order for possession or to adjourn the proceedings, even on condition of payment of instalments and/or arrears, if the lender does not agree.[3] (The court's normal powers to adjourn in the ordinary course of proceedings, for instance if one party is unable to attend, are not affected.)[4] The court may adjourn for a short time to afford the borrower a chance to pay the whole of the mortgage, if there is a reasonable prospect of him being able to do so.[5] If the mortgaged property is entirely non-residential, the court will either grant a short adjournment or make an order for possession.

Residential land

15.18 In cases where the mortgaged property consists of or includes a dwelling-house, the court has powers under ss 36, 38A and 39 of the Administration of Justice Act 1970 and s 8 of the Administration of Justice Act 1973 which, if exercised, will mean that no immediately enforceable order for possession is made. The relevant date for determining whether the

---

[1]   That date will be not less than 28 days from issue; the standard period between issue and the claim form will be not more than 8 weeks: CPR, r 55.5.

[2]   *Greyhound Guaranty Ltd v Caulfield* [1981] CLY 1808.

[3]   *Birmingham Citizens Permanent Building Society v Caunt* [1962] Ch 883.

[4]   *Hinkley v South Leicestershire Permanent Benefit Building Society v Freeman* [1941] Ch 32; as explained in *Birmingham Citizens Permanent Building Society v Caunt* [1962] Ch 883.

[5]   *Birmingham Citizens Permanent Building Society v Caunt* [1962] Ch 883.

property consists of or includes a dwelling-house is the date on which the claim is commenced. It is not necessary that the property consisted of or included a dwelling-house at the time the mortgage was granted.[1] These powers do not apply where the mortgage is a regulated consumer credit agreement.[2]

What are the court's powers?

15.19 The powers of the court under s 36(2) of the Administration of Justice Act 1970 are to adjourn the proceedings (ie not to make a possession order at all on that day), or, if it does make an order, to stay the order, suspend it, or postpone the date for delivery of possession for such period or periods as it thinks reasonable. The adjournment, stay, suspension or postponement may be subject to such conditions with regard to payment by the borrower of any sum secured by the mortgage or the remedying of any default as the court thinks fit. These powers are not only exercisable on the first hearing: any order made may be varied or revoked at any time before the warrant is executed. Any stay, suspension or postponement must relate to the *whole* mortgaged property: there is no power to stay an order for possession in respect of part only of the mortgaged property.[3]

Of what must the court be satisfied before exercising powers?

15.20 The court's powers under s 36(2) arise only if it is satisfied that in the event of it exercising the power, the borrower is likely to be able within a reasonable period to pay any sums due under the mortgage or to remedy a default consisting of a breach of any other obligation arising under or by virtue of the mortgage.[4]

Extension of court's powers

15.21 Most mortgages contain a provision making the whole principal sum payable in the case of default. The courts interpreted s 36 of the Administration of Justice Act 1970 as meaning that the court had to be convinced that the borrower would be able to pay off not only the arrears, but the whole of the principal sum, within a reasonable period.[5] Section 36 was therefore in practice only of assistance in a very small number of cases 'for, if the mortgagor was already in difficulties with his instalments, the chances of his being able to pay off the whole principal as well as in a reasonable time must be considered fairly slim'.[6]

---

1   *Royal Bank of Scotland v Miller* [2001] EWCA Civ 344, [2002] QB 255.
2   Administration of Justice Act 1970, s 38A.
3   *Barclays Bank Plc v Alcorn* [2002] All ER (D) 146 (Mar), ChD; see also [2002] EWCA Civ 87.
4   Administration of Justice Act 1970, s 36(1).
5   *Halifax Building Society v Clark* [1973] Ch 307.
6   *Habib Bank Ltd v Tailor* [1982] 1 WLR 1218, at 1222, per Oliver LJ.

15.22 The court's powers were accordingly extended by s 8 of the Administration of Justice Act 1973, with the intention in the case of an instalment mortgage of enabling the court to defer possession if it was satisfied that there was a reasonable prospect of the borrower paying off the arrears within a reasonable period.

Application of section 8

15.23 In order for s 8 of the Administration of Justice Act 1973 to apply, two provisions must appear either in the mortgage, or in a collateral agreement between the parties.[1] First, the borrower must be entitled to pay the principal by instalments or to defer payment in some other way. A bank overdraft which is repayable on demand will not fall within s 8.[2] An endowment mortgage where the obligation to repay the principal does not arise until the end of the term except in the case of default, on the other hand, does fall within s 8.[3] An indulgence given by the lender to the borrower, unsupported by consideration, does not bring the borrower within the section since this is not 'an agreement'.[4] Secondly, it must be a term of the contract that the principal is payable earlier in case of default by the borrower, or demand by the lender, or otherwise.

Combined test under sections 36 and 8

15.24 Where the possession proceedings are brought on the basis of arrears of mortgage the court must be satisfied that it is likely that the borrower will be able to pay the required sums within a reasonable period. Whether or not the borrower is likely to be able to pay is a question of fact to be decided on the evidence. Where the proceedings are founded on breach of some other obligation under the mortgage, the court must be satisfied that the borrower is likely to be able to remedy the default within a reasonable period. The burden of proof is on the borrower.

What sums is the borrower required to show he can pay?

15.25 The sums that the borrower must show he is likely to be able to pay are the sums due under the mortgage, but where the principal has become repayable immediately by reason of the default, it is to be treated for the purposes of this test as if it were not so payable. The sums are therefore likely to include arrears of interest and instalments of principal, plus the continuing interest and instalments of principal.

---

[1]   *Centrax Trustees Ltd v Ross* [1979] 2 All ER 952.
[2]   *Habib Bank Ltd v Tailor* [1982] 1 WLR 1218, [1982] 1 All ER 561.
[3]   *Bank of Scotland v Grimes* [1985] 1 QB 1179, [1985] 2 All ER 254. See also *Royal Bank of Scotland v Miller* [2001] EWCA Civ 344, [2002] QB 255.
[4]   *Rees Investments Ltd v Groves* [2001] All ER (D) 292 (June), Neuberger J.

What is a reasonable period?

15.26 The starting point in determining the reasonable period, in the absence of unusual circumstances, is the outstanding term of the mortgage.[1]

Exercise of discretion

15.27 The court will take into account the following questions when exercising its discretion:[2]

(1)   How much can the borrower reasonably afford to pay, both now and in the future?
(2)   If the borrower has a temporary difficulty in meeting his obligations, how long is the difficulty likely to last?
(3)   What was the reason for the arrears that have accumulated?
(4)   How much remains of the original term?
(5)   What are relevant contractual terms, and what type of mortgage is it, ie when is the principal due to be repaid?
(6)   Is it a case where the court should exercise its power to disregard accelerated payment provisions (s 8 of the 1973 Act)?
(7)   Is it reasonable to expect the lender, in the circumstances of the particular case, to recoup the arrears of interest (a) over the whole of the original term, or (b) within a shorter period, or even (c) within a longer period, ie by extending the repayment period?
(8)   Is it reasonable to expect the lender to capitalise the interest?
(9)   Are there any reasons affecting the security which should influence the length of the period for payment?

LENDER'S EVIDENCE

15.28 Given the now comprehensive nature of the information required to be included in the particulars of claim (verified by a statement of truth), it is unlikely that much additional information will be required by way of witness statement. However, if the particulars of claim do not detail arrears and interest up to the date of the hearing (usually from the issue of the claim form), additional evidence in respect of these amounts (and any recent payments made by the borrower) may be adduced orally or in writing on the day of the hearing.[3]

15.29 However, most importantly, the lender must produce evidence, by way of a witness statement, that the notification of the hearing has been sent to the

---

[1]   *Cheltenham and Gloucester Building Society v Norgan* [1996] 1 WLR 343, [1996] 1 All ER 449.
[2]   *Cheltenham and Gloucester Building Society v Norgan* [1996] 1 WLR 343, at 357.
[3]   CPR, PD55, para 5.2.

occupiers of the property.[1] The witness statement should exhibit the notice sent and the witness should (if possible) be the person responsible for sending the notice.

15.30 CPR PD55 para 5.5 makes reference to s 113 of the Land Registration Act 1925. The equivalent provision is now s 120 of the Land Registration Act 2002. The effect of this provision is that any copy of a charge lodged at the Registry is conclusive as between lender and the borrower. The lender need only produce a copy of the Registry's document, as evidence of the existence of the charge, rather than the original. The copy should be attached as an exhibit to the particulars of claim.

15.31 In the authors' experience, the lender's representative should be in a position to give the district judge the figures in relation to (a) the current monthly instalment, (b) the total arrears, (c) the redemption figure, and (d) the remaining term of the mortgage (in months). Some district judges put cases to the back of their lists if representatives do not have this information immediately to hand.

BORROWER'S EVIDENCE

15.32 The court may, in its discretion, exercise its powers on the basis of informal material:

> 'It must be open to [judges] to act without evidence, especially where … the mortgagor is present in court and available to be questioned, and no objection to the reception of informal material is made by the mortgagee.'[2]

15.33 Having said that, it is clearly advisable and better practice to prepare a detailed witness statement on behalf of the borrower at the earliest opportunity, setting out in detail his present and projected financial circumstances and demonstrating that he is likely to be able to pay the required sums within the required period, or, in a case where he will have to sell, whether or not there is negative equity, and the period of time which a sale is likely to take.

15.34 The draftsman of the witness statement should bear in mind the factors the court will take into account in exercising its discretion, and should seek to address each of the questions set out in **15.27** in the statement.

15.35 In addition, if relevant, the statement should set out:

---

[1]   CPR, r 55.10(4).
[2]   *Cheltenham & Gloucester Building Society v Grant* (1994) 26 HLR 703.

(a)   the amount of any outstanding social security or housing benefit relevant to the mortgage arrears;

(b)   the status of any claims for social security or housing benefit about which a decision has not yet been made; and

(c)   any applications to appeal or review a social security or housing benefit decision where that appeal has not yet been concluded.[1]

ORDER OF THE COURT

Stay, suspension or postponement

15.36 If the court stays or suspends an order for possession, the period of stay or suspension must be defined in the order, or be ascertainable from it.[2] Similarly, an order which provides that possession is not to be given if the borrower pays arrears should specify the precise amount of the arrears, if necessary by a formula.[3] The standard forms of order in the county court are Forms N29 and N31.

Application of combined test where borrower not able to pay except by selling property

15.37 The court may decide in its discretion and in the light of all the circumstances what is a reasonable period to adjourn or to stay, suspend or postpone the order.[4]

Cases where the test is not met

15.38 Where there is negative equity, and the borrower has no assets with which to make up the shortfall on sale, the court should not purport to exercise the power with the object of giving the borrower the conduct of the sale.[5] Where the test is not met, the position is the same as in relation to non-residential property: the court may adjourn or stay only for valid case management reasons.[6]

Human Rights Act 1998

15.39 There is no inconsistency between the common law, as mitigated by s 36 of the Administration of Justice Act 1970 and s 8 of the Administration of Justice Act 1973, and Art 8 of the European Convention on Human Rights (right to respect for private and family life, home and correspondence), or

---

1   CPR, PD55, para 5.3.
2   *Royal Trust Co of Canada v Markham* [1975] 1 WLR 1416, [1975] 3 All ER 433.
3   *Rees Investments Ltd v Groves* [2001] All ER (D) 292 (June), Neuberger J.
4   *Bristol & West Building Society v Ellis* (1996) 73 P&CR 158.
5   *Cheltenham and Gloucester Building Society v Krausz* [1997] 1 WLR 1558, [1997] 1 All ER 21.
6   *State Bank of New South Wales v Carey Harrison III* [2002] EWCA Civ 363.

Art 1 of the First Protocol to the Convention (entitlement to peaceful enjoyment of possessions).[1]

COSTS OF PROCEEDINGS

Liability for costs

15.40 The recovery of its costs by a lender is usually governed by the mortgage deed.[2] Lenders will seek to add the costs of taking (or defending) proceedings to the amount secured by the mortgage, in respect of which no specific order for costs is required. The costs legitimately so added will be those actual costs, charges and expenses reasonably incurred and reasonable in amount.

15.41 If the lender is unsuccessful in the proceedings/application, or an adjournment is caused by the lender's default, the borrower will usually (and should) seek an order that the lender 'be not at liberty to add any costs to the security' in relation to the costs of those proceedings or that hearing.

Amount of costs

15.42 The borrower may challenge the amount of the lender's costs as excessive by seeking:

(a) a summary or detailed assessment of the costs at the hearing.[3] There is county court authority to the effect that such an assessment can only be carried out where the court has actually made an order for costs at the lender's request.[4] Any assessment carried out will be on the basis specified in the deed, or otherwise on the standard basis;

(b) a detailed assessment of the lender's solicitor's costs.[5] The county court has jurisdiction only in respect of sums not exceeding £5,000 and in respect of work wholly or partly carried out in the county court;

(c) an account of the amount the lender seeks to add to the security.[6] At this point, the court is not bound by the contractual provisions and may determine that the amount added to the security is excessive.[7]

---

[1]   *Barclays Bank plc v Alcorn* [2002] EWCA Civ 87.

[2]   If it is not, an order for costs and assessment occurs in the usual way.

[3]   Pursuant to CPR, r 48.3 and PD48; *Gomba Holdings v Minories Finance (No 2)* [1993] Ch 171.

[4]   *Bank of Ireland Home Mortgages Ltd v Bissett* [1999] 11 CL 53.

[5]   Solicitors Act 1974, s 70.

[6]   The court may direct the lender to file an account: CPR, r 25.1(l)(n).

[7]   CPR, PD48.1, para 50.4.

EXECUTION

15.43 An order for possession may not lawfully be enforced other than by warrant for possession in the county court[1] (or by writ of possession in the High Court[2]). Once the date for giving up possession has expired, a warrant for possession may be issued. The appropriate forms are N325 (request for warrant of possession), N49 (warrant of possession) and N50 (warrant of restitution).[3]

15.44 Where possession was ordered unconditionally on a particular day, the request for issue of a warrant must certify that the land has not been vacated in accordance with the order.[4]

15.45 Where the order has been suspended on terms as to payment of a sum of money by instalments, the lender must certify in his request the amount of money remaining due under the judgment or order, and that the whole or part of any instalment due remains unpaid.[5]

15.46 The borrower or other occupants of the mortgaged property should (as a matter of court practice) receive notice of the warrant before it is executed in Form N54.[6]

15.47 An unexecuted warrant remains in force for one year, subject to renewal, year by year, by leave of the court.[7]

15.48 A warrant may not be issued without permission more than 6 years after the order for possession.[8] A warrant obtained after the expiry of 6 years without permission is an abuse of process which cannot be cured by the application of CPR, r 3.10. In such circumstances, the defendant will be entitled to have it set aside.[9]

15.49 If the land is re-entered after possession has been obtained by eviction by warrant of possession, a warrant of restitution may be issued in the county court (writ of restitution in the High Court) to recover possession once more.[10]

---

[1]   CCR, Ord 26, r 17.
[2]   RSC Ord 45, r 3.
[3]   CPR, PD4.
[4]   CCR, Ord 26, r 17(2).
[5]   CCR, Ord 26, r 17(3A).
[6]   *Southwark London Borough Council v St Brice* [2001] EWCA Civ 1138, [2002] 1 WLR 1537.
[7]   CCR, r 26.6; applied by Ord 26, r 17(6).
[8]   CCR, Ord 26, r 5(1)(a).
[9]   *Hammersmith and Fulham London Borough Council v Hill* (1995) 27 HLR 368, CA; *Hackney London Borough Council v White* (1995) 28 HLR 219, CA.
[10] CCR, Ord 26, r 17(4) and (5).

OTHER REMEDIES OF MORTGAGEE

Action for breach of covenant to pay

15.50 Mortgages normally create a contract requiring the borrower to make repayment to the lender. The lender may bring an action to recover principal and interest on failure to pay any of the instalments or upon demand. In practice, this does not happen very often since the enforcement of lender's security provides a much more reliable method of recovering the outstanding sums.

15.51 However, a lender may still need to have recourse to action in circumstances where there is a shortfall between the amount of the proceeds of sale and that outstanding on the account. For the purposes of limitation,[1] time begins to run from the date of the breach of the covenant to pay by the borrower. The borrower has 12 years from such a breach (if the mortgage is by deed) to recover the principal, and 6 years to recover outstanding payments of interest (whether or not the power of sale has been exercised).[2]

Appointment of receiver

15.52 Many mortgages specifically provide that a lender has the power to appoint a receiver to collect the income from property in the event of a breach of the obligations under the mortgage, eg the non-payment of instalments. Such provisions usually provide for the receiver to benefit from extensive powers of management.

15.53 Even where no such specific power exists, s 109 of the LPA 1925 permits the lender to appoint a receiver. This statutory power is exercisable only where the mortgage was made by deed or the money under the mortgage is due and one of the following three events has occurred, namely:

(a) notice requiring payment of the mortgage money has been served on the borrower and default has been made in payment of part or all of it for 3 months thereafter;
(b) some interest under the mortgage is 2 months or more in arrear;
(c) there has been a breach of some provision of the LPA 1925 or of the mortgage deed.

15.54 The statutory power usually makes it unnecessary to apply to the court for an appointment of a receiver, although the High Court can appoint one where it is thought just and convenient to do so.[3] The advantage of applying

---

[1] Limitation Act 1980, s 20 (relating to actions for money secured by mortgage).
[2] *Bristol and West Plc v Bartlett* [2003] 1 WLR 284, CA; *Scottish Equitable v Thompson* [2003] HLR 48.
[3] Supreme Court Act 1981, s 37.

to the court[1] is that it can deal with questions of a receiver's remuneration and the preparation of accounts.

15.55 The receiver acts as the agent of the borrower, not of the lender,[2] and so is not under a strict duty to account in the same way as if the receiver were the lender's agent. The receiver is under a duty to ensure that he creates a situation in which the interest and debt can be repaid. He is also required to manage the property with due diligence and to act in good faith.[3] However, there is no duty to maximise the value of the asset prior to sale.[4]

Foreclosure

15.56 Foreclosure is rarely employed as a mode of enforcement for two reasons:

(a)   a foreclosure decree does not guarantee that the lender can sell the property; and
(b)   lenders have other more certain remedies available to them.

15.57 Foreclosure is the process by which the borrower's equitable right to redeem the mortgage is declared by the court to be extinguished and the lender becomes the owner of the property. A right to foreclose arises where:

(a)   the date for the redemption of the mortgage has passed and the debt (or part of it) remains outstanding;
(b)   if there is no such date, or prior to such date, where there is a breach of an obligation under the mortgage, eg for the payment of an instalment of interest or principal.

15.58 Foreclosure proceedings are commenced by CPR Part 8 claim form. An interim order is made requiring payment of the sums due by a fixed day, in default of which the mortgage will be foreclosed. In the absence of an order for sale (which may be made where the foreclosing lender would obtain a property worth in excess of the debt), a disclosure order absolute is made. However, the foreclosure may be opened (or 'reopened') where, for instance, a mortgagor, through no fault of his own, is not in funds prior to the date fixed in the order.

---

[1]   CPR, Part 69.
[2]   *Gaskell v Gosling* [1896] 1 QB 669; *Medforth v Blake* [2000] Ch 86.
[3]   Ibid.
[4]   *Silven Properties v Royal Bank of Scotland Plc* [2004] 1 WLR 997 (no requirement to apply for planning permission for development prior to sale).

Power to sell mortgaged property

15.59 Most modern mortgages provide the lender with the power to sell. In the event that there is no such express power, and in the absence of contrary intention, s 101 of the LPA 1925 gives rise to a power of sale if:

(a)   the mortgage was made by deed (as all legal mortgages must be);

(b)   the mortgage money is due (ie the legal date for redemption has passed).

15.60 If the above conditions are satisfied, the power to sell is available to the lender. However, this power only becomes exercisable in one or more of the circumstances (described above) in which the right to appoint a receiver is triggered.[1]

15.61 Apart from the statutory power of sale, the court can order sale of the mortgaged property on application[2] of anyone interested in the mortgage money/equity of redemption.[3] It may also make order for possession or for receipt of rents and profits as an adjunct of an order for sale.[4] The court[5] has ordered a sale on the application of a borrower, although such an order is probably exceptional.[6]

---

[1]   See **15.53**.

[2]   Pursuant to CPR, r 40.16.

[3]   LPA 1925, s 91.

[4]   CPR, r 40.17.

[5]   The jurisdiction of the county court is limited to circumstances where the amount due under the mortgage does not exceed £30,000: LPA 1925, s 91(8).

[6]   *Palk v Mortgage Services Funding Plc* [1993] Ch 330, CA.

Chapter 16

LANDLORD AND TENANT

Edward Denehan

INTRODUCTION

16.1 Landlord and tenant proceedings are not exclusively Chancery matters. Save to a limited extent, landlord and tenant proceedings may be commenced in the Chancery Division or the Queen's Bench Division of the High Court.[1] Landlord and tenant proceedings may also be commenced in the county court, and the vast majority are.

16.2 In the High Court, only proceedings under Part I of the Landlord and Tenant Act 1927 (LTA 1927), Part II of the Landlord and Tenant Act 1954 (LTA 1954), the Landlord and Tenant Act 1987 (LTA 1987) and the Leasehold Reform Act 1967 (LRA 1967) must be commenced in the Chancery Division.[2] Other landlord and tenant claims within CPR Part 56 may be made in the Chancery Division or the Queen's Bench Division. Where the Chancery Division does not have exclusive High Court jurisdiction, as between the Chancery Division and the Queen's Bench Division, the former is usually the appropriate venue for landlord and tenant claims.

16.3 Further, the Chancery Division has exclusive High Court jurisdiction in landlord and tenant proceedings that arise in the context of the insolvency of companies[3] and individuals.[4]

16.4 This chapter is concerned, for the most part, with proceedings under Part II of the LTA 1954, and under ss 182 and 320 of the Insolvency Act 1986 (IA 1986), these being the most common landlord and tenant proceedings within the exclusive High Court jurisdiction of the Chancery Division and which can therefore properly be called Chancery matters, whether they are dealt with in the High Court or the county court. In addition,

---

[1] For the jurisdiction of the Chancery Division and the Queen's Bench Division generally, see s 61(1) of, and paras 1 and 2 of Sch 1 to, the Supreme Court Act 1981. Whilst landlord and tenant matters issues arise in family proceedings, it is not appropriate to commence such proceedings in the Family Division. For the jurisdiction of the Family Division see s 61(1) of, and para 3 of Sch 1 to, the 1981 Act.

[2] Chancery Guide, para 18.1(15).

[3] Ibid, para 18.1(10) and Chapter 20.

[4] Ibid, para 18.1(5) and Chapter 19.

this chapter contains some short observations on landlord and tenant claims generally in the context of the new CPR applicable thereto.

LANDLORD AND TENANT CLAIMS GENERALLY

CPR Part 56

16.5   CPR Part 56 is concerned with 'landlord and tenant claims'.[1] CPR Part 56 came into force on 15 October 2001,[2] and applies to all landlord and tenant claims issued after that date.[3] *Practice Direction: Landlord and Tenant Claims and Miscellaneous Provisions About Land* (the Practice Direction) supplements CPR Part 56.

16.6   Landlord and tenant claims within CPR Part 56 are those made under the LTA 1927, the Leasehold (Property) Repairs Act 1938 (L(P)RA 1938), the LTA 1954,[4] the LTA 1985 and the LTA 1987.[5]

16.7   Only claims under ss 24(1) and 29(2) of the LTA 1954 benefit from discrete treatment in CPR Part 56[6] and the Practice Direction.[7] Provisions particular to the other landlord and tenant claims are found in the Practice Direction only,[8] save for claims under the L(P)RA 1938, which are not dealt with specifically in the Practice Direction.[9]

16.8   Further, CPR, r 56.1 provides that 'a practice direction' may set out special provisions with regard to claims under: the Chancel Repairs Act 1932 (CRA 1932), the LRA 1967, the Access to Neighbourhood Land Act 1992 (ANLA 1992), the Leasehold Reform, Housing and Urban Development Act

---

[1]   CPR, r 56.1(1).

[2]   Civil Procedure (Amendment) Rules 2001, SI 2001/256, r 1(d). CPR Part 56 was amended, as from 1 June 2004, by the Civil Procedure (Amendment) Rules 2004, SI 2004/1306, r 15 to accommodate the substantive amendments made to the LTA 1954 by the Regulatory Reform (Business Tenancies) (England and Wales) Order 2003, SI 2003/3096, which also came into effect on 1 June 2004.

[3]   Civil Procedure (Amendment) Rules 2001, SI 2001/256, r 31. The amendments made to CPR Part 56 by the 2004 Rules do not apply where the landlord has given a tenant a notice under s 25, or the tenant has made a request in accordance with s 26, before 1 June 2004. See r 20(1)(a) of the 2004 Rules. In such circumstances, CPR Part 56 continues to apply on and after 1 June 2004 as if the amendments made by the 2004 Rules had not been made. See r 20(1)(b) of the 2004 Rules and Art 29(1) of the 2003 Order.

[4]   Note, CPR, Part 56 applies to applications under both Part I and Part II of the LTA 1954.

[5]   CPR, r 56.1(1)(a)–(e).

[6]   In CPR, r 56.3.

[7]   Practice Direction, para 3.

[8]   Ibid, para 4 is concerned with claims under Part I of the LTA 1954; para 5 is concerned with claims under the LTA 1927; para 6 with claims under the LTA 1985; paras 7, 8, 9 and 10 with certain claims under the LTA 1987.

[9]   Practice Direction, para 2, which is concerned with 'starting the claim', applies to all landlord and tenant claims.

1993 (LRHUDA 1993) and the Commonhold and Leasehold Reform Act 2002 (CLRA 2002).

16.9 It is doubtful whether claims under the CRA 1932, the ANLA 1992 or the CLRA 2002 can be properly called landlord and tenant claims in the strict sense, but they are nevertheless dealt with in CPR Part 56. The Practice Direction contains perfunctory provisions concerning the ANLA 1992,[1] the CRA 1932,[2] the LRA 1967,[3] the LRHUDA 1993,[4] and the CLRA 2002.[5]

16.10 It will be seen that the bulk of the landlord and tenant claims are now dealt with in CPR Part 56, although the coverage is uneven. This reflects the incidence of landlord and tenant claims: by far the greatest number of landlord and tenant claims within CPR Part 56 arise under Part II of the LTA 1954.

16.11 Save where specific provision is made in CPR Part 56 and/or the Practice Direction, a landlord and tenant claim falls to be prosecuted in accordance with the CPR generally.

CPR Part 55

16.12 Claims for possession of land and/or buildings, which often involve landlords and tenants, are dealt with by CPR Part 55,[6] which also came into force on 15 October 2001. CPR Part 55 is not considered in this chapter as, for the most part, its operation is clear.

VESTING ORDERS UNDER IA 1986

16.13 Applications under the IA 1986 for vesting orders in respect of leasehold property are not dealt with in CPR Part 56.[7] Instead, they are dealt with under the Insolvency Rules 1986 (the Rules),[8] which became operative on 29 December 1986. However, r 7.51 of the Rules, as amended, provides that the CPR, the practice and procedure of the High Court and of the county court (including any practice direction), apply to insolvency proceedings with any necessary modifications except so far as inconsistent with the Rules.

---

[1]   Practice Direction, para 11.
[2]   Ibid, para 12.
[3]   Ibid, para 13.
[4]   Ibid, para 14.
[5]   Ibid, para 15.
[6]   As are claims by tenants for relief from forfeiture, claims by mortgagees for possession, claims by licensors for possession and claims for possession made against trespassers: CPR, r 55.2(1).
[7]   CPR, r 2.1 provides that the CPR, do not apply to insolvency proceedings.
[8]   SI 1986/1925.

CLAIMS UNDER PART II OF LTA 1954

Tribunal

16.14 CPR Part 56 applies both to claims in the High Court and the county court.[1] Accordingly, the procedure is the same in both. Where it is appropriate to commence a claim under the LTA 1954 in the High Court (which will not usually be the case), the claim must be made in the Chancery Division.[2]

16.15 Some county courts operate 'Chancery Lists', pursuant to which certain cases are listed to appear before circuit judges or recorders with experience of Chancery matters, including landlord and tenant claims. Substantial landlord and tenant claims will usually be entered in the Chancery List in the county court, if such a list is maintained.

16.16 Certain claims can be made under Part II of the LTA 1954. These are:

(a) a claim for an order for a new tenancy under s 24(1);
(b) a claim for the determination of an interim rent under s 24A;
(c) a claim for a declaration pursuant to s 31(2);[3]
(d) a claim for a certificate under s 37(4);[4]
(e) a claim for the revocation of an order granting a new tenancy;[5]
(f) a landlord's application for an order for the termination of a tenancy to which Part II of the LTA 1954 applies.[6]

16.17 Of these, by far the most common are substantive claims under s 24(1). The ability of a landlord to make an application under s 29(2), item (g) above, is new, having been introduced by the Regulatory Reform (Business Tenancies) (England and Wales) Order 2003[7] (the 2003 Order), which came into force on 1 June 2004. It is likely that applications under s 29(2) will be popular, as a landlord who wishes to oppose a tenant's application under s 24(1) is likely to make an application under s 29(2), and therefore such

---

[1] CPR, r 2.1(a) and (b).
[2] Chancery Guide, para 18.1(15).
[3] Ie a declaration that one of the grounds of opposition contained in s 30(1)(e), (f) or (g) would have been made out if a longer period had been specified in the s 25 notice or s 26 request.
[4] Ie the court certifying the grounds upon which it was precluded from granting a new tenancy.
[5] Made pursuant to s 36(2).
[6] Made pursuant to s 29(2), a new subsection inserted by Art 5 of the 2003 Order. Such applications can only be made where the s 25 notice, or s 26 request, as the case may be, is served after 1 June 2004 and only then if the landlord states that he is to oppose any application by the tenant for a new tenancy. See Art 29(1) of the 2003 Order and s 29(2).
[7] SI 2003/3096. The 2003 Order was made on 1 December 2003 and came into force on 1 June 2004: (Art 1(3)). The 2003 Order applies only where the landlord has given a s 25 notice, or the tenant has served a s 26 request, after 1 June 2004 (Art 29(1)). Accordingly, in respect of notices and requests served before 1 June 2004, Part II of the 1954 Act in its unamended form applies, so that for approximately one year after 1 June 2004, two regimes will be in operation.

applications, together with substantive applications under s 24(1), and claims for the determination of interim rents, will be considered here.

COMMENCING CLAIM UNDER LTA 1954, SECTIONS 24(1) AND 29(2)

Right to apply

16.18 As originally enacted, Part II of the LTA 1954 gave only tenants the right to apply to the court for a new tenancy.[1] The right to apply for a new tenancy under s 24(1) is extended by amendments to s 24 introduced by Art 3(1) of the 2003 Order. If a s 25 notice, or s 26 request, is served after 1 June 2004, either the tenant or the landlord may apply for a new tenancy.[2] Only a landlord can make an application under s 29(2), and only then if he is opposed to the grant of a new tenancy to the tenant.

16.19 The right of both tenants and landlords to make claims under s 24(1), and the right of a landlord to make an application under s 29(2), means that in theory there could be competing claims. The Practice Direction provides for this possibility.[3] Where more than one application to the court under s 24(1) or s 29(2) is made,[4] the following rules apply:

(a)   Once an application to the court under s 24(1) has been served on a defendant, no further application to the court in respect of the same tenancy whether under s 24(1) or s 29(2) may be served by that defendant without the permission of the court.[5]

(b)   If more than one application to the court under s 24(1) in respect of the same tenancy is served on the same day, any landlord's application is stayed until further order of the court.[6]

(c)   If applications to the court under both s 24(1) and 29(2) in respect of the same tenancy is served on the same day, any tenant's application under s 24(1) is stayed until further order of the court.[7]

(d)   If a defendant is served with an application under s 29(2) which was issued at a time when an application to the court had already been made by that defendant in respect of the same tenancy under s 24(1), the service of the s 29(2) application shall be deemed to be a notice under

---

[1]   LTA 1954, s 24(1).

[2]   Ibid, s 24(1), as amended by Art 3(1) of the 2003 Order. Both cannot apply: see s 24(2A), inserted by Art 3(2) of the 2003 Order.

[3]   Practice Direction, para 3.2.

[4]   A landlord cannot make an application under s 29(2) if he or the tenant has made an application under s 24(1) (see s 29(3) of the LTA 1954), and neither the landlord nor the tenant can make a claim under s 24(1) if the landlord has made an application under s 29(2) (see s 24(2B) of the LTA 1954).

[5]   Practice Direction, para 3.2(1).

[6]   Ibid, para 3.2(2).

[7]   Ibid, para 3.2(3).

CPR Part 7, r 7.7 requiring service or discontinuance of the s 24(1) application within a period of 14 days after service of the s 29(2) application.[1]

Jurisdiction

16.20 Both the Chancery Division of the High Court and the county court have unlimited jurisdiction to hear a claim under s 24(1) and under s 29(2),[2] but the inevitable, and sensible, practice of most practitioners has been to make claims in the county court, since the claim will be determined more quickly, and at less expense.

16.21 This practice is reflected in CPR Part 56. A claim under s 24(1) and under s 29(2) must be started in the county court for the district in which the land is situated, save in exceptional circumstances.[3] Those circumstances are described in the Practice Direction[4] as being where there are complicated disputes of fact[5] or where there are points of law of general importance.[6] The facts of a claim under s 24(1) or under s 29(2) are usually well within the understanding of a circuit judge, and for the most part the substantive principles of law that arise are well known and straightforward.

16.22 Paragraph 2.5 of the Practice Direction provides that the value of the property, and the amount of any financial claim per se will not normally justify commencing the claim in the Chancery Division, but the value of the property may be a relevant circumstance to be taken into account. A claim with an estimated value of less than £50,000 is generally thought to be suitable for determination in the county court.[7] However, having regard to para 2.5 of the Practice Direction, it is not safe to assume that claims under s 24(1) where, for example, the difference between the parties as to the new s 34 rent, and/or the level of interim rent, exceeds £50,000, are suitable for determination in the Chancery Division.

16.23 The amount in issue will probably need to be well in excess of six figures before a claim under s 24(1) is suitable for determination in the Chancery Division. Further, if, for example, a landlord makes an application under s 29(2) relying on the ground of opposition contained in s 30(1)(f), and the development the landlord proposes is substantial, this may be sufficient to justify the claim being made in the Chancery Division provided the issues are

---

[1] Practice Direction, para 3(2) and(4).
[2] LTA 1954, s 63(2), as amended by the High Court and County Courts Jurisdiction Order 1991, SI 1991/724.
[3] CPR, r 56.2(1); PD56, para 2.2.
[4] CPR, PD56, para 2.4.
[5] CPR, PD56, para 2.4(1).
[6] CPR, PD56, para 2.4(2).
[7] CPR, PD56, para 2.2, which supplements CPR, Part 29.

sufficiently complex. If both sides agree that the claim is suitable for determination in the Chancery Division, that constitutes some assistance when trying to justify the decision to issue the claim in the High Court, but it is very far from being determinative of the point.

16.24 If the tenant's adviser takes the view that it is appropriate to begin the claim in the Chancery Division, the claim form must be accompanied by a certificate stating the reasons for bringing the claim there, which certification must be verified by a statement of truth in accordance with CPR, r 22.1(1).[1]

16.25 It is important that the tenant's advisor makes the right decision in this regard. If the claim is begun in the Chancery Division, and it should have been started in the county court, the master[2] 'will normally' strike out the claim or transfer it to the county court of his own initiative.[3] Nothing is said in CPR Part 56 or the Practice Direction as to what happens if the claim is commenced in the county court and the district judge thinks that it should have been started in the Chancery Division. One assumes there will be a transfer upward.[4]

16.26 The Practice Direction states that if the Chancery Division exercises this power, there are likely to be delays, and the cost of beginning the claim in the Chancery Division, plus the cost of any transfer, will be disallowed.[5] It is self-evident that there will be delays, and if the tenant issues in the wrong court, as a matter of principle he should pay any costs thrown away. There may be scope for a different order for costs in the event that the parties had agreed that the claim should be issued in the Chancery Division, and the master disagrees. In such circumstances it can be said that both sides are to blame.

16.27 Section 29A(1) of the LTA 1954 provides, that subject to agreement between the parties,[6] the court shall not entertain an application under s 24(1) or under s 29(2) if it is made after the end of the statutory period. The statutory period means a period ending on the date of termination specified in a s 25 notice, or the date before the date specified for the commencement of a new tenancy in a s 26 request, as the case may be. This is a statutory time-limit; as a result it must be strictly observed. Section 29A(1) provides, in effect,

---

1   CPR, r 56.2(2).
2   If the claim is made in the district registry, the district judge will be concerned with the claim. However, for the sake of brevity, in the context of claims made in the Chancery Division, references herein will be to the master, whether the proceedings are in London or in a district registry.
3   Practice Direction, para 2.3.
4   Pursuant to the County Courts Act 1984, s 42.
5   County Courts Act 1984, s 42.
6   For which see s 29B of the LTA 1954.

a statutory limitation period which cannot be extended by the court under CPR Part 3 or at all.[1]

16.28 There is a further time-limit which applies where a tenant has made a request under s 26. In such a case the court shall not entertain an application under s 24(1) which is made before the end of the period of 2 months beginning with the date of the making of the request.[2] In other words, if a tenant services a s 26 request, the parties must wait 2 months before an application to the court under s 24(1) can be made, thus giving the parties some breathing space within which to negotiate. There is an exception to this. If the landlord gives notice to the tenant under s 26(6),[3] the application can be made immediately after the notice is given; there is no need to wait for 2 months. The rationale is that if the landlord is to oppose the application to the court under s 24(1), there is no point in waiting 2 months in circumstances where negotiations are unlikely.

16.29 It is not hard to imagine a case where a claim under s 24(1) or s 29(2) is made in the Chancery Division very shortly before the expiration of the statutory period prescribed by s 29A(1). The master may strike out the claim because it should have been commenced in the county court. The tenant, or landlord, as the case may be, is then out of time to make a second claim to the county court. It seems the defendant may waive the requirement that the claim be made within the statutory period,[4] but it will be a rare case where a waiver can be found, and the right of the parties to agree extensions of time under s 29B seemingly does not survive the expiration of the statutory period, or such period as extended, so there cannot be a retrospective agreement under s 29B.[5]

16.30 In view of the overriding objective,[6] in the vast majority of cases the master will not strike out a claim because it is issued in the wrong court; rather, he will simply transfer the claim. A decision to strike out rather than transfer should be the subject of an appeal.

---

[1]   *Hodgson v Armstrong* [1967] 2 QB 300; *Chabba v Turbogame Ltd* 82 P&CR DG24.

[2]   See s 29A(3).

[3]   Ie a notice specifying a statutory ground of opposition.

[4]   *Kammins Ballroom Limited v Zenith Investments (Torquay) Limited* [1971] AC 850. This was a case decided prior to the amendments made by the 2003 Order, but there are no obvious reasons why the same principles should not apply.

[5]   It seems a little odd that one can waive the time-limit, but cannot agree to extend it once a time-limit has expired, but that seems to be the effect of s 29B.

[6]   For which see CPR, r 1.1(1) and (2)(b).

LEVEL OF JUDICIARY

16.31 In the Chancery Division, a master may not make final orders under the LTA 1954 without the consent of the Vice-Chancellor,[1] except:

(a)   by consent;

(b)   the order is for the determination of an interim rent under s 24A.

16.32 Whether it will be suitable to agree that a master determine a substantive claim under s 24(1) or s 29(2) turns on the issues involved. Even if the parties do not consent, and insist upon a judge, it is likely that, save in complex claims, a deputy High Court judge will hear the substantive claim. In all other aspects, the master will be very much involved in the prosecution of a claim under s 24(1). In all other respects, the master will be very much involved in the prosecution of claims under ss 24(1) and 29(2). In particular, he will give important directions for the further conduct of the claim.

16.33 In the county court, although claims under s 24(1) may be reallocated to the fast track,[2] only circuit judges may hear them.[3] In the county court a district judge performs the same functions as the master in the Chancery Division.

THE CLAIM FORM

16.34 A distinction must be drawn between what is called 'an unopposed claim' and 'an opposed claim'. An unopposed claim means a claim for a new tenancy under s 24(1), made by either a tenant or a landlord, where the claim is not opposed by the landlord.[4] An opposed claim means a claim for a new tenancy under s 24(1) where the claim is opposed, or a claim under s 29(2).[5] It must be remembered that although in the vast majority of opposed claims, the landlord can only oppose on one of the statutory grounds of opposition described in s 30(1) of the LTA 1954, it sometimes happens that a landlord may oppose the application on some other ground. For example, the landlord may take a jurisdictional point, and allege that the current tenancy is not one to which the LTA 1954 applies, or he may take some procedural point. The existence of such extra-statutory grounds of opposition is reflected in the Practice Direction. Paragraph 3.1(3) of the Practice Direction provides that 'grounds of opposition' means not only the s 30(1) statutory grounds, but also

---

[1]   At the date of writing no such consent has been given.

[2]   Pursuant to CPR, r 26.10. This is a question of reallocation since all CPR, Part 8 claims are allocated to the multi-track in the first instance: see CPR, r 8.9(c).

[3]   CPR, Part 2; PD2B, para 11.1(a)(ii).

[4]   CPR, r 56.3(2)(b).

[5]   CPR, r 56.3(2)(c).

any other basis on which the landlord asserts that a new tenancy ought not to be granted.

16.35 Where the claim is an unopposed claim, the claimant must use the CPR Part 8 procedure[1] save that:

(a) The claimant is not required to file his written evidence with the claim form, and the defendant, as a consequence, does not have to file his written evidence in reply.[2]

(b) As a result, the prohibition on the reliance on evidence not served in accordance with CPR, r 8.5 has no application.[3]

(c) The claim form must be served within 2 months after the date of issue and CPR, rr 7.5 and 7.6 are modified accordingly.[4]

(d) The court will give directions about the future management of the claim following receipt of the acknowledgement of service.[5]

16.36 Where the claim is an opposed claim, the claimant must use the CPR Part 7 procedure, but the claim form must be served within 2 months after the date of issue, and CPR, rr 7.5 and 7.6 are modified accordingly.[6]

16.37 Where a claim under s 24(1) is made by a tenant, the proper defendant is the competent landlord.[7] However, para 4.1 of the Practice Direction provides that in addition to the competent landlord, a mesne landlord, whose consent is sought under para 4(2) of Sch 6 to the LTA 1954[8] must also be a defendant if an issue arises as to the reasonableness of the mesne landlord withholding consent, or imposing conditions, which issue is determined by the court pursuant to para 4(3) of Sch 6. In practice, the circumstances in which it is necessary to joint a mesne landlord rarely arises. Where a landlord makes a claim under s 24(1) or s 29(2), the defendant will be the tenant under the current tenancy.

16.38 The claim, whether under s 24(1) or s 29(2), is made using Form N208.[9] The particulars which the claim form must contain varies, but in every case the claim form must contain details of:[10]

---

1   CPR, r 56.3(3)(a) and Practice Direction, para 2.1.
2   CPR, r 56.3(3)(a)(i), excluding CPR, r 8.5.
3   CPR, r 56.3(3)(a)(ii), excluding CPR, r 8.6.
4   CPR, r 56.3(3)(b).
5   CPR, r 56.3(3)(c).
6   CPR, r 56.3(4)(a), (b) and Practice Direction, para 2.1A.
7   For which see s 44 of, and Sch 6 to, the LTA 1954: Practice Direction, para 3.3.
8   Ie consent to the service of a notice by the competent landlord on the tenant: see LTA 1954, Sch 6, para 3(1).
9   An example of this form is on the CD-ROM which accompanies this book. This claim form must be used even if the CPR Part 7 procedure is applicable because the claim is an opposed claim.
10   These particulars should be given in the section of the claim form entitled 'details of claim'.

(a)   The property to which the claim relates.

(b)   The particulars of the current tenancy (including date, parties and duration), the current rent (if not the original rent) and the date and method of termination.

(c)   Every notice or request given or made under ss 25 or 26 of the LTA 1954.

(d)   The expiry date of the statutory period under s 29A(2) of the LTA 1954 or any agreed extended period made under s 29B(1) or (2) of the LTA 1954.[1]

16.39   Where the tenant is making a claim under s 24(1), in addition to the details described in para **16.34** above, the claim form must also contain the following details:[2]

(a)   The nature of the business carried on at the property.

(b)   Whether the tenant relies upon ss 23(1A), 41 or 42 of the LTA 1954 and, if so, the basis on which he does so.[3]

(c)   Whether the tenant relies upon s 31A of the LTA 1954 and, if so, the basis on which he does so.[4]

(d)   Whether any, and if so what part, of the property comprised in the tenancy is occupied neither by the claimant nor by a person employed by the claimant for the purpose of the claimant's business.

(e)   The tenant's proposed terms of the new tenancy.

(f)   The name and address of:

   (i)   anyone known to the tenant who has an interest in the reversion in the property (whether immediate or in not more than 15 years) on the termination of the claimant's current tenancy and who is likely to be affected by the grant of a new tenancy; or

   (ii) if the tenant does not know of any such person, anyone who has a freehold interest in the property.

The claim form must be served on the persons referred to in (f)(i) or (f)(ii) above, as appropriate.[5]

16.40   Where the claimant is a landlord making a claim for a new tenancy under s 24(1), in addition to the details described above, the claim form must contain details of:[6]

---

[1]   Practice Direction, para 3.4.
[2]   Ibid, para 3.5.
[3]   Section 23(1A) is concerned with the occupation, or the carrying on of a business, by a company in which the tenant has a controlling interest, or where the tenant is a company, by a person with a controlling interest in the company. Section 41 is concerned with trusts, and s 42 with groups of companies.
[4]   Section 31A is concerned with the grant of a new tenancy in some cases where s 30(1)(f) of the LTA 1954 applies.
[5]   Practice Direction, para 3.6.
[6]   Ibid, para 3.7.

(a)   The landlord's proposed terms of the new tenancy.

(b)   Whether the landlord is aware that the tenant's tenancy is one to which
         s 32(2) applies[1] and, if so, whether the landlord requires that any new
         tenancy shall be a tenancy of the whole of the property comprised in
         the tenant's current tenancy or just of the holding.

(c)   The name and address of:

         (i)   anyone known to the landlord who has an interest in the reversion
                in the property (whether immediate or in not more than 15 years)
                on the termination of the tenant's current tenancy and who is
                likely to be affected by the grant of a new tenancy; or

         (ii)   if the landlord does not know of any such person, anyone who has
                a freehold interest in the property.

The claim form must be served on the persons referred to in para (c)(i) or
(c)(ii) as appropriate.[2]

16.41   Finally in respect of claim forms, where the claimant is a landlord
making an application under s 29(2), in addition to the details described above,
the claim form must also contain the following details:[3]

(a)   The landlord's ground of opposition.[4]

(b)   Full details of those grounds of opposition.

(c)   The terms of a new tenancy that the landlord proposes in the event that
         the application under s 29(2) fails.

16.42 The claim is made using Form N208,[5] and the following particulars
must be included therein:[6]

(a)   details of the property to which the claim relates;

(b)   the nature of the business carried on in the property;

(c)   particulars of the current tenancy, including date, parties and duration,
         the current rent (if not the original rent) and the date and method of
         termination;

(d)   whether any part of the property is not comprised in 'the holding';[7]

(e)   particulars of any notice given under s 25 or s 26;

(f)   the name and address of anyone known to the tenant who:

         (i)   has an interest in the property on the termination of the current
                tenancy, whether or not that interest is immediate or one that will
                vest within 14 years;

---

[1]   Section 32(2) applies where the property comprised in the current tenancy includes other property
      besides the holding, for which see s 23(3) of the LTA 1954.

[2]   Practice Direction, para 3.8.

[3]   Practice Direction, para 3.9.

[4]   For which see s 30(1) of the LTA 1954.

[5]   An example of this form is on the CD-ROM which accompanies this book.

[6]   These particulars should be given in the section of the claim form entitled 'details of claim'.

[7]   For which, see s 23(3).

(ii)   is likely to be affected by the grant of a new tenancy, save for freeholders.[1]

16.43 Despite use of the word 'must' in paras 3.4, 3.5, 3.7 and 3.9 of the Practice Direction, the better view is that if a claimant fails to provide the relevant details, the claim will not be a nullity.[2] Instead the court will make an order to remedy the error. Having said that, it is advisable and desirable to include all the required particulars in the first instance. As a general rule, as much detail as possible should be provided. Thus, when describing the property to which the claim relates, the description in the parcels clause of the current lease can be used unless it is clearly too vague,[3] or the postal address has changed since the date of the grant. Where the claimant is required to describe his proposals for the terms of the new tenancy, the greater the detail the better. It is good practice to append a draft form of lease to the claim form. It is a new requirement that a landlord specify the details of his ground of opposition in a claim form issued under s 29(2). Where the ground of opposition is that contained in s 30(1)(f), demolition and reconstruction, full particulars should be given at this early stage.

16.44   As stated, the claim form must be served within 2 months after the date of issue. The position is not entirely clear where the landlord is out of the jurisdiction. Under CPR, r 7.5(c) a claimant has 6 months within which to serve a claim form on a defendant out of the jurisdiction. There is nothing in CPR, r 56.3(2) which deals specifically with r 7.5(c). As stated, it merely provides that the whole of r 7.5 is to be modified accordingly. It is best to assume that even overseas landlords must be served within 2 months of the date of issue of the claim form.

16.45 The claim form must be served on the persons named therein, and those referred to at **16.34**(f).[4]

16.46 A claim form under CPR Part 8 is automatically allocated to the multi-track.[5] However, as indicated above, when the claim comes before the master or district judge it may be reallocated to the fast track where the claim is likely to last less than one day and the expert evidence, if any, is not extensive. CPR Part 7 procedure applies to an opposed claim, and therefore there will have to be an allocation by the master or district judge. In the majority of cases, an opposed claim will justify allocation to the multi track.

---

[1]   CPR,PD56, para 3.2.
[2]   See *William v Hillcroft Garage Limited* (1971) 22 P&CR 402; and CPR, r 3.10.
[3]   For example, where the property is described in the current lease as 'factory premises to the north of the High Street, Anytown'.
[4]   CPR, PD56, para 3.3.
[5]   CPR, r 8.9(c).

THE DEFENDANT'S RESPONSE

16.47 The Practice Direction describes the means by which the defendant, who may be a landlord or a tenant, must respond to the service of a claim form. There are four possible types of claims. They are:

(a)   A claim by a tenant which is unopposed.
(b)   A claim by a tenant which is opposed.
(c)   A claim by a landlord which is unopposed.[1]
(d)   A claim by a landlord under s 29(2).

How a defendant to each of these claims must respond is as follows.

Acknowledgment of service in a tenant's claim under section 24(1) which is unopposed

16.48 A landlord, faced with a claim by a tenant under s 24(1), which he does not oppose, must nevertheless serve an acknowledgement of service. It must be in form N210,[2] and must state with particulars:[3]

(a)   Whether, if a new tenancy is granted, the defendant objects to any of the terms proposed by the claimant and if so:
    (i)   the terms to which he objects; and
    (ii)   the terms that he proposes in so far as they differ from those proposed by the tenant.
(b)   Whether the tenant is a tenant under a lease having less than 15 years unexpired at the date of the termination of his current tenancy and, if so, the name and address of any person who, to the knowledge of the landlord, has an interest in the reversion in the property expectant (whether immediate or in not more than 15 years from that date) on the termination of the tenant's tenancy.
(c)   The name and address of any person having an interest in the property who is likely to be affected by the grant of a new tenancy.
(d)   If the tenant's current tenancy is one to which s 32(2) applies, whether the defendant requires that any new tenancy shall be a tenancy of the whole of the property comprised in the tenant's current tenancy.

Acknowledgment of service in a landlord's claim under section 24(1) which is unopposed

16.49 In these circumstances it is of course the tenant who is the defendant. He must serve and file an acknowledgement of service which again must be in form N210, and which must contain the following particulars:[4]

---

[1]   A landlord will hardly oppose his claim under s 24(1), he will simply make a claim under s 29(2). Accordingly there is no provision made for a claim by a landlord which is opposed.
[2]   An example of this form is on the CD-ROM which accompanies this book.
[3]   CPR, PD56, para 3.10.
[4]   Ibid, para 3.11.

(a)   The nature of the business carried on at the property.

(b)   If the tenant relies on ss 23(1A), 41 or 42 of the LTA 1954, the basis on which he does so.

(c)   Whether any, and if so what part, of the property comprised in the tenancy is occupied neither by the tenant nor by a person employed by him for the purpose of the business.

(d)   The name and address of:

   (i)   anyone known to the tenant who has an interest in the reversion in the property (whether immediate or in not more than 15 years) on the termination of the current tenancy and who is likely to be affected by the grant of a new tenancy; or

   (ii)   if the tenant does not know of any such person, anyone who has a freehold interest in the property.

(e)   Whether, if a new tenancy is granted, the tenant objects to any of the terms proposed by the landlord and, if so:

   (i)   the terms to which he objects; and

   (ii)   the terms that he proposes in so far as they differ from those proposed by the landlord.

Acknowledgment of service and defence where the tenant is the claimant and the claim is opposed

16.50 As stated above, in a case such as this, CPR Part 7 procedure must be used, and it is the landlord who is the defendant. In such a case, the acknowledgement of service must be in Form N9 and in his defence the landlord must state with particulars:[1]

(a)   The grounds of opposition, which having regard to the definition of that expression in Practice Direction para 3.1(3), are not limited to the statutory grounds described in s 30(1) of the LTA 1954.

(b)   Full details of those grounds of opposition.

(c)   Whether, if a new tenancy is granted, the landlord to any of the terms proposed by the tenant and, if so, the terms to which he objects; and the terms that he proposes in so far as they differ from those proposed by the tenant.

(d)   Whether the tenant is a tenant under a lease having less than 15 years unexpired at the date of the termination of the current tenancy and, if so, the name and address of any person who, to the knowledge of the landlord, has an interest in the reversion in the property expectant (whether immediately or in not more than 15 years from that date) on the termination of the tenant's tenancy.

(e)   The name and address of any person having an interest in the property who is likely to be affected by the grant of a new tenancy.

(f)   If the tenant's current tenancy is one to which s 32(2) of the LTA 1954 applies, whether the landlord requires that any new tenancy shall be a

---

[1]   Practice Direction, para 3.12.

tenancy of the whole of the property comprised in the tenant's current tenancy.

Acknowledgement of service and defence where the landlord is the claimant making an application under section 29(2)

16.51 In such cases, the tenant will be the defendant, and the acknowledgement of service must be in Form N9, and in his defence the tenant must state with particulars:

(a)   Whether he relies on ss 23(1A), 41 or 42 of the LTA 1954 and, if so, the basis on which he does so.

(b)   Whether the tenant relies on s 31A of the LTA 1954 and, if so, the basis on which he does so.

(c)   The terms of the new tenancy that the tenant would propose in the event that the landlord's claim to terminate the current tenancy fails.

16.52 The observations made in para **13.36** above in respect of the claim form apply equally to the content of the acknowledgement of service and the defence, if any. Prior to the amendments to CPR Part 56 introduced by the 2004 Rules on 1 June 2004, there was some doubt as to the form of acknowledgement of service which should be used. Thankfully any doubt has now been removed. Importantly, it will be noted that the landlord's right to apply for an automatic stay under CPR, r 56.3(4) has been removed by the amendments made by the 2004 Rules.

16.53 Previously it was held that where a landlord failed to serve an answer in the county court, he was prevented from opposing the claim for the grant of a new tenancy, but was still entitled to be heard as to the terms of the new lease to be granted to the tenant.[1] The position under the CPR now is that if a defendant, be it a landlord or tenant, fails to serve and file an acknowledgement of service, and the time for so doing has expired, he is not entitled to take part in the hearing unless the court gives permission, although the defendant may attend the hearing.[2]

16.54 Unless the claimant will suffer some substantial prejudice which is not capable of being compensated in costs, the court will probably permit a defendant who has failed to serve an acknowledgement of service to take full part in the proceedings. In many cases the appropriate order is for an adjournment of the claimant's application so that the defendant can serve an acknowledgement of service setting out his case in accordance with the rules.

---

[1]   *Morgan v Jones* [1960] 1 WLR 1220.

[2]   CPR, r 8.4.

EVIDENCE

16.55 CPR, r 56.3(3)(a) excludes the provisions in CPR, rr 8.5 and 8.6 for the filing and service of evidence in claims within the CPR Part 8 procedure. Accordingly, specific provisions are contained in CPR, r 56 dealing with evidence, both in opposed and unopposed claims. The amendments to CPR Part 56 introduced by the 2004 Rules have had a dramatic impact. Where the claim is unopposed, no evidence need be filed unless and until the court directs it to be filed.[1] Accordingly, the requirement to front load with evidence is removed, thus saving costs in claims where, in the first instance at least, the parties should be able to agree the terms of the new tenancy.

16.56 In opposed claims, evidence, including expert evidence, must be filed by the parties as the court directs, and the landlord, whether he is a claimant or defendant, shall be required to file his evidence first.[2] The requirement that the landlord file his evidence first in opposed claims reflects the facts that the bulk of the evidence in such claims will be directed towards the landlord's ground of opposition, and there is frequently little the tenant can say until he knows what the landlord's case is; even then there is often not much the tenant can say to counter the landlord's evidence.

16.57 As to the orders the court might make as to evidence once the claim is before the master or district judge, that will turn on what is in issue between the parties. In unopposed claims, there is frequently a need for expert evidence as to the new s 34 rent and, perhaps, the appropriate rent review pattern and of the market generally. If a party, usually a landlord, wishes to make changes to the terms of the current tenancy, the burden is on that party to justify the changes.[3] Accordingly, evidence will be needed to justify the changes sought save to the extent that they are cosmetic.

16.58 In opposed cases there will usually need to be extensive evidence, both factual and expert, dealing with the landlord's grounds of opposition, particularly if he is relying upon the grounds described in s 30(1)(f) or (g). As the landlord has only one opportunity to make out his ground of opposition,[4] it is important that the evidence filed and served by him is complete. It is impossible to provide guidance in the abstract as to what the evidence should contain. However, it is vital that the grounds of opposition are considered carefully, and each element thereof addressed in the landlord's evidence.

16.59 If the claim is opposed, the grounds of opposition have inevitably been determined as a preliminary point, thereby avoiding costs incurred in respect

---

[1] Practice Direction, para 3.14.
[2] Practice Direction, para 3.15.
[3] See *O'May v City of London Real Property Co Ltd* [1983] AC 726.
[4] Namely at the hearing.

of evidence which may never be relied upon. It is now expressly provided in the Practice Direction, in para 3.16, that grounds of opposition shall be tried as a preliminary issue, unless the circumstances are such that it is unreasonable to do so. It will be an exceptional case where it will be unreasonable to do so.

16.60 In addition to giving the important directions as to evidence, the master or district judge will give more general directions for the further prosecution of the claim. The nature of the directions which may be made is considered further below.

DIRECTIONS

16.61 When the claim gets before the master or, more likely, the district judge, in the manner described above, he will give directions for the further prosecution of the claim. The precise nature of the directions depend upon what is in issue between the parties. If, for example, the only issues concern the terms of the new tenancy, the directions will be very different from those required in a case where the landlord opposes the application for a new tenancy on one or more of the statutory grounds.

16.62 Since July 2002 a pilot scheme has operated in the Central London County Court and the West London County Court, where a post-action protocol has been adopted.[1] The protocol has no formal status under the CPR, but has been adopted to reflect the fact that claims under the LTA 1954 are unlike most other litigation.

16.63 The post-action protocol provides two 'menus of directions'. One menu applies to cases where the landlord does not oppose the grant of a new tenancy, and the issues between the parties concern the terms of the new lease; the second menu applies where the landlord opposes the application for a new tenancy either on one or more of the statutory grounds of opposition, or on some jurisdictional or procedural ground.

16.64 These menus of directions, although not prescriptive, are extremely helpful and provide for almost every eventuality in claims for a new tenancy under the LTA 1954. When acting for a landlord or tenant in a claim under s 24(1) or s 29(2), these directions should be used, modified as appropriate to the particular case.[2]

---

[1] No pre-action protocol has been approved for use in connection with landlord and tenant claims.
[2] The menus of directions are on the CD-ROM which accompanies this book.

DISCONTINUANCE OF CLAIM

16.65 By virtue of CPR, r 38.2(1), a tenant or landlord may discontinue a claim under s 24(1) or s 29(2) of the LTA 1954 as of right. Exceptions to this general statement are contained in CPR, r 38.2(2), but these exceptions are unlikely to arise in the context of claims under s 24(1) or s 29(2). It is not uncommon for landlord and tenants to change their minds about wanting a new tenancy or about opposing an application for a new tenancy.[1] A downturn in business, a realisation that the rent is likely to increase dramatically, may cause a tenant to change his mind. A downturn in the property market, and a drop in rents may have the same effect on a landlord.

16.66 A claim under s 24(1) or s 29(2) may be discontinued by the filing of a notice of discontinuance, and serving a copy of it on the other party to the proceedings.[2] The discontinuance takes effect on the date on which the notice of discontinuance is served on the defendant.[3]

16.67 If a claim is discontinued, then, unless the court orders otherwise, the claimant will be liable for the defendant's costs incurred on or before the date on which the notice of discontinuance is served on the defendant.[4]

16.68 If a tenant discontinues his claim under s 24(1) in a case where the landlord is opposing the application on a ground which entitles the tenant to claim compensation under LTA 1954, s 37 if the ground is made out, the right to such compensation is not lost by the discontinuance of the claim.[5]

SUMMARY JUDGMENT

16.69 Unlike the position under the old rules of court, the parties to a claim under s 24(1) and under s 29(2) can apply for summary judgment pursuant to CPR, r 24.3(1). The application cannot be made until such time as the acknowledgement of service has been served, unless the court otherwise gives permission.[6] The application is made in accordance with CPR Part 23.

16.70 The court will grant summary judgment if it considers that the claimant has no real prospect of succeeding on the claim, or if the defendant has no

---

[1]   For an interesting case decided under the old rules of court in which both the landlord and the tenant changed their minds, see *Bacchiocchi v Academic Agency Ltd* [1998] 1 WLR 1313.

[2]   CPR, r 38.3(1).

[3]   CPR, r 38.5(1).

[4]   CPR, r 38.6(1). CPR, r 44.12 provides for the basis of assessment where a right to costs arises on discontinuance.

[5]   LTA 1954, s 37(1). See also *Bacchiocchi v Academic Agency Limited* [1998] 1 WLR 1313, referred to at footnote 1 above.

[6]   CPR, r 24.4(1).

real prospect of successfully defending the claim, and there are no other compelling reasons why there should be a hearing.[1]

16.71 However, it is difficult to imagine a situation where an application for summary judgment will be appropriate. It is submitted that the summary procedure may be available to a landlord who seeks to oppose the claim, or who has applied to the court under s 29(2), and whose case is very strong. Thus, it is usually fairly easy to establish the ground of opposition contained in s 30(1)(g). Provided the landlord can prove that he has a genuine intention to occupy the holding for his own business purposes, or to reside there, there is very little a tenant can argue to the contrary.

16.72 It is more difficult to imagine circumstances in which a landlord successfully applies for summary judgment where he is relying on the ground of opposition contained in s 30(1)(f).

16.73 In conclusion, it will probably very rarely be appropriate to apply for summary judgment in the context of a claim under s 24(1) or under s 29(2).

THE HEARING

16.74 Once the directions given by the master or district judge have been complied with, the claim is ready for trial. Unless the parties agree otherwise, the substantive claim, and/or a preliminary point, will be heard by a judge.

CLAIM FOR INTERIM RENT

16.75 The amendments to the LTA 1954 introduced by the 2003 Order have had a dramatic impact on the issue of interim rents. Provided a landlord has served a s 25 notice, or a tenant has made a s 26 request, on or after 1 June 2004, either of them may make an application to the court to determine an interim rent which the tenant is to pay while the current tenancy continues by virtue of s 24.[2] The 2004 Rules amended the Practice Direction to accommodate the substantive changes to the LTA 1954 concerning with interim rents.[3]

16.76 Before considering the procedure, two points of substance. First, neither the tenant nor the landlord may make an application for an interim rent if the other has made such an application and has not withdrawn it.[4]

---

[1]   CPR, r 24.2.
[2]   Section 24A(1) of the LTA 1954.
[3]   Practice Direction, paras 3.17, 3.18 and 3.19.
[4]   See s 24A(2).

Secondly, and most importantly, no application under s 24A(1) for an interim rent shall be entertained if it is made more than 6 months after the termination of the current tenancy.[1] Use of the expression 'shall not be entertained' means that the court does not have jurisdiction to determine an interim rent if the application is not made within the prescribed time-limit.

16.77 The Practice Direction makes provision for situations where proceedings have already commenced, either under s 24(1) or s 29(2), and situations where proceedings have yet to be commenced, or have been disposed of.[2]

16.78 Where proceedings are extant, the claim for an interim rent under s 24A(1) must be made in those proceedings in the claim form, if made by the claimant, in the acknowledgement of service, if made by the defendant, or by an interim application in accordance with CPR Part 23, which interim application may be made by either party.[3] There is no obvious reason why one would not make the claim for an interim rent in the claim form or acknowledgement of service, and accordingly that is where the claim should be made.[4] The ability to apply pursuant to CPR Part 23 is nevertheless useful. A decision not to apply for the determination of an interim rent may be revisited if the market changes, and CPR Part 23 is available in such circumstances.[5]

16.79 The timing of the claim for an interim rent is not as important as it once was. Prior to 1 June 2004, a delay in making a claim for an interim rent resulted in the landlord losing out. Now, the interim rent is payable from the earliest date that could have been specified in a landlord's notice under s 25 of the LTA 1954, or the earliest date that could have been specified in the tenant's s 26 request, as the case may be.[6] This is the case no matter when the claim for an interim rent is made, provided it is made before the expiration of the 6-month period prescribed by s 24A(3).

16.80 Where a claim under s 24(1) or s 29(2) has yet to be commenced, or where such a claim has been disposed of, a party who wishes to make a claim for an interim rent must commence proceedings in accordance with CPR Part 8.[7] As the date from which the interim rent is payable is, in effect, set by the LTA 1954, in the vast majority of cases there will be no reason why a landlord or tenant should initiate proceedings for the sole purpose of applying

---

[1] See s 24A(3).

[2] Practice Direction, paras 3.17 and 3.18.

[3] Practice Direction, para 3.17.

[4] If the application is made pursuant to CPR Part 23, a fee is payable when the application notice is issued. A good reason to make the claim in the claim form or acknowledgement of service.

[5] Although it would need to be a dramatic and unanticipated change in the market to produce such a change of mind.

[6] See s 24B of the LTA 1954. These dates are, in effect, the earliest dates in which the current tenancy would have come to an end at common law.

[7] Practice Direction, para 3.19.

for an interim rent. If such proceedings are issued and served, the claim form must include details of:

(a)   The property to which the claim relates.

(b)   The particulars of the relevant tenancy (including date, parties and duration) and the current rent (if not the original rent).

(c)   Every notice or request given or made under ss 25 or 26 of the LTA 1954.

(d)   If the current tenancy has terminated, the date and mode of termination.

(e)   If the relevant tenancy has been terminated and the landlord has granted a new tenancy of the property to the tenant:
    (i)   particulars of the new tenancy (including date, parties and duration) and the rent; and
    (ii)   in a case where s 24C(2) of the LTA 1954 applies[1] but the claimant seeks a different rent under s 24C(3),[2] particulars and matters on which the claimant relies as satisfying s 24C(3) of the LTA 1954.[3]

A final point on interim rents. If a court makes an order for the payment of an interim rent under s 24C, but the order for the grant of a new tenancy is not acted upon by the landlord and the tenant, or the order is revoked under s 36(2) of the LTA 1954,[4] then the landlord or tenant can apply to the court to determine an interim rent in accordance with s 24C(1) and (2).[5] If such an application is made, it must be made on an application under CPR Part 23 in the original proceedings, and not by the commencement of new proceedings.[6] Such application will not be common.

APPLICATIONS FOR VESTING ORDERS IN RESPECT OF LEASEHOLD INTERESTS

Introduction

16.81 Both liquidators and trustees in bankruptcy may disclaim onerous property upon giving appropriate notice.[7] Leases are often onerous property in the hands of an insolvent tenant, and may be disclaimed. Indeed, the

---

1   That is where the interim rent will be the same as the s 34 rent.

2   A different rent because the interim rent will be substantially different from the s 34 rent.

3   Practice Direction, para 3.19. Section 24C(3) may be satisfied if the terms of the new tenancy differ substantially from the terms of the current tenancy so that the differences in lease terms result in a substantial difference between the interim rent and the s 34 rent.

4   A tenant may apply under s 36(2) to the court for an order revoking an order for the grant of a new tenancy to him if the tenant changes his mind and does not want a new tenancy. The application must be made within 14 days of the making of the order for the grant of a new tenancy.

5   See s 24D(3) of the LTA 1954.

6   Practice Direction, para 3.18.

7   IA 1986, ss 178(2) and 315(1).

IA 1986 makes specific provision for the disclaimer of leasehold interests in the context of both corporate and personal insolvency.[1]

16.82 The effect of a disclaimer is complicated, but in broad terms it brings to an end the relationship of landlord and tenant, thus releasing an insolvent tenant from all future liability under the terms of the disclaimed lease.[2] However, the disclaimer will not affect the rights and liabilities of any other person save to the extent that it is necessary for the purpose of releasing the insolvent tenant. Thus, although the lease seems to end as between the landlord and the tenant, it may still exist in relation to other parties.

16.83 Therefore, an original tenant under a lease made before 1 January 1996,[3] an assignee who has directly covenanted with the landlord, and sureties for the assignee and/or the insolvent tenant, remain liable.[4] Any of these persons are entitled to apply for a vesting order, which will have the effect of vesting the lease in the successful applicant. Further, it is possible for a landlord to apply to have a vesting order made in respect of another person, or example a sub-tenant or mortgagee.[5] Anyone with an interest in the relevant property, or who remains under a liability notwithstanding the disclaimer, or, where the property is a dwelling house, any person living in, or entitled to live in, the dwelling house at the date the bankruptcy petition was presented,[6] may apply for a vesting order.[7]

Tribunal

16.84 An application for a vesting order must be made in the court in which the winding-up or bankruptcy proceedings have been issued. Accordingly, the tribunal will not be a matter for the person seeking the vesting order. There is a financial limit on the county court's jurisdiction in winding-up proceedings.[8] Thus, in larger liquidations an application for a vesting order will be made to the Chancery Division, whereas in more modest liquidations, the application will be to the county court. The High Court and the county court have the same jurisdiction in respect of personal insolvency;[9] as such, an application for a vesting order may have to be made in either the Chancery Division or the county court. Except as otherwise stated, the procedure and practice described below applies to applications in the Chancery Division and in the county court.

---

[1]   IA 1986, ss 179 and 317.
[2]   Ibid, ss 178 and 315.
[3]   Ie a tenant of an old tenancy within the meaning of the Landlord and Tenant (Covenants) Act 1995.
[4]   *Hindcastle v Barbara Attenborough Associates Limited* [1997] AC 70.
[5]   *Re Baker ex parte Lupton* [1901] 2 KB 628.
[6]   There is no equivalent provision in corporate insolvency.
[7]   IA 1986, ss 181(2) and 320(2).
[8]   Ibid, s 117(2).
[9]   Ibid, s 373(1).

Timing

16.85 An application for a vesting order must be made within 3 months of the applicant becoming aware of the disclaimer, or of receiving a copy of the liquidator's or trustee's notice of the disclaimer, whichever is the earlier.[1] The court has power to extend the period of 3 months.[2] An appropriate case for extending time would be where an applicant did not receive the notice of disclaimer and was not otherwise aware of it.

Form and content of application

16.86 Since the application for a vesting order will be made in proceedings pending before the court, the application is made by way of an 'ordinary application'.[3] The form of the application must be in a form appropriate to the application concerned.[4] An application notice in Form N244[5] is appropriate for these purposes. The application must contain:

(a)   the names of the parties;
(b)   the nature of the order referred applied for;
(c)   the names and addresses of the person (if any) on whom it is intended to serve the application, or that no person is intended to be served;
(d)   where the IA 1986 or the 1986 Rules require that notice of the application is to be given to specified persons, the names and addresses of all those persons (so far as they are known to the applicant);
(e)   the applicant's address for service.[6]

16.87 The application must also be signed.[7] It is advisable to make all interested parties defendants to the application. Thus, if a sub-tenant is making an application, the landlord and any mortgagee should be joined.

16.88 The application must be supported by an affidavit,[8] or witness statement verified by a statement of truth,[9] which must be filed at court at the same time as the application. The affidavit or witness statement must:[10]

(a)   state whether the application is based on IA 1986, s 181(2)(a) or (b), or s 320(2)(a) or (b), as the case may be;

---

[1]   IR 1986, rr 4.194(2) and 6.186(2).
[2]   *WH Smith Ltd v Wyndham Investments Ltd* [1994] BCC 699.
[3]   IR 1986, r 7.2(1).
[4]   Ibid, r 7.2(2).
[5]   In the High Court, Form PF244 is used.
[6]   IR 1986, r 7(3)(1).
[7]   Ibid, r 7.3(3).
[8]   Ibid, rr 4.194 and 6.186(3).
[9]   Ibid, r 7.57(5).
[10]   Ibid, rr 4.194(3) and 6.186(3).

(b)   specify the date on which the applicant received a copy of the notice of disclaimer, or otherwise became aware of the disclaimer;

(c)   specify the grounds of the application and the order which the applicant desires the court to make.

16.89 Grounds are described in IA 1986, ss 181(2) and 320(2) and should be expanded upon in the support affidavit or witness statement as appropriate. Thus, if the application is being made on the ground that the applicant has an interest in the disclaimed lease, for example as a sub-tenant, full details of the sub-tenancy should be given.

The hearing

16.90   In the first instance, an application for a vesting order must be made to the registrar or district judge and will be heard in chambers.[1] In a proper case, an application can be made directly to the judge,[2] but, save in exceptional circumstances, should be made to the registrar or district judge.

16.91   The court will fix a date and venue for the hearing of the application and, not later than 7 days before the date fixed, the applicant must give to the liquidator or the trustee in bankruptcy, as the case may be, notice of the venue, together with copies of the application and affidavit or witness statement in support.[3]

16.92   If, on the hearing of the application, the registrar or district judge takes the view that the application is better dealt with by a judge, he will refer the application to the judge, who will deal with it or refer it back to the registrar or district judge with directions.[4] Further, if the registrar or district judge is of the view that other persons should be sent or given notice of the application, he will make directions to that effect.[5]

16.93   Provided all those with an interest have been served, there is no reason why the registrar or district judge will not make an order in accordance with ss 182 and 321 of the IA 1986. Once an order is made, the court will

---

[1]   IR 1986, r 7.6(1) and (3); Practice Direction, paras 5.2 and 9.2.
[2]   Ibid, r 7.6(4).
[3]   Ibid, rr 4.194(4) and 6.186(4).
[4]   Ibid, r 7.6(3).
[5]   Ibid, rr 4.194(5) and 6.186(5).

send sealed copies to the applicant, and the liquidator or trustee, as the case may be.

16.94   If an order is made in favour of the applicant, the lease will vest in him without any conveyance, assignment or transfer.[1]

---

1   IA 1986, ss 181(6) and 320(6).

Chapter 17

STATUTORY APPEALS (INCLUDING TAX APPEALS)

Daniel Bromilow & John Smart

SCOPE OF CHAPTER

17.1 This chapter concerns appeals from various tribunals which are required to be brought in the Chancery Division. While this chapter does not deal with appeals from county courts, or appeals from the Court of Protection, it should be remembered that the High Court deals with increasing numbers of appeals from the county courts, as to which CPR Part 52 and its Practice Direction are applicable. County court cases with a Chancery flavour are best brought to the Chancery Division, although there seems to be no restriction imposed by Part 52 in this regard. This chapter outlines the procedures generally applicable,[1] and then concentrates on some of the important features applicable to tax appeals, as to which the general procedures are somewhat modified. The importance of adhering to time-limits and the peculiarities of the case-stated procedures are emphasised.

17.2 In most, but not all, revenue appeals, the parties will have had the opportunity of calling evidence from witnesses, and adducing documentary evidence at a hearing before a specialist tribunal. As will be discussed at **17.6–17.7**, whether the appellant is the taxpayer, the Inland Revenue or Customs and Excise, these appeals to the Chancery Division are limited to appeals on points of law, and (save in the increasingly rare case of a stamp duty appeal) in tax appeals fresh evidence is never adduced before the Chancery judge.

---

[1] Practitioners should be aware that the PD to Part 52 has been amended with effect from 1 July 2004. For a summary of the changes see *Scribes West Limited v Relsa Ansalt* [2004] EWCA (Civ) 835.

APPEALS WHICH MUST BE BROUGHT TO THE CHANCERY DIVISION

17.3 Any appeal or case stated under the following enactments will be referred to the Chancery Division:

- Law of Property Act 1922, Sch 15, para 16;
- Industrial Assurance Act 1923;
- Land Registration Act 1925;
- Water Resources Act 1991, s 205(4);
- Clergy Pensions Measure 1961, s 38(3);
- Industrial and Provident Societies Act 1965;
- Pension Schemes Act 1993, ss 151, 173;
- Pensions Act 1995, s 97;
- Charities Act 1993;
- Stamp Act 1891, ss 13, 13B;
- Income and Corporation Taxes Act 1988, s 705A;
- General Commissioners (Jurisdiction and Procedure) Regulations 1994,[1] reg 22;
- Taxes Management Act 1970, ss 53, 56A, 100C(4);
- Inheritance Tax Act 1984, ss 222(3), 225, 249(3), 251;
- Stamp Duty Reserve Tax Regulations 1986,[2] regs 8(3), 10;
- Land Registration Act 2002.[3]

This list, which is contained in the Practice Direction to CPR Part 52 (PD52), is expressed to be 'not exhaustive'. Where any relevant Practice Direction or statute requires a statutory appeal or appeal by way of case stated to be heard in the Chancery Division, the matter should be commenced in the Chancery Division. However, there may be cases where a statute provides for a right of appeal to the High Court but does not specify in which division the appeal should be heard, and there is no Practice Direction specifying the proper forum for the hearing. The old rules of court provided that statutory appeals would be heard in the Queen's Bench Division unless a relevant statute or Practice Direction stated otherwise.[4] However, there is no equivalent 'default' position in the CPR. In cases where the statute providing the right of appeal is silent as to what division is appropriate and where there is no Practice Direction on this point, it seems that this is a matter for the discretion of the appellant. Where the subject matter of the appeal is within the Chancery Division's area of expertise, it may be appropriate for the appeal to be issued in the Chancery Division.

---

[1]   SI 1994/1812.
[2]   SI 1986/1711.
[3]   CPR, PD52, para 23.2.
[4]   RSC Ord 55, r 2 and Ord 56, r 1.

17.4　CPR PD52 also contains specific procedural rules for appeals heard under the following enactments, all of which must also be heard in the Chancery Division:

- Inheritance Tax Act 1984, s 222.
- Taxes Management Act 1970, ss 53, 100C(4);
- Inheritance Tax Act 1984, ss 249(3), 251;
- Taxes Management Act 1970, s 56A, Inheritance Tax Act 1984, and Stamp Duty Reserve Tax Regulations 1986, reg 10;
- Industrial Assurance Act 1923, s 17;
- Friendly Societies Act 1974, Friendly Societies Act 1992, Industrial Assurance Act 1923, and Industrial and Provident Societies Act 1965;
- Tribunals and Inquiries Act 1992, s 11(1) in relation to appeals against a decision of a Value Added Tax and Duties Tribunal;
- Commons Registration Act 1965;
- an order or decision of the Charity Commissioners;
- Land Registration Act 2002, s 111.

Where the appeal is made under any of the above statutory provisions, the relevant procedural rules in Section III of CPR PD52 should be complied with.

INTRODUCTION

17.5　This chapter does not cover judicial review. It should be remembered that in relation to some bodies and tribunals which exercise quasi-judicial functions a relevant statute may state that any decision of the tribunal is to be final, which may preclude the possibility of an appeal to a court. But the jurisdiction of the courts to supervise the functions of such bodies will rarely be wholly ousted by such words, as the courts will generally accept jurisdiction to intervene in the affairs of the body or tribunal by way of judicial review.[1]

17.6　In some instances an appeal can only be brought on a point of law, but that does not wholly exclude the possibility of an appeal on the basis that the tribunal has reached an unreasonable decision. A party to an appeal heard by the General Commissioners can appeal if he is dissatisfied with their final determination as erroneous in point of law.[2] Similarly, s 56A of the Taxes Management Act 1970 (TMA 1970) gives a right of appeal against decisions of the Special Commissioners either finally determining the appeal, or decisions 'in principle' on one or more issues, typically leaving figures to be agreed, if a party is dissatisfied in point of law. In inheritance tax cases, s 222 of the

---

[1]　*Anisminic v Foreign Compensation Commission* [1969] 2 AC 147.
[2]　General Commissioners (Jurisdiction and Procedure) Regulations 1994, SI 1994/1812, reg 20.

Inheritance Tax Act 1984 (ITA 1984) permits an appeal against the Special Commissioners' determination if a party is 'dissatisfied in point of law' with their determination. There is a similar right of appeal under reg 10 of the Stamp Duty Reserve Tax Regulations 1986. In VAT cases, s 11(1) of the Tribunals and Inquiries Act 1992 and CPR PD52, para 23.8 provide for appeals from a VAT and Duties Tribunal if a party is dissatisfied with a decision in point of law.

17.7   The losing party may wish to attack certain findings of fact. In order to succeed, it is not enough to argue that a finding is against the weight of the evidence. Whether a finding of primary fact is involved or an inference drawn from the findings of fact is being questioned, it has been held[1] that the court cannot disturb such findings save on the basis of principles set out in *Edwards v Bairstow*.[2] As indicated by Lord Radcliffe,[3] factual conclusions set out in a case stated (or, where relevant, a decision) can be challenged if 'the case contains anything ex facie which is bad law' or 'no person acting judicially and properly instructed as to the relevant law could have come to the determination under appeal'. The courts do not need to impose any exceptional restraints on themselves because they are dealing with cases that arise out of facts found by commissioners:

> 'Their duty is to examine those facts with a decent respect for the tribunal appealed from and if they think that the only reasonable conclusion on the facts found is inconsistent with the determination come to, to say so without more ado.'[4]

PROCEDURE GENERALLY

17.8   The procedure to be adopted in statutory appeals and appeals by way of case stated is now largely set out in Part 52 of the CPR and the accompanying Practice Direction, which apply to all appeals in which the appellant has filed either a notice of appeal or applied for permission to appeal on or after 2 May 2000.[5] Specific provisions dealing with statutory appeals and appeals by way of case stated are found in Section II of CPR PD52.

17.9   To determine the proper procedure for a particular appeal, it is necessary to consider the rules setting out the general procedure as defined above, any other relevant rule of court, and the enactment providing the right

---

[1]   For example in cases such as *Ransom v Higgs* [1974] 50 TC 1 and *Furniss v Dawson* [1984] AC 474.
[2]   [1956] AC 14.
[3]   Ibid, at 37.
[4]   Ibid, at 39.
[5]   Civil Procedure (Amendment) Rules 2000, SI 2000/221, r 39; as amended by Civil Procedure (Amendment No 2) Rules 2000, SI 2000/940.

of appeal. Only when all these sources are considered can a full and proper picture of the procedure to be followed be seen.

TYPES OF APPEAL

17.10 There are two basic types of statutory appeal:

(a)   a 'standard' statutory appeal – throughout this chapter, where the term 'statutory appeal' is used rather than 'appeal by way of case stated' it is the former which is being referred to;

(b)   an appeal by way of case stated.

Slightly different procedures apply to statutory appeals and appeals by way of case stated. As such, they will be considered separately here. The case stated procedure is something of a relic from the past,[1] and may well be phased out. A case stated is a document embodying the findings of fact made by the tribunal and its conclusions of law thereon. The idea is that it is self-contained, although that does not preclude documents being annexed. The notes taken by the tribunal stating a case are not produced at the hearing of the appeal (unlike the position in many statutory appeals) and even if the parties have, unusually, gone to the expense of having the proceedings transcribed, the court hearing an appeal by way of case stated will not allow itself to have regard to the transcript of the 'raw' evidence. Thus, if asked to do so, the General Commissioners must set out verbatim any important pieces of evidence upon which they have relied in the case stated itself.[2]

STATUTORY APPEALS

17.11 Statutory appeals are defined in CPR PD52 as being any instance where 'under any enactment an appeal (other than by way of case stated) lies to the court from a Minister of State, government department, tribunal or other person ("statutory appeals")'.[3]

17.12 As a general rule, appeals from a tribunal or person other than a court, such as appeals provided for by statute, do not require permission. CPR, r 52.3(1) provides that permission is required for an appeal from either the High Court or the county court, but does not extend this provision to appeals from other bodies. An appeal is brought by way of an appellant's

---

[1]   Deriving from criminal proceedings governed by the Summary Jurisdiction Act 1857.
[2]   *Hitch v Stone* [2001] STC 214, at 225d; and *Bradley (Inspector of Taxes) v London Electric plc* [1996] STC 231, at 233f.
[3]   CPR, PD52, para 17.1(1).

notice,[1] and Form N161 should be used for this purpose. The general principle is that an appellant's notice must be filed with the appeal court within 14 days of the date of decision of the body whose decision is being challenged[2] unless the body or tribunal making the decision orders otherwise.[3] However, in the case of statutory appeals this is extended to 28 days after the decision is made.[4] Where the decision is made on a certain date but a statement of the reasons for the decision is given at a later date, then the 28-day period will start to run when the statement of the reasons for the appeal is received by the appellant.[5]

17.13 Where the appellant's notice is not served within the 28-day time-limit, an extension of time can be granted by the court. There is a general provision that the parties may not by agreement extend any time-limit imposed by the rules in CPR Part 52, CPR PD52, or any order of either the lower court or the appeal court.[6] An application for such an extension must be made in the appellant's notice.[7] There appears to be no way in which an appellant, anticipating that it will not be possible to file the appellant's notice in time, can make a pre-emptive application for time to be extended. Where an application for an extension of time is made, the appellant's notice must state the reason for the delay and the steps taken before the application was made.[8] The respondent is entitled to be heard at the application for an extension of time and must be provided with a copy of the appeal bundle.[9] However, it is specifically stated that where a respondent unreasonably objects to an extension of time being granted, he may be ordered to pay the costs of the application.

17.14 The appellant's notice may also include other applications, such as an application for security for costs or for an interim remedy, although these may be made by way of an application notice under CPR Part 23.[10] The grounds of appeal should set out clearly the reasons why r 52.11(3)(a) or (b) is said to apply and specify in respect of each ground whether the ground raises an appeal on a point of law or an appeal against a finding of fact.[11]

17.15 Certain documents must be filed with the appellant's notice. They are:[12]

---

[1]   CPR, PD52, para 5.1.
[2]   CPR, r 52.4(2)(b).
[3]   CPR, r 52.4(2)(a).
[4]   CPR, PD52, para 17.3.
[5]   CPR, PD52, para 17.4
[6]   CPR, r 52.6(2).
[7]   CPR, PD52, para 5.2.
[8]   CPR, PD52, para 5.2.
[9]   CPR, PD52, para 5.3.
[10] CPR, PD52, para 5.5.
[11] CPR, PD52, para 3.2.
[12] CPR, PD52, paras 5.6, 5.6A.

- two additional copies of the appellant's notice for the appeal court;
- one copy of the appellant's notice for each of the respondents;
- one copy of the skeleton argument for each copy of the appellant's notice that is filed;
- a sealed copy of the order being appealed;
- a copy of any order giving or refusing permission to appeal, together with a copy of the reasons for that decision;
- any witness statements or affidavits in support of any application included in the appellant's notice;
- an appeal bundle, the contents of which is prescribed and listed below. Note that all documents which are extraneous to the issues to be considered on the application or appeal must be excluded.[1] The appeal bundle must contain a certificate signed by the appellant's solicitor, counsel or other legal representative to the effect that he has read and understood para (2) and that the composition of the appeal bundle with it.[2]

Contents of the appeal bundle:

(a)   a sealed copy of the appellant's notice;

(b)   a sealed copy of the order being appealed;

(c)   a copy of any order giving or refusing permission to appeal, together with a copy of the judge's reasons for allowing or refusing permission to appeal;

(d)   any affidavit or witness statement filed in support of any application included in the appellant's notice;

(e)   a copy of his skeleton argument;

(f)   a transcript or note of judgment (see para 5.12), and in cases where permission to appeal was given by the lower court or is not required those parts of any transcript of evidence which are directly relevant to any question at issue on the appeal;

(g)   the claim form and statements of case (where relevant to the subject of the appeal);

(h)   any application notice (or case management documentation) relevant to the subject of the appeal;

(i)   in cases where the decision appealed was itself made on appeal (eg from district judge to circuit judge), the first order, the reasons given and the appellant's notice used to appeal from that order;

(j)   in the case of judicial review or a statutory appeal, the original decision which was the subject of the application to the lower court;

(k)   in cases where the appeal is from a Tribunal, a copy of the Tribunal's reasons for the decision, a copy of the decision reviewed by the

---

[1]   CPR, PD 52, para 5.6A(2).

[2]   Ibid, para 5.6A(3).

Tribunal and the reasons for the original decision and any document filed with the Tribunal setting out the grounds of appeal from that decision;

(l)   any other documents which the appellant reasonably considers necessary to enable the Appeal Court to reach its decision on the hearing of the application or appeal; and

(m)   such other documents as the court may direct.

Where any of these documents cannot be included in the bundle, the appellant must indicate which documents have not yet been filed and the reasons why they are not currently available.[1]

17.16 The skeleton argument can be part of the appellant's notice itself, included in the bundle as a separate document, or filed and served on all the other parties up to 14 days after the appellant's notice is filed if it is impracticable for it to be filed with the appellant's notice.[2] Skeleton arguments must contain a numbered list of points on which the appeal is brought, each dealt with in no more than a few sentences and with cross-references to the documents filed.[3] A chronology of events should normally be included with the skeleton argument, and a list of the persons involved in the case and a glossary of technical terms used when appropriate.[4] Where authorities are referred to on points of law, the specific pages of the authority dealing with the point in question should be stated.[5] The cost of non-compliant or late filed skeleton arguments will not be allowed save to the extent that the court otherwise directs.[6]

17.17 In the case of appeals from a tribunal, it is provided that a sealed copy of the tribunal's reasons for the decision should be provided.[7] Where evidence before the lower body or tribunal is relevant to the appeal, then either an official transcript,[8] or a 'typed version of the judge's note of evidence' where there is no official transcript available,[9] should be obtained. In the context of statutory appeals, this reference to a 'judge' should presumably be read as a reference to whatever body or tribunal heard the evidence in question.

---

[1]   CPR, PD52, para 5.7. The appellant must provide a reasonable estimate of when the missing documents can be filed, and must file them as soon as possible.

[2]   CPR, PD52, para 5.9(2).

[3]   CPR, PD52, para 5.10.

[4]   CPR, PD52, para 5.11.

[5]   CPR, PD52, para 5.10(3). Note that the specific proposition must be identified. If more than one authority is cited the reasons should be stated in terms of relevance and necessity for a proper presentation of the argument: CPR, PD52, para 5.10(4), (5).

[6]   CPR, PD52, para 5.10(6).

[7]   CPR, PD52, para 5.12(4).

[8]   CPR, PD52, para 5.15.

[9]   CPR, PD52, para 5.16.

17.18 Once the appellant's notice and skeleton argument are filed they must be served not only on the respondent[1] but also on the body, person or tribunal whose decision is being appealed against.[2] Where the 'lower court' is a tribunal, the notice must be served on the tribunal's chairman. Service must be made as soon as is practicable after the notice is filed, but in any event within 7 days of filing.[3] A copy of the appeal bundle which has to be filed with the appellant's notice must only be served with the appellant's notice where permission to appeal does not need to be sought or has been granted by a lower court.[4]

17.19 Once the appellant's notice has been filed with the appeal court, the court will send the parties notification of a 'listing window' during which the appeal is likely to be heard, along with any other directions ordered by the court.[5]

17.20 If the respondent also wishes to appeal against the decision of the body or tribunal which gave the decision, he may do so by filing and serving a respondent's notice, although this is not necessary where the respondent merely wishes to have the original decision upheld.[6] Note that in appeals from the General Commissioners it may also be necessary or desirable for the winning party to have cross-appealed by way of case stated: see **17.35**. Form N162 should be used for the respondent's notice, which may include an application for interim relief or security for costs in the same manner as an appellant's notice may include such an application.[7] If the respondent does not file and serve a respondent's notice he cannot advance any argument not relied upon before the lower tribunal.[8] The respondent's notice must be filed within 14 days of the date on which the respondent is served the appellant's notice[9] and must be served on the appellant and any other respondent as soon as possible and in any event within 7 days of it being filed.[10]

17.21 The respondent must file with his respondent's notice two additional copies of the notice for the Appeal Court and one additional copy for the appellant and any other respondents.[11] The skeleton argument may be

---

[1] CPR, PD52, para 5.21.
[2] CPR, PD52, para 17.5.
[3] CPR, r 52.4(3).
[4] CPR, PD52, para 5.24. Where permission to appeal needs to be sought the appeal bundle should not be sent with the appellant's notice unless the court directs: CPR, PD52, para 5.24(1).
[5] CPR, PD52, para 6.3.
[6] CPR, PD52, para 7.2.
[7] CPR, PD52, para 7.9.
[8] CPR, PD52, para 7.3(2).
[9] CPR, r 52.5(4) and (5): this is the general rule, where permission to appeal is not rejected or has been granted by the lower courts.
[10] CPR, r 52.5(6).
[11] CPR, PD52, para 7.10(1).

included within the respondent's notice itself,[1] but if it is not included in the notice it may be filed and served within 14 days of the respondent filing the notice.[2] A respondent who does not file a respondent's notice should file and serve a skeleton argument, in all cases where he wishes to address the court, at least 7 days before the appeal hearing.[3] Where appropriate, the respondent's argument should deal with the arguments advanced in the appellant's argument. Where the respondent wishes to rely on documents not included in the appellant's bundle of documents, he should try and agree amendments to the appeal bundle or else he may prepare a supplemental bundle and file this with the respondent's notice.[4] Any bundle should be served on the appellant and any other respondents at the same time as they are served with the respondent's notice or, if none is filed, within 21 days after service of the appeal bundle. The appellant's notice and the respondent's notice may be amended after they have been filed and served[5] but only with the permission of the court.[6]

17.22 As a general rule the hearing of the appeal will be limited to a review of the lower tribunal's decision rather than a full rehearing.[7] However, this will not be the case if the enactment providing for the appeal requires the contrary, where the decision made by the lower tribunal was held without a hearing or was held at a hearing where the procedure did not allow for a consideration of the evidence,[8] or where the court considers that it is in the interests of justice to hold a re-hearing.[9] None of the parties are entitled to rely on any matter which is not contained in the appeal notice unless the appeal court gives permission.[10] At the hearing of the appeal, the court can exercise any of the powers which the lower tribunal could have exercised,[11] and may:

(a)   affirm, set aside or vary any order or judgment made or given by the lower court;

(b)   refer any claim or issue for determination by the lower tribunal;

(c)   order a new hearing;

(d)   make orders for the payment of interest; and

(e)   make a costs order.[12]

---

[1]   CPR, PD52, para 7.6.
[2]   CPR, PD52, para 7.7(1)(b).
[3]   CPR, PD52, para 7.7(2).
[4]   CPR, PD52, paras 7.11, 7.12.
[5]   CPR, PD52, para 5.25.
[6]   CPR, r 52.8.
[7]   CPR, r 52.11(1).
[8]   CPR, PD52, para 9.1.
[9]   CPR, r 52.11(1).
[10]   CPR, r 52.11(5).
[11]   CPR, r 52.10(1).
[12]   CPR, r 52.10(2).

17.23 Where the appeal is from a decision of a minister of state or from a government department, the minister or department is entitled to attend the hearing and to make representations.[1] The appeal court will not receive oral evidence or evidence which was not before the lower court unless it orders otherwise.[2] In practice this almost never happens. However, the appeal court may draw any inference of fact which it considers justified on the evidence,[3] even if this is contrary to any inference drawn by the lower court. It is possible for new evidence to be allowed in support of an argument that the tribunal misconducted itself at the hearing or to show fraud or perjury by a party to the proceedings.[4]

17.24 The appeal court will allow an appeal where the decision of the lower tribunal is found to have been wrong or unjust because of a serious procedural or other irregularity in the proceedings before it.[5]

APPEALS BY WAY OF CASE STATED

17.25 As with statutory appeals, CPR Part 52 will apply with amendments.[6] As such, the majority of the procedure set out above will apply equally to appeals by way of case stated. Most of the differences relate to the need to have the case stated before the appeal procedure itself can commence. The procedure for having the case stated may be set out either in the enactment providing for the right of appeal or in any Practice Directions applying to the tribunal.[7] Where no prescribed procedure exists, a request for a case to be stated should be sent to the tribunal. The case stated should be signed, in the case of a decision by a tribunal, by the chairman of the tribunal and, in the case of a decision by any other person, by that person or by any person authorised to sign the case on his behalf.[8] Where a minister or tribunal states a case, the case stated must be served by the minister or tribunal on the person who made the request for the case to be stated.[9] Where the minister or tribunal states a case or refers a question of law to the appeal court without a request being made, the minister or tribunal must serve a copy of the case stated on those parties which the minister or tribunal consider appropriate, and all other parties must be notified both of the fact that the stated case has been served on that party and the date on which it was served.[10] If the lower

---

1   CPR, PD52, para 7.16.
2   CPR, r 52.11(2).
3   CPR, r 52.11(4).
4   *R v Secretary of State for the Environment ex parte Powis* [1981] 1 WLR 584.
5   CPR, r 52.11(3).
6   CPR, PD52, para 18.2.
7   CPR, PD52, para 18.7.
8   CPR, PD52, para 18.8.
9   CPR, PD52, para 18.9.
10   CPR, PD52, para 18.10.

body or tribunal refuses to state a case, the appellant must apply to the court for an order requiring the body or tribunal to state a case.

17.26 Once a case has been stated, whether by virtue of an application under CPR Part 23 or otherwise, the person who has had the stated case served upon him must file an appellant's notice along with a copy of the stated case and serve a copy of both documents on the tribunal (whose decision is being appealed against) and on every party to the proceedings within 14 days of receiving the stated case.[1] If the person on whom the stated case has been served does not file an appellant's notice within 14 days, any other party to the proceedings may file an appellant's notice[2] within a period of 14 days following the last day on which the person on whom the stated case was served had to file an appellant's notice.[3] The rules require that person to file and serve with the appellant's notice a copy of the case stated[4] although the new appellant will not have had a copy of the stated case served on him by the minister or tribunal stating the case, and a copy of the stated case must therefore be requested from the minister or tribunal. A copy of both the appellant's notice and the stated case must be served on the tribunal whose decision is being appealed against and on every party to the proceedings. Where a case has been stated by a minister or tribunal without a request for any of the parties, the minister or tribunal must file an appellant's notice and a copy of the stated case, and serve those documents on all persons notified of the case having been stated, again within 14 days of the case having been stated.[5]

17.27 The stated case may be amended by the court, or the court may return the stated case to the Minister or tribunal and require them to amend it. Further, the appeal court may draw inferences of fact from the facts set out in the stated case.[6]

17.28 The procedure relating to the documents to be filed and served with the appellant's notice and the conduct of the appeal following the filing and service of the appellant's notice are the same as for statutory appeals as set out above.

---

1   CPR, PD52, para 18.11.
2   CPR, PD52, para 18.13.
3   CPR, PD52, para 18.14.
4   CPR, PD52, para 18.13(2).
5   CPR, PD52, para 18.12.
6   CPR, PD52, para 18.15.

TAX APPEALS

Time-limits and procedure for commencing an appeal to the Chancery Division

(1)   Appeals from the General Commissioners by way of case stated

17.29 The final determination of an appeal heard by the General Commissioners is given at the end of the hearing orally or may be reserved and, in either case, is required to be recorded in a document which is signed and dated by the General Commissioners.[1] The clerk to the General Commissioners is required to send each party a notice setting out the final determination as so recorded. Except where the final determination is given at the end of the hearing, it is treated as having been made on the date on which the clerk to the General Commissioners sends the parties the notice.[2]

17.30 Within 30 days after the final determination (or a decision varying it or substituting for it a new final determination[3]), any party may, if dissatisfied with it as erroneous in point of law, require the General Commissioners to state and sign a case for the opinion of the High Court. A fee of £25 must be paid to the clerk before the appellant is entitled to have the case stated.[4]

17.31 The absence in the General Commissioners (Jurisdiction and Procedure) Regulations 1994[5] of any provision for appeals solely from decisions 'in principle' compared with the specific provisions in the Special Commissioners (Jurisdiction and Procedure) Regulations 1994[6] for decisions in principle suggests that there is no jurisdiction on the part of the General Commissioners to state a case before the final determination of the appeal. Thus, it appears that the chargeable gain or income assessable must be determined before a right to appeal arises. This may be inconvenient and if both parties are content to have a case stated before the figures have been agreed or determined then the court may still entertain such a case stated.[7]

17.32 After the case has been stated and signed, the clerk to the General Commissioners will send it to the party who required the case and notify the other party or parties that the case has been sent to that party. The party requiring the case must transmit the case to the High Court within 30 days of

---

[1]   General Commissioners (Jurisdiction and Procedure) Regulations, 1994, SI 1994/1812, reg 16(2).
[2]   Ibid, reg 16(4).
[3]   Under ibid, reg 17, on the application of a party on the grounds, broadly speaking, of (a) administrative error in the final determination, (b) excusable failure to appear at the hearing, or (c) failure of documents sent to the Commissioners or to the Revenue to arrive until after the hearing.
[4]   TMA 1970, s 56(3).
[5]   SI 1994/1812.
[6]   SI 1994/1811: see reg 18(5)(a). See also TMA 1970, s 56A.
[7]   *Maclaine & Co v Eccott (HMIT)* [1926] 10 TC 481.

receiving it and at or before such time send notice of the fact that the case has been stated on his application together with a copy of the case to the other party or parties.[1] The most important point to note is that it was held under the previous legislation,[2] and it is still the case,[3] that whereas the requirement to notify the other parties and send them a copy of the case stated is directory,[4] the requirement to transmit the case to the High Court is mandatory and the time-limit *cannot be extended* by the High Court.[5]

17.33 Under CPR Part 52 the appellant must file an appellant's notice and the case stated at the High Court (Chancery Chambers), and serve copies of the notice and case stated on the General Commissioners and every other party in the proceedings to which the case relates. In general, the time-limit specified is within 14 days after the case stated was served on the appellant.[6] However, the general requirements are subject to any provision in any enactment[7] and so it is thought that the correct procedure is to ensure that the appellant's notice is filed and served within 30 days of receipt of the case stated.

(2) Action of respondent

17.34 The winning party may wish to cross-appeal in relation to part of the determination of the Commissioners in order to protect the respondent's position if the appellant wins before the judge on a particular point but the respondent suspects that the appellant would lose the appeal on a different point on which the respondent lost before the Commissioners. Each party, including the winning party, is entitled to have its own case stated.[8] The Commissioners may consolidate the cases into one document. If separate appeals have been heard together, whether against separate assessments issued against the same taxpayer or against different taxpayers, this may cause no difficulty. However, where more than one party wishes to appeal it is essential to ensure that each party transmits the document sent to that party by the clerk to the General Commissioners to the High Court (even though this would appear to amount to pointless duplication). Otherwise the court will have no jurisdiction to hear the appeal by the party which has not transmitted its case.[9]

---

1   General Commissioners (Jurisdiction and Procedure) Regulations 1994, reg 22(4).
2   Before these Regulations had application, such appeals by way of case stated were governed by, inter alia, TMA 1970, s 56(4) and (5), which were in similar terms to reg 22(4).
3   *New World Medical Ltd v Cormack (Inspector of Taxes)* [2002] STC 1245.
4   *Hughes v Viner* [1985] STC 235.
5   See *Valleybright v Richardson* [1985] STC 70; *Brassington v Guthrie* [1992] STC 47; *Petch v Gurney* [1994] STC 689.
6   CPR, PD52, para 18.11.
7   CPR, PD52, para 18.1.
8   This is what happened in *Countess Fitzwilliam v IRC* [1990] STC 65, 68e–f; although see dicta to the effect that a separate case stated is unnecessary in *Muir v IRC* [1966] 1 WLR 1269, 1281, 1286.
9   *Petch v Gurney* [1994] STC 689. See also *IRC v McGuckian* [1994] STC 888 (Court of Appeal in Northern Ireland); [1997] 1 WLR 991, HL, where it was held that there was no jurisdiction to hear the taxpayer's

17.35 A respondent who wishes to contend that the Commissioners erred in law in some respect or to advance a new point on appeal to the High Court should consider whether the General Commissioners should be required to state a case and whether he should not rely solely on the filing and service of a respondent's notice in response to the original appellant's notice. The risk of simply relying on a respondent's notice is that the court may refuse to allow the point to be taken (because had the point been taken earlier, evidence might have been adduced relevant to the point) and refuse in its discretion to order the case to be remitted to enable the Commissioners to make further findings of fact.[1] During the process of having the case stated the Commissioners should be asked to make any findings of fact that are relevant to the new point and covered by the evidence adduced before them. CPR, r 52.5 requires a respondent who wishes to ask the appeal court to uphold the orders of the lower court for reasons different from or additional to those given by the lower court, to file and serve a respondent's notice. Such notice must be filed within 14 days after the date on which the respondent is served with the appellant's notice.[2] The notice should be served on the appellant and any other respondent as soon as is practicable and in any event not later than 7 days after it is filed.[3]

(3) Stamp duty land tax appeals

17.36 Stamp duty land tax is a new tax introduced by Part 4 of the Finance Act 2003. Whereas stamp duty (which is still in force in certain cases) was essentially a tax on documents, stamp duty land tax is a tax on land transactions.[4] It replaces stamp duty on most land transactions dated on or after 1 December 2003, although transitional provisions deal with contracts entered into earlier. The Revenue must be notified of certain categories of land transaction, most acquisitions of what are termed 'chargeable interests' in land being notifiable. The tax must be paid before registration can take place at the Land Registry. Some transactions can be self-certified and the self-certificate produced to the Land Registry. Where tax is payable it must be paid by the purchaser at the same time as a land transaction return is made in respect of the transaction.[5] Provision exists for interest to be payable if tax is paid late, and there is a regime of penalties applicable.[6]

---

appeals from the Special Commissioners when the taxpayer failed to transmit a copy of the single document embodying cases stated at the request of the taxpayer and the Revenue.

[1] See *Leisureking v Cushing* [1993] STC 46, at 51; and *Parmar and others (t/a Ace Knitwear) v Woods (Inspector of Taxes)* [2002] STC 846, at 869–870.

[2] See CPR, r 52.5(4)(b). There is also provision in r 52.5(4) for the 'lower court' to give a direction for the time-limit for filing a respondent's notice.

[3] See CPR, r 52.5(6)(b).

[4] Finance Act 2003, s 42.

[5] Ibid, s 86(1), and in particular reg 25.

[6] See ibid, s 99 and Sch 14.

17.37 It is outside the scope of this chapter to go into the substantive law relating to stamp duty land tax appeals. Under the Stamp Duty (Appeals) Regulations 2004[1] the provisions of the TMA 1970 relating to appeals to the General and Special Commissioners are applied with suitable modifications. Thus, if a stamp duty land tax appeal has been heard by the General Commissioners, an appeal to the High Court will be by way of case stated (see **17.29–17.35**). The usual procedure applicable to appeals from the Special Commissioners (see **17.41–17.48**) is followed. The CPR PD52 has not yet been amended to provide for appeals to the High Court in stamp duty land tax appeals to be assigned to the Chancery Division, but it is thought highly unlikely that such appeals will be assigned elsewhere.

(4)   Stamp duty appeals by way of case stated

17.38 Stamp duty appeals to the Chancery Division (except those which relate only to the penalty on late stamping in relation to instruments executed after 30 September 1999) are the exception to the rule that oral evidence is excluded on appeals by way of case stated. The Commissioners of Inland Revenue do not hear evidence or argument before stating a case. Although such appeals do not usually involve the adducing of evidence, and are not restricted to appeals on points of law, oral evidence has been adduced in a few reported cases.

17.39 A person who is dissatisfied with a decision of the Commissioners on an adjudication may appeal within 30 days of notice of the decision being given, but only on payment of the duty. Any penalty in conformity with the Commissioners' decision and any interest that is in conformity with that decision is payable on stamping the instrument on the day on which the appeal is brought. An appeal which relates only to the penalty payable on late stamping is to the Special Commissioners under s 13A of the Stamp Act 1891. Thereafter, appeal can be made to the High Court on a point of law or the amount of any penalty. Any other appeal is by way of case stated in accordance with s 13B of the Stamp Act 1891, pursuant to which the case stated should be set down for hearing within 30 days of its being delivered to the appellant.

17.40 The appellant is also obliged[2] to file at court an appellant's notice with his case stated and serve copies of the notice (and skeleton argument) and case stated on the Commissioners. The general time-limit for doing so is within 14 days after the case stated was served on him. However, the general requirements are subject to any provision in any enactment[3] and so it is

---

[1]   SI 2004/1363.
[2]   According to CPR, PD52, para 18.11, which imposes a general requirement to this effect in appeals by way of case stated.
[3]   CPR, PD52, para 18.1.

thought that the appellant's notice should be filed (and served on the Revenue with a copy of the case stated) within 30 days.

(5) Appeals from the Special Commissioners

17.41 The final determination of an appeal heard by the Special Commissioners is given at the end of the hearing orally or (more usually) may be reserved, and in either case is required to be recorded in a document which is signed and dated by the Special Commissioners.[1] Unlike decisions of the General Commissioners, decisions of the Special Commissioners must contain a statement of the facts found by them and the reasons for the determination.[2] Where the final determination is reserved, the Special Commissioners may give a written decision in principle on one or more issues arising in the proceedings and adjourn the making of the final determination until after their decision in principle has been issued and such further questions arising from that decision have been agreed by the parties or, failing agreement, decided by them after having heard the parties.[3]

17.42 The clerk to the Commissioners is required to send each party a copy of a decision in principle or document recording the final determination.[4] Except where it is given at the end of the hearing, the final determination is treated as having been made on the date on which the clerk to the Special Commissioners sends the document recording the final determination to the parties.[5] Presumably, a decision in principle is also treated as made when sent.

17.43 An appellant wishing to exercise the right to appeal conferred by s 56A(1) of the TMA 1970 against a decision in principle, a decision finally determining an appeal or a decision given varying a decision or final determination,[6] may do so by appealing within 56 days after the date of determination or other decision against which the appeal is brought.[7] It is necessary to file the appellant's notice and the documents required by CPR PD52, para 5.6 (see para **17.15** above) and then to serve a sealed copy (and the skeleton argument and a copy of the bundle) on the respondent and on the Special Commissioners. It is difficult to see what point there is in serving the Commissioners with a bundle of documents, and it seems that they may properly be asked to give a dispensation in this respect. Service should be effected as soon as is practicable and in any event not later than 7 days after

---

[1] Special Commissioners (Jurisdiction and Procedure) Regulations 1994, reg 18(4).
[2] Ibid.
[3] Ibid, reg 18(5).
[4] Ibid, reg 18(8).
[5] Ibid, reg 18(9).
[6] Under ibid, reg 19.
[7] CPR, PD52 para 23.5(1)(c).

the appellant's notice is filed.[1] CPR PD52 refers to serving the 'chairman' of the tribunal rather than the clerk to the Commissioners.[2]

17.44 CPR, PD52, para 17.4 states that where the statement of the reasons for a decision is given later than the notice of that decision, the period for filing the appellant's notice is calculated from the date on which the statement is received by the appellant. However, as in most cases the Special Commissioners reserve their decision in principle or final determination, which is then sent out, there will be no early notice of the decision, so that para 17.4 would seem to be of little assistance. The crucial date appears to be the date of sending the decision or final determination by the clerk to the Special Commissioners. It is unfortunate that CPR PD52, para 23.5 refers to the date of the decision, which may not be the same thing as the date of sending.

17.45 The right to appeal to the Chancery Division in an inheritance tax matter heard by the Special Commissioners, following the issuing of a notice of determination under s 221 of the ITA 1984, is contained in s 225 of that Act. The appeal is against the 'determination' by the Special Commissioners, and the same 56-day time-limit is applicable for filing the appellant's notice.[3]

17.46 Unlike s 56A of the TMA 1970, there is no specific reference in s 222 of the ITA 1984 to appeals against decisions given in principle, or following a review of a decision or final determination. The Special Commissioners (Jurisdiction and Procedure) Regulations 1994 do not restrict the Special Commissioners' powers to give such decisions, or their powers of review in inheritance tax cases, and it seems unlikely to have been intended that either party should be unable to appeal in such circumstances. It is odd that the statutory instrument which substituted both sections (in relation to cases to which the Regulations apply) should have made different provision.[4]

17.47 In stamp duty reserve tax cases, reg 10 of the Stamp Duty Reserve Tax Regulations 1986[5] is drafted in almost identical terms to s 225 of the ITA 1984. The appeal is against the 'determination' of the appeal by the Special Commissioners, and the same 56-day time-limit applies for serving the appellant's notice.

17.48 Unlike the position with appeals by way of case stated, in an appropriate case an extension of time may be sought by including an

---

[1]   CPR, r 52.4(3) and CPR, PD52, paras 5.21 and 17.5.
[2]   CPR, PD52, para 17.5.
[3]   CPR, PD52, para 23.5(1)(c).
[4]   General and Special Commissioners (Amendment of Enactments) Regulations 1994, SI 1994/1813.
[5]   SI 1986/1711, as amended.

application for an extension of time in the appellant's notice.[1] The notice should state the reason for the delay and the steps taken prior to the application being made.[2] In practice, evidence by witness statement will be required. It appears that in an appropriate case an extension of time may be sought by applying, on notice to the respondent, to the Chancery interim applications judge. The procedure set out in CPR Part 23 and PD23 is rendered applicable by PD52, para 11.1. The court must consider the overriding objective set out in CPR Part 1 in deciding whether to grant an extension of time.[3] Lightman J held in *Commissioners of Customs and Excise v Eastwood Care Homes (Ilkeston) Limited*[4] that whereas there had only been a slim chance before the Woolf Reforms of obtaining an extension of time where the delay was due to inadvertence, the position was fundamentally changed by the CPR. Each application must be viewed by reference to the criterion of justice. Among the facts which must be taken into account are the length of the delay, the explanation for the delay, the prejudice caused by the delay to the other party, the merits of the appeal, the effect of the delay on public administration, the importance of compliance with time-limits (bearing in mind that they were to be observed), and the resources of the parties, which might be relevant, in particular to the question of prejudice. On the facts, the judge granted an extension of time where notice of appeal was served 3 days late. A condition of payment into court might conceivably be imposed[5] as the price of a successful application.

(6)   Appeals from the VAT and Duties Tribunal

17.49 Appeals to the VAT and Duties Tribunals are governed by the VAT Tribunals Rules 1986.[6] At the conclusion of the hearing, the chairman may give or announce the decision of the tribunal. In a 'mitigation appeal'[7] or a 'reasonable excuse appeal'[8] the chairman may ask the parties present whether they require the decision to be recorded in a written document, and if none of the parties requires this, there are 14 days in which to request this in writing.[9] In other cases the decision must be recorded in a document containing the findings of fact and reasons for the decision.[10] Every decision (and each copy

---

[1]   CPR, PD52, paras 5.2–5.4 and Form N161.
[2]   CPR, PD52, para 5.2.
[3]   The power to do so is contained in CPR, r 3.1(2)(a).
[4]   [2001] STC 1629.
[5]   Under CPR, r 3.1(3).
[6]   SI 1986/590, as amended.
[7]   See the definition contained in r 2 of the VAT Tribunals Rules 1986, SI 1986/590: these appeals are against the amount of certain penalties imposed by Customs and Excise and/or interest.
[8]   See the definition contained in r 2 of the VAT Tribunals Rules 1986: these appeals are against liability to pay certain penalties, or as to the amount of the penalty, and, for example, the obligation to pay default surcharge in circumstances where a person must establish a reasonable excuse for a failure to comply with his obligations in order to appeal successfully.
[9]   VAT Tribunals Rules 1986, r 30(8).
[10]   Ibid 1986, r 30(1).

thereof which is sent to the parties) must bear the date when the copies are released to the parties.

17.50 The time-limit for appealing is 56 days from the date of the decision or determination against which the appellant wishes to appeal.[1] CPR, PD52, para 17.4 states that where a statement of the reasons for a decision is given later than the notice of that decision, the period for filing the appellant's notice is calculated from the date on which the statement is received by the appellant. The procedure is then the same as appeals from the Special Commissioners.[2]

(7) *Leapfrog appeals direct to the Chancery Division in inheritance tax and stamp duty reserve tax cases*

17.51 It is possible to 'leapfrog' the Special Commissioners direct to the High Court in an inheritance tax or stamp duty reserve tax appeal. This must be agreed between the Inland Revenue and the taxpayer, or the taxpayer may make an application to the High Court for permission to bring an appeal on the grounds that the matters to be decided are likely to be substantially confined to questions of law.[3] The provisions are infrequently invoked. Similarly, in stamp duty reserve tax cases,[4] if the taxpayer and the Inland Revenue agree or the High Court, on an application made by the taxpayer, is satisfied that the matters to be decided on the appeal are likely to be substantially confined to questions of law and gives leave, appeal may be made to the High Court. It has been held that there must be some special circumstance before the procedure can be adopted. It is a precondition that the matter involves a point of law. If the point is one of novelty or importance this may be a ground for proceeding direct to the High Court.[5]

17.52 The initial time-limit for appealing against an inheritance tax determination by the Inland Revenue is 30 days from the service of the notice of determination,[6] although there is provision for an appeal out of time with the consent of the Inland Revenue or the Special Commissioners.[7] In stamp duty reserve tax cases, the time-limit for appealing is 30 days from the date of the notice of determination issued under reg 6, and similar provision is made for late appeals by reg 9, of the Stamp Duty Reserve Tax Regulations 1986. The notice of appeal given in the first instance is the same sort of notice as is

---

1   CPR, PD52, para 23.8(2).
2   See **17.41–17.48**.
3   ITA 1984, s 222(3).
4   Under reg 8 of the Stamp Duty Reserve Tax Regulations 1986.
5   *Bennett v IRC* [1995] STC 5.
6   Under ITA 1984, s 221.
7   By ITA 1984, s 223(a), the Inland Revenue is obliged to consent if it is satisfied that there was a reasonable excuse for not bringing the appeal within the time limited, and that the application to it for consent was made thereafter without unreasonable delay; if it is not so satisfied it must refer the matter to the Special Commissioners: s 223(b).

given in a case where the appellant wishes to appeal to the Special Commissioners, and it must specify the grounds of appeal.

17.53 In both cases, the appeal to the Chancery Division is brought by means of an appellant's notice. At the time of filing the appellant's notice, the appellant must file in Chancery Chambers two copies of the notice of determination, and two copies of the notice of appeal given (referred to at **17.52**). An application for permission to appeal direct to the High Court is required to be contained in the appellant's notice.[1] Evidence in support of the application must be prepared, and generally this will be contained in a separate witness statement (rather than the appellant's notice itself) setting out the grounds on which it is alleged that the matters to be decided on the appeal are likely to be substantially confined to questions of law.[2]

17.54 The appellant's notice must be filed and served on the Inland Revenue (with a copy of the written evidence referred to above) within 30 days of the date on which the appellant gave notice of appeal or, if the Revenue or the Special Commissioners have given consent to the appeal being brought out of time, within 30 days of the date on which such consent was given.[3] These requirements are in addition to the usual documents required for appeals.

(8) *Appeals against penalties*

17.55 Section 53 of the TMA 1970 confers a right of appeal to the High Court against the summary determination of penalties by the General and Special Commissioners pursuant to their powers under the relevant regulations. Section 251 of the ITA 1984 confers a similar right of appeal from penalties imposed by the Special Commissioners in inheritance tax cases. Under s 249(3) of the ITA 1984 there is an appeal from penalties imposed by the Special Commissioners after penalty proceedings have been instituted by the Inland Revenue.[4] Where penalty proceedings have been instituted before the General or Special Commissioners for certain penalties,[5] a right of appeal from the Commissioners arises under s 100C(4) of the ICTA 1988.

17.56 Under CPR PD52, para 23.4 the appellant's notice must be filed at Chancery Chambers within 30 days from the decision, award or determination. It is necessary to file the appellant's notice and the documents required by CPR PD52, and then to effect service of sealed copies of the appellant's notice, skeleton argument and bundle. Service should be effected

---

[1]   CPR, PD52, para 23.3(2)(c).
[2]   CPR, PD52, para 23.3(3)(c).
[3]   CPR, PD52, para 23.3(4).
[4]   For example, under s 245 for failure to account or provide a return.
[5]   Under ICTA 1988, s 100C(1) these are penalties to which s 100(1) does not apply by reason of s 100(2).

as soon as is practicable and in any event not later than 7 days after the appellant's notice is filed.[1]

Content of case stated in appeals from General Commissioners: remission

17.57 A case stated by the General Commissioners must set out the facts and the final determination of the Commissioners, who may require the question of law to be identified within 28 days.[2]

17.58 The Commissioners must send a draft case within 56 days of receipt of the appellant's written notice requesting the case (and their fee of £25) or within 56 days of the identification to their satisfaction of the point of law involved. Any party then has 56 days to make written representations on the draft to the clerk.[3] Copies of the representations must be sent at the same time to the other parties.[4] There are 28 days to make further representations to the clerk (which must also be sent to the other parties) on the draft in response to the representations.[5]

17.59 As soon as possible after the latest date on which representations may be made, the Commissioners must state and sign the case, taking into account any representations made by the parties.[6]

17.60 The Commissioners are not obliged to set out the whole of the evidence for and against a particular finding of fact, but only the evidence which supports the conclusion of fact reached. Such evidence must be set out fairly, that is to say truly and accurately, and must be credible, in the sense that a reasonable man could accept that evidence as the truth.[7] It is permissible to set out the evidence relied upon verbatim for the purpose of clarity.

17.61 The court is likely to be unwilling, in the absence of fraud, dishonesty or a change in the law, to remit a case stated in order for the Commissioners to make further findings of fact (which may or may not involve the calling of fresh evidence) on matters which could have been raised at the hearing.[8] CPR PD52, para 18.16 permits the appeal court to draw inferences but it is consistent with CPR PD52, para 18.1 that such a power is 'subject to any provision about a specific category of appeal in any enactment(s)'. The nature of appeals on a point of law is such that the power to draw inferences of fact

---

[1]   CPR, PD52, paras 5.21 and 17.5; CPR, r 52.4(3).
[2]   General Commissioners (Jurisdiction and Procedure) Regulations 1994, reg 20(2) and (3).
[3]   Ibid, reg 21(2).
[4]   Ibid, reg 21(2).
[5]   Ibid, reg 21(3).
[6]   Ibid, reg 22(1).
[7]   *Tersons Limited v Stevenage Development Corporation* [1965] 1 QB 37; *Johnson v Scott* (1981) 52 TC 383.
[8]   *Yuill v Wilson* (1981) 52 TC 674; *Bradshaw v Blunden (No 2)* (1960) 39 TC 73.

on appeal will be exercised sparingly. Remission back for a total rehearing is possible, although this is likely to be rare.[1] The case stated should deal with all the issues of fact (and preferably all the legal arguments which were presented to the Commissioners), even if an appeal is decided on one ground alone, making the other arguments irrelevant. It is possible to argue points of law not advanced before the Commissioners in the High Court,[2] but the factual foundation for such points must be found in the case stated.[3] Where an opportunity to make points on the draft case was not taken, it has been held to be 'totally out of the question' to remit the case.[4]

17.62 Remission back under s 56(6) of the TMA 1970 for a supplemental case to be stated (or under s 56(7) for amendment of the case stated, after which the case returns to the High Court and judgment is delivered) is possible in order for the Commissioners to make further findings if an application is made promptly and:

(a) the findings are material to some tenable argument;
(b) the findings are reasonably open on the evidence that has been adduced; and
(c) the findings asked for are not inconsistent with the findings already made.[5]

17.63 Remission of the case stated before the hearing of the appeal should be obtained by applying to the Chancery interim applications judge by application notice[6] in accordance with the procedure set out in CPR Part 23 and PD23.

Powers of court hearing tax appeals

17.64 In appeals governed by a combination of reg 22(4) of the General Commissioners (Jurisdiction and Procedure) Regulations 1994 and s 56 of the

---

1   *Rose v Humbles* (1971) 48 TC 103, CA where, inter alia, there was a misunderstanding about whether two taxpayers' appeals were being heard at the same time; and *Ottley v Morris* (1981) 52 TC 375 where an adjournment was requested by the taxpayer by letter but refused, and allegations of fraud had been made against the taxpayer.

2   TMA 1970, s 56(6).

3   See, for example, *Muir v IRC* (1966) 43 TC 367.

4   *Jeffries v Stevens* (1982) 56 TC 134, per Vinelott J. But see the approach of Scott J in *Consolidated Goldfields v IRC* [1990] STC 357. See also *Euro Fire Limited v Davison (Inspector of Taxes)* [1999] STC 1050, including the remarks by Robert Walker LJ concerning the applicability of judicial review at p 1053G.

5   *Consolidated Goldfields v IRC* [1990] STC 357, where it was stated by Scott J that the Commissioners are to be protected from 'nit-picking': if the case stated is full and fair in that its findings broadly cover the territory desired to be dealt with by the proposed additional findings then the court should be slow to send the case back, particularly if it appears that the Commissioners had the proposed additional findings in mind when settling the final form of the case stated.

6   See Chapter 3.

TMA 1970[1] (and also in appeals from s 705A of the ICTA 1988 tribunal[2]) the court may determine any question of law arising on the case stated, and has the power[3] to reverse, confirm or amend the determination in respect of which the case has been stated, remit the matter to the Commissioners with the opinion of the court thereon, or may make such other order in relation to the matter as it may seem fit. The court also has the power[4] to remit the case back to the Commissioners or the tribunal for amendment and to give judgment after the case stated has been amended.

17.65 In appeals from the Special Commissioners under TMA 1970, s 56A, ITA 1984, s 225 and the Stamp Duty Reserve Tax Regulations 1986, reg 10, the legislation is very similar. The court is given power to reverse, affirm or 'vary' (rather than 'amend') the decision, although it is thought that little turns on this. The court can vary the 'determination' appealed against or remit the matter to the Commissioners with the opinion of the court thereon, or make such other order in relation to the matter as it thinks fit.

17.66 In VAT cases, reference should be made to CPR, r 52.10.

17.67 In stamp duty appeals in relation to instruments executed after 30 September 1999, the court must determine the questions submitted and may give such directions as it thinks fit with respect to the repayment of any duty or penalty paid by conformity with the Commissioners' decision.[5]

17.68 In leapfrog appeals, it appears that the court should act in a similar fashion to the Special Commissioners and should confirm the determination unless satisfied that it ought to be varied or quashed.[6]

17.69 In penalty proceedings where penalties have been determined otherwise than by proceedings instituted before the Commissioners, appeals[7] lie to the relevant Commissioners in the first instance, and a subsequent appeal to the High Court is possible either by way of case stated or by appellant's notice as appropriate. An appeal also lies to the High Court against the amount of the penalty. The High Court now has the same jurisdiction as the Commissioners

---

[1]   Ie by way of case stated from decisions of the General Commissioners.

[2]   Ie by way of case stated from the tribunal set up under the provisions relating to the cancellation of tax advantages from transactions in securities set out in ICTA 1988, Part XVII.

[3]   Under ICTA 1988, s 56(6) or 705A(6).

[4]   Ibid, s 56(7) or 705A(7).

[5]   Stamp Act 1891, s 13B(4).

[6]   Although there is no express statutory provision to this effect, it would be surprising if the position were otherwise: see ITA 1984, s 224(5), and the Stamp Duty Reserve Tax Regulations 1986, reg 8(4D).

[7]   See TMA 1970, s 100B(3) which also provides for appeals to lie to the High Court against the amount of a penalty determined under s 100 or s 100B by the Commissioners on appeal to them, and it is provided that on such an appeal the court has the same jurisdiction as the Commissioners.

under s 100B(2) of the TMA 1970. Thus,[1] in such appeals, the court is not limited to looking at whether the penalty is disproportionate or plainly wrong. Before amendments made to s 100 of the TMA 1970 in 1989, it was held by the Court of Appeal in *Salmon v General Commissioners for Havering and IRC*,[2] that the court could interfere with the amount of the penalty awarded after a hearing before the Commissioners only when 'plainly something had gone wrong'. Citing this decision, Vinelott J seems to have held in *QT Discount v Warley General Commissioners*,[3] that the power of the court under s 53 of the TMA 1970 was wider (at least so far as the admissibility of evidence on appeal was concerned). It is difficult to see how this emerges from the wording of s 53(2) which still states that the court can confirm or reverse the decision of the Commissioners or reduce or increase the sum awarded.

17.70 In penalty proceedings determined under s 100C(4) of the TMA 1970 there is a right for either party to appeal on a question of law and for the defendant to appeal against the amount of the penalty. The court can set the determination aside where it appears that no penalty has been incurred. It can confirm the determination if it is appropriate, reduce it if it is excessive, or, increase it if it is insufficient. Section 53 of the TMA 1970 and ss 249 and 251 of the ITA 1984 give similar powers to confirm, reduce or increase the penalties (summarily assessed), although there is no specific reference in ss 53 and 251 to appeals on questions of law. Leaving aside the possibility of remitter and the possibility of adducing evidence on appeal, the re-hearings by the court are not *de novo*, and the onus is on the appellant to show that a smaller penalty should have been awarded.[4]

Remission after hearing of appeal

17.71 There is a significant amount of case-law relating to remission back to the Commissioners or VAT and Duties Tribunal. As with remission on an interlocutory application, the court will be reluctant to order a further hearing at which evidence may be adduced unless there is a good reason why the party did not adduce the evidence initially. Typically the decision or case stated will be remitted so that figures can be agreed. In *IRC v McGuckian*[5] the Court of Appeal in Northern Ireland ordered the remission to the Special Commissioners of a case stated with a direction to treat an assessment as having been made under s 470 of the ICTA 1970 (rather than under s 478 of that Act). Leave to cross-appeal to the House of Lords was granted against this decision, but in the event it was unnecessary to consider the point because the Inland Revenue won its appeal on a different point. It is thought that

---

[1] According to DC Potter QC and KJ Prosser *Tax Appeals* (Sweet & Maxwell, 1991), at p 137.

[2] [1968] 45 TC 77.

[3] [1982] STC 40.

[4] *Delapage v Highbury General Commissioners* [1992] STC 290, per Mummery J.

[5] [1994] STC 888.

McGuckian was wrongly decided on this point. Section 29(6) of the TMA 1970 only permits alteration of assessments in accordance with the express provisions of the Taxes Acts, and s 50(6) and (7) of the TMA 1970 provides for increases or reductions if the Commissioners consider an appellant to have been undercharged or overcharged. *Bath & West Counties Property Trust Limited v Thomas*,[1] relied upon by the Court of Appeal (Northern Ireland), was probably wrongly decided because Walton J did not consider the point; s 56(6) does not contain any express provision for amendment of an assessment. In *Foulsham v Pickles*[2] the possibility of remitter with a direction to the Commissioners to make a proper assessment under a different case within Sch D was mentioned but reliance on this by the Court of Appeal in *McGuckian* was misplaced because the Special Commissioners were both an assessing body and an appellate body at the time when *Foulsham* was decided. The power to assess passed to the inspectors of taxes when the Income Tax Management Act 1964 came into force.

Costs

17.72 Costs usually follow the event, although occasionally the Inland Revenue agrees at the outset not to ask for costs if it wins (or even agrees to bear the taxpayer's costs) in cases where important points of law are involved. Unless the court specifically directs the Commissioners or the relevant tribunal to give a further decision or to state a further case (or to amend a case) the question of costs should be dealt with as soon as judgment is given at the conclusion of the appeal.

17.73 The court may direct the parties to agree and sign a statement of the terms of the order made by it. In cases of dispute or difficulty, it is possible to arrange to 'mention'[3] the matter to the judge.

---

[1]   [1977] 1 WLR 1423.

[2]   [1925] AC 458.

[3]   By way of a short hearing on the same or a later date, when convenient to the judge and the parties.

PROCEDURAL TABLE

Statutory Appeal		
Filing appellant's notice	Notice in Form N161 should be used. The appellant's notice must be filed within 28 days of the decision being appealed against. Where the reasons for the decision are given after the decision, the notice must be filed within 28 days of the reasons being received by the appellant.	PD52, para 5.1 PD52, para 17.3 PD52, para 17.4
Applying for extension of time if necessary	If the appellant's notice has not been served within the 28-day period, the appellant's notice should include an application for an extension of time. The documents filed with the appellant's notice should include any documents relied upon in support of the application.	PD52, para 5.2 PD52, para 5.6
Filing documents in support of appeal	Prepare and file appeal bundle with preamble and contents; exclude all documents extraneous to appeal; certify compliance with PD52, para 5.6A(2). Lodge with appeal bundle two additional copies of Appellant's Notice for court, one for each respondent, one copy of skeleton argument for each copy of the appellant's notice.	PD52, para 5.6 PD52, para 5.6A
Skeleton argument	Documents filed with the appellant's notice should include skeleton argument and, where necessary, a chronology and list of persons. If it is impractical to file a skeleton argument with the appellant's notice it can be filed and served within 14 days of filing the appellant's notice.	PD52, para 5.9 PD52, para 5.11
Serving appellant's notice	The appellant's notice, skeleton argument and (once permission to appeal has been granted, where permission is required) the appeal bundle must be served on all respondents and the body or tribunal whose decision is being appealed against as soon as practically possible, but in any event within 7 days of the appellant's notice being filed.	PD52, para 5.21, 5.24 CPR, r 52.4(3) PD52, para 17.5
Notifying hearing date	Once the appellant's notice has been filed, the court will inform the parties of a listing window during which the appeal will be heard.	PD52, para 6.3

Response		
Filing respondent's notice	This is not necessary if the respondent merely wishes to have the original decision upheld. If the respondent wishes to have the original decision varied in any way or have the original decision upheld on different grounds, a respondent's notice must be filed within 14 days of the respondent receiving the appellant's notice.	PD52, para 7.2 CPR, r 52.5(2)
Applying for extension of time	If the respondent fails to file a notice within the 14-day time-limit, an application for an extension of time must be included in the notice, along with the reasons for the failure to comply with the time-limits.	PD52, para 7.5
Skeleton argument	A skeleton argument must be filed and served even where a respondent's notice is not filed if the respondent wishes to address the appeal court. The skeleton argument may be included in the respondent's notice or filed and served within 14 days of the respondent receiving the appellant's notice. If no respondent notice is being served, file and serve skeleton arguments at least 7 days before hearing at the appeal.	PD52, para 7.6 PD52, para 7.7
Documents	If the respondent wishes to rely on any documents other than those in the appellant's bundle, he should make every effort to agree amendments to the appeal bundle with the appellant; otherwise he should prepare a supplemental bundle, which must be filed and served with the respondent's notice, or, if notice is served, within 21 days of service of the appeal bundle.	PD52, paras 7.11, 7.12
Appeals by way of case stated		
Case stated	The appellant should ask the minister or tribunal whose decision is being challenged to state a case.	
Applying for order to state case	If the relevant minister or tribunal refuses or fails to state a case, the appellant should apply for an order requiring the minister or tribunal to state a case within 14 days of the refusal to state a case.	PD52, paras 18.17–18.20
Filing appellant's notice	The appellant's notice must be filed and served with a copy of the stated case on all parties to the case and on the minister or tribunal which stated the case within 14 days of the appellant receiving the stated case. NB any time-limits for lodging the case stated at court are likely to be mandatory and incapable of being extended.	PD52, para 18.11
	Subject to the above, the procedure applicable to statutory appeals generally should be adopted, including the filing and service of documents in support of the appeal	PD52, para 18.2

Forms
Form N161
Form N162

Part 2

PROCEDURAL GUIDES

Procedural Guide 1
Commencement of proceedings (CPR Part 7 or Part 8 procedure)

Preliminary		
Which court	If the value of the claim is less than £15,000, the claim must be started in the county court.	CPR PD7, para 2.1
	If the value of the claim or the value of the property is more than £30,000 and the claim would fall within its equity jurisdiction, if heard in the county court, then the claim must be started in the High Court.	CCA 1984, s 23
	Generally, where a relevant statute, rule or Practice Direction specifies the use of a particular form then this form should be used.	
Which claim form	If the proceedings are to be issued in the county court, and are contained in Table 3 of CPR PD4, use the form referred to in that Practice Direction.	CPR PD4, Table 3
	If the proceedings are contained in any of the Tables in CPR PD8B and the requirements of the section in question are met, use a Part 8 claim form (Form N208).	CPR PD8B
	If the proceedings are unlikely to involve significant disputes of fact, use a Part 8 claim form (Form N208).	CPR, r 8.1(2)(a)
	In all other proceedings in which the use of a particular form of originating process is not required by statute or a relevant Practice Direction, use a Part 7 claim form (Form N1).	CPR PD7, para 3.3
CPR Part 7 procedure Issue	A claim form is completed and lodged with or sent to the court office.	CPR, r 7.2(1)
	The claim form must be verified by a statement of truth.	CPR, r 22.1(1)
	Particulars of claim may be served with the claim form or endorsed on it and any particulars of claim must be verified by a statement of truth.	CPR, r 7.4(1) CPR, r 22.1(1)
Service	Service will normally be effected by the court and the claim form will need to state the defendant's address.	CPR, r 6.3(1) CPR, r 6.13
	If the claimant wishes to effect service, he must inform the court and must file a certificate of service following service of the claim form.	CPR, r 6.3(1)(b) CPR, r 6.14(2)(a)

	If difficulties are faced in serving the claim form, the court can direct an alternative form of service on the application of the claimant.	CPR, r 6.8
Particulars of claim	If particulars of claim were not endorsed on, or served with, the claim form, the defendant must be served with them by the claimant within 14 days of service of the claim form on him and in any event no later than the latest date for service of the claim form.	CPR, r 7.4(1)(b) CPR, r 7.4(2)
Responding to claim form	Upon service of the particulars of claim, the defendant may: (1) file a defence; (2) file an admission; or (3) file an acknowledgement of service.	CPR, Part 10 CPR, Part 14 CPR, Part 15
	If the defendant wishes to dispute the claim, he must serve a defence. The defence must be served with 14 days of service of the particulars of claim.	CPR, r 15.4(1)(a)
	If the defendant cannot serve a defence within 14 days, he may file an acknowledgement of service within 14 days of service of the particulars of claim. A defence must then be filed within 28 days of service of the particulars of claim.	CPR, r 10.1(3)(a) CPR, r 10.3(1) CPR, r 15.4(1)(b)
	If the defendant wishes to dispute the jurisdiction of the court to hear the claim, he must file an acknowledgement of service within 14 days of service of the particulars of claim.	CPR, r 10.1(3)(b)
	If the defendant admits the claim then he should file an admission within 14 days of service of the particulars of claim.	CPR, r 14.2

CPR Part 8 procedure

Issue	A claim form is completed and lodged with or sent to the court office.	CPR PD7, para 3.1 CPR, r 7.2(1)
	The claim form must state that the Part 8 procedure applies to the claim.	CPR, r 8.2(a)
	The claim form must be verified by a statement of truth.	CPR, r 22.1
	The claimant must file with his claim form any written evidence on which he intends to rely.	CPR, r 8.5(1)
Service	Service is effected in the same way as a Part 7 claim form, save that the written evidence filed by the claimant must be served with the claim form.	CPR, r 8.5(2)

Responding to claim form	The defendant must file an acknowledgement of service with the court and serve the acknowledgement of service on all the other parties within 14 days after service of the claim form.	CPR, r 8.3(1)
	The acknowledgement of service must state whether the defendant contests the claim. If the defendant seeks a remedy other than that set out in the claim form, the acknowledgement of service must state what that remedy is.	CPR, r 8.3(2)
	The defendant must file and serve with the acknowledgement of service any written evidence on which he intends to rely.	CPR, r 8.5(3)
Response by claimant	The claimant may serve evidence in reply to the defendant's evidence within 14 days of service of the defendant's evidence and any such evidence in reply must be filed and served on all the other parties.	CPR, r 8.5(5)

Procedural Guide 2
Summary judgment

When	Unless the claim includes claim for specific performance of an agreement for the sale, purchase, exchange, mortgage or charge of any property, or for the grant or assignment of a lease or tenancy of any property or for the rescission of such an agreement, or for the forfeiture or return of any deposit made under such an agreement a claimant can only apply after acknowledgement of service of the particulars of claim.	CPR, r 24.4(1) CPR PD24, para 7.1
	The respondent must be given at least 14 days' notice of the hearing and of the issues which the court will decide at the hearing.	CPR, r 24.4(3)
Which form	Form N244. The application notice must include a statement that the application is for summary judgment made under Part 24.	CPR PD24, para 2.2
Service of evidence	Applicant's evidence should be served with the application notice, which should identify clearly all the evidence upon which the applicant is relying.	CPR PD24, para 2.4
	In the case of specific performance, the claim form must have a copy of the order sought attached to it.	CPR PD24, para 7.2
Respondent's evidence	The respondent must file and serve copies of his witness statement at least 7 days before the hearing.	CPR, r 24.5(1)
Applicant's evidence in response	The applicant may serve evidence in response no less than 3 days before the hearing.	CPR, r 24.5(2)
When	The summary procedure for obtaining possession of land against trespassers may only be used where the land is occupied by persons (not tenants or sub-tenants) who entered or remained without the consent of a person entitled to possession.	CPR, r 55.1(b)
Which court	Possesion proceedings must be started in the county court for the district unless there are exceptional circumstances or it does not have jurisdiction.	CPR, PD55, para 1.1

Application	Form N5 for a claim against trespassers. The Particulars of Claim are in Form N121 and must be filed and served with the claim.	CPR PD15, para 1.5 CPR, r 55.4
	Where the claimant does not know the name of a person in occupation or possession the claim must be brought against 'persons unknown' as well as any named defendants.	CPR, r 55.3(4)
Hearing date	The court fixes the hearing date when the claim form is issued	CPR, r 55.5(1)
Service	Service on named persons is effected in the normal way.	CPR, r 6.12 et seq
	Service on persons unknown is either by fixing copies of the documents to the main door or other conspicuous part of the land and, if practicable, posting them in a transparent envelope through the letter box or by attaching copies to stakes in the land.	CPR, r 55.6
	Service must be effected (for residential property) not less than 5 days and (for other land) not less than 2 days before the hearing. The court may extend or shorten this time-limit.	CPR, r 55.5(2) CPR, r 3.1(2)(a)
Interim possession orders	Claim must be by Form N5 and the application by Form N130 which incorporates a witness statement.	CPR PD55, para 9.1
	The application must be made within 28 days of when the claimant first knew or ought reasonably to have known that any defendant was in occupation.	CPR, r 55.21(1)(c)
Service	Service must take place within 24 hours of the issue of the application for the interim possession order.	CPR, r 55.23(1)
	Service must be effected by fixing the documents to the door or other conspicuous part of the property and, if practicable, by posting them in a transparent envelope through the letter box addressed to 'the occupiers' .	CPR, r 55.23(2)
Certificate of service	At or before the hearing, the claimant must file a certificate of service.	CPR, r 55.23(3)
After interim possession order is granted	On making the interim possession order the court will set a date for the hearing of the claim not less than 7 days after the interim order is granted	CPR, r 55.25(4)

	The interim possession order (together with the claim form and the written evidence in support) must be served within 48 hours after the order is sealed by fixing the documents to the main door or other conspicuous part of the property and, if practicable, by posting them through the letter box.	CPR, r 55.26
Return date	Before the return date the claimant must file a certificate of service relating to the service of the interim possession order.	CPR, r 55.27(1)
	At the hearing, the court may make a final order for possession, dismiss the claim, give directions for it to proceed under CPR, r 55, Section I or enforce any of the claimant's undertakings.	CPR, r 55.27(3)

Procedural Guide 3
Interim remedies

Legal background
Part 25 and the Practice Directions which supplement it make provision for the application for granting a wide range of interim remedies including freezing injunctions (*Mareva* orders) and search orders (*Anton Piller* orders). Additional provisions are made in other Rules and the Practice Directions to them in respect of some of the remedies.

This guide deals with applications for:

– interim remedies between parties in existing proceedings;
– orders relating to property, in existing proceedings, against non-parties; and
– orders relating to property in anticipation of proceedings.

Part 23 contains general rules about applications.

General considerations and requirements

The court's powers	The court may grant the following:
	(1) an interim injunction;
	(2) an interim declaration;
	(3) an order for:
	    (a) the detention, custody or preservation of relevant property,
	    (b) the inspection of relevant property,
	    (c) the taking of a sample of relevant property,
	    (d) the carrying out of an experiment on or with relevant property,
	    (e) the sale of relevant property which is of a perishable nature or which for any other good reason it is desirable to sell quickly,
	    (f) the payment of income from relevant property until a claim is decided, and
	    (g) authorisation of a person to enter any land or building in the possession of a party to the proceedings for the purposes of carrying out any such order;
		CPR, r 25.1(1)

	(4) an order to deliver up goods;	Torts (Interference with Goods) Act 1977, s 4
	(5) an order (a 'freezing injunction') restraining a party from removing assets from the jurisdiction or from dealing with any assets wherever located;	

	(6) an order directing a party to provide information about the location of relevant property or assets, or about relevant property or assets which are or may be the subject of an application for a freezing injunction;	
	(7) a 'search order' requiring a party to admit another party to premises for the purpose of preserving evidence, etc;	CPA 1997, s 7
	(8) an order for disclosure of documents or inspection of property before a claim has been made;	SCA 1981, s 33 or CCA 1984, s 52
	(9) an order for disclosure of documents or inspection of property against a non-party;	SCA 1981, s 34 or CCA 1984, s 53
	(10) an order for an interim payment;	
	(11) an order for a specified fund to be paid into court or otherwise secured;	
	(12) an order permitting a party seeking to recover personal property to pay money into court pending the outcome of the proceedings and directing that, if he does so, the property shall be given up to him;	
	(13) an order directing a party to prepare and file accounts; and	
	(14) an order requiring an account to be taken or enquiries to be made.	CPR, r 25.1(1)
	This list is not exhaustive.	CPR, r 25.1(3)
	An interim remedy may be granted irrespective of the final remedy claimed.	CPR, r 25.1(4)
Time for applying	Subject to any rule, Practice Direction or enactment, an application for an interim remedy may be made:	CPR, r 25.2(2)(a)
	(1) before the proceedings are started;	
	(2) during proceedings; or	
	(3) after final judgment has been given.	CPR, r 25.2(1)

	However, a defendant may not apply without the court's permission before he has filed an acknowledgement of service or a defence.	CPR, r 25.2(2)(c)
Applications before proceedings	The court may only grant an interim remedy before the start of proceedings if the matter is urgent or it is otherwise in the interests of justice.	CPR, r 25.2(2)
	When granting such an application, the court may give directions which include a direction that a claim be commenced.	CPR, r 25.2(3)
Applications without notice	An application may be made without notice if there are good reasons not to give notice.	CPR, r 25.3(1)
	Evidence in support of the application must state those reasons.	CPR, r 25.3(3)
Applications where there is no related claim	An application for: (1) an interim remedy relating to a claim or a prospective claim in a foreign court; or (2) the inspection, preservation, custody, etc of property before commencement of proceedings under SCA 1981, s 33, or CCA 1984, s 52; is made by application notice, not by issuing a claim.	CPR, r 25.4
Evidence	An application for an interim remedy must be supported by evidence unless the court orders otherwise.	CPR, r 25.3(2)
	Evidence in respect of an application under SCA 1981, ss 33(1) and 34(3), or CCA 1984, ss 52(1) or 53(3), should show, in addition to any other matters, that the property is or may become the subject-matter of, or be relevant to the issues in, proceedings or prospective proceedings.	CPR, r 25.5(2)

**Injunctions – including freezing injunctions
and search orders**

Which judge	Freezing injunctions and search orders may be made by a High Court judge or any other duly authorised.	CPR PD25, para 1.1
	Where the court has made a freezing order and has ordered a person to make a witness statement or affidavit about his assets and to be cross-examined on its contents, unless the judge directs otherwise, the cross-examination will take place before a Master or a district judge, or if the Master or district judge directs, before an examiner of the court.	CPR PD2B, para 7
	In the High Court, Masters and district judges may grant injunctions: (1) by consent; (2) in connection with charging orders and appointments of receivers; or (3) in aid of execution of judgments.	CPR PD25, para 1.2
	Otherwise, in the High Court, any judge who has trial jurisdiction in the matter may grant an injunction.	CPR PD25, para 1.3
	In the county court, any judge who has jurisdiction to conduct the trial of the action may grant an injunction.	CPR PD25, para 1.3
	A district judge may also grant an injunction in a money claim before allocation if the amount claimed does not exceed the fast-track limit or in a matter which a district judge has jurisdiction to hear.	CPR PD2B, para 8.1(a), (b)
	A Master or district judge may vary or discharge an injunction granted by any judge with the consent of all the parties.	CPR PD2B, paras 2.4 and 8.2 CPR PD25, para 1.4
The application notice	The application notice must state the order sought. Evidence in support and a draft of the order, if possible, should be filed with it.	CPR PD25, paras 2.1, 2.2 and 2.4
	In the Royal Courts of Justice, a disk containing the draft order in WordPerfect 5.1 should also be supplied if possible.	
	Enquiry should be made at other courts to ascertain whether this would be of assistance. Not all courts will have the facilities to use such a disk.	

	The document file format used should be that of WordPerfect 5.1.	CPR PD25, para 2.4
Evidence	Applications for freezing orders and search orders must be supported by affidavit evidence. Otherwise the general rules as to evidence apply.	CPR PD25, para 3.1
Urgent applications	The application notice, evidence in support and draft order should where possible be filed 2 hours before the hearing.	CPR PD25, para 4.3(1)
	If the application is heard before issue of the application, a draft order should be produced at the hearing and the application notice and evidence in support should be filed the same day or the next working day, or as the court orders.	CPR PD25, para 4.3(2)
	Unless there is a need for secrecy, the applicant should inform the respondent of the application informally.	CPR PD25, para 4.3(3)
	In the case of urgent applications made before issue of the claim, where possible, the claim form should be served with any order made.	CPR PD25, para 4.4(2)
	If an applicant is legally represented, an urgent application may be made by telephone where a hearing cannot be obtained. The Practice Direction contains details of how this may be arranged. A draft order should be faxed to the judge if possible, and the application and evidence in support must be filed the same or the next working day, or as the judge orders.	CPR PD25, para 4.5
What the order must contain	An injunction order must: (1) set out clearly what the respondent must do or not do; and	CPR PD25, para 5.3
	(2) unless the court orders otherwise, contain an undertaking by the applicant to the court to pay any damages which the respondent(s) (or any other party served with or notified of the order) sustain which the court considers the applicant should pay. An injunction order made before issue of the claim form:	CPR PD25, para 5.1(1)

	(1) should state in the title after the names of the applicant and respondent 'the Claimant and Defendant in an Intended Action'; and	CPR PD25, para 4.4(3)
	(2) unless the court orders otherwise, must contain *either* an undertaking by the applicant to the court to issue a claim form and pay the appropriate fee immediately *or* directions for the commencement of the claim.	CPR PD25, paras 4.4(1) and 5.1(5)
	An injunction order made before the issue of an application notice must, unless the court orders otherwise, contain an undertaking to file and pay the appropriate fee on the same or next working day.	CPR PD25, para 5.1(4)
	An order made without notice must unless the court orders otherwise contain:	
	(1) an undertaking by the applicant to the court to serve on the respondent the application notice, evidence in support and any order made as soon as practicable; and	CPR PD25, para 5.1(2)
	(2) a return date for a further hearing at which the other party can be present.	CPR PD25, para 5.1(3)
	An injunction order which is made in the presence of all parties to be bound may be expressed to be effective until trial or further order.	CPR PD25, para 5.2
Effect of a stay	If the claim is stayed while an interim injunction is in force, the injunction is set aside unless the court orders otherwise.	CPR, r 25.10
Effect of claim being struck out for non-payment of fee	If a claim is struck out under r 3.7, an interim injunction ceases to have effect after 14 days unless the claimant applies within that time to reinstate the claim.	CPR, r 25.11
Special provisions relating to search orders	Applications for a search order in intellectual property cases should be made to the Chancery Division.	CPR PD25, para 8.5
	Supervising solicitor	
	The affidavit in support of the application must name a supervising solicitor, his firm and its address and his experience.	CPR PD25, para 7.3(1)

	He must be experienced in the operation of search orders and must *not* be a member of the applicant's firm of solicitors.	CPR PD25, para 7.2 CPR PD25, para 8.1
	A supervising solicitor may be contacted either through the Law Society or, for the London area, through the London Solicitors Litigation Association.	CPR PD25, para 7.2
	The supervising solicitor is responsible for the general conduct of the order, including the listing of any items removed, and must report on the carrying out of the order to the applicant's solicitors. (A copy of the report must be filed and served on the respondent.)	CPR PD25, para 7.5(6) CPR PD25, para 7.5(11) CPR PD25, para 7.5(12)
	Service	
	The supervising solicitor must serve the order personally, unless the court orders otherwise, in which case the order should so provide and explain why.	CPR PD25, para 7.4(1) CPR PD25, para 8.2
	Search and custody of materials	
	The Practice Direction makes detailed provision as to what documents should be served with or accompany the order and who may or should accompany the supervising solicitor when he serves.	CPR PD25, para 7.4
	The Practice Direction makes detailed provision as to what may be removed, what may be searched, and as to the custody, safekeeping and insurance of removed items.	CPR PD25, para 7.5
	Any items removed must be listed and the respondent must have the opportunity to check the list before removal of any items, unless this is impracticable.	CPR PD25, para 7.5(6), (7) CPR PD25, para 7.5(13)
Specimen orders	Examples of freezing and search orders are annexed to the Practice Direction.	CPR PD25, Annex

Interim payments

Conditions to be satisfied before an order may be made	The court may make an order for an interim payment if: (1) the applicant has obtained judgment for, or the respondent has admitted liability to pay, damages to be assessed or some other sum of money (if the court has ordered an account and the evidence on the application for	CPR, r 25.7(1)(a), (b)

interim payment shows that the
account is bound to result in a payment
to the applicant then the court will
order that the applicant be paid 'the
amount shown by the account to be
done' before making an order for
interim payment);

(2) it is satisfied that the claimant
would obtain judgment for a
substantial amount of money against a
defendant from whom the payment is
sought; or

CPR, r 25.7(1)(c)

(3) where the applicant is seeking an
order for the possession of land, at trial
the defendant would be ordered to pay
the claimant for the use and
occupation of the land.

CPR, r 25.7(1)(d)

Matters to be taken into account when making the order	The court must take into account contributory negligence and any relevant set off or counterclaim, and may only award a reasonable proportion of the amount likely to be awarded on final judgment.	CPR, r 25.7(5) CPR, r 25.7(4)
Children and patients	The court's permission must be obtained before making a voluntary interim payment to a child or patient.	CPR PD25B, para 1.2
The application	The application notice and supporting evidence must be served 14 clear days before the hearing.	CPR, r 25.6(3)
	No application may be made before the time for acknowledging service has expired.	CPR, r 25.6(1)
Evidence	The application must be supported by evidence dealing with: (1) the amount sought; (2) the items in respect of which it is sought; (3) the likely amount of final judgment; and (4) the pre-conditions for the granting of an interim payment (see above); (5) any other relevant matters.	CPR, r 25.6(3)(b) CPR PD25B, para 2.1
	Documents in support, including medical reports, should be exhibited.	CPR PD25B, para 2.2
	The respondent must file and serve his evidence 7 clear days before the hearing. The applicant must file and serve evidence in reply 3 clear days before the hearing.	CPR, r 25.6(4) CPR, r 25.6(5)

	Any evidence which has already been filed and served may also be relied upon.	CPR, r 25.6(6)
Instalments	The court may order an interim payment to be paid in instalments. If it does so, the order must set out:	CPR, r 25.6(7)
	(1) the total amount of the payment; (2) the amount of each instalment; (3) the amount and date for payment of each instalment; and (4) the payee.	CPR PD25B, para 3
The court's power to adjust the order	The court has a general power to adjust an interim payment order. The order may be to vary or discharge the payment, or for its repayment in whole or in part.	CPR, r 25.8(1), (2)
	The court may order a defendant to reimburse, in whole or in part, another defendant who has made an interim payment if:	CPR, r 25.8(2)(c)
	(1) the latter has made a Part 20 claim against the former in the proceedings; and	
	(2) if the claim (or part) to which the payment relates is continuing, the pre-conditions set out above concerning making an interim payment order are met.	CPR, r 25.8(3)
No disclosure to trial judge	Unless the defendant agrees, the fact of any interim payment should not be disclosed to the trial judge until liability and quantum have been decided.	CPR, r 25.9
Adjustment on final judgment	The court may make an adjustment order of its own motion when finally disposing of a claim or part of it.	CPR, r 25.8(4)
	Where an interim payment has been made, the final judgment must set out the total amount awarded and the amount(s) and date(s) of the interim payment(s). Judgments should be entered for the amount of the award less any interim payment(s) already paid.	CPR PD25B, para 5.2 CPR PD25B, para 5.3
	If the amount of the interim payment(s) exceed(s) the amount of the judgment, the court should then make an adjustment order under CPR, r 25.8(5). The court has power to	CPR PD25B, para 5.4 CPR, r 25.8(5) CPR PD25B, para 5.5

	award interest to the defendant; the power should be exercised.	
Court fees	On an application made in existing proceedings (or an undertaking to issue them):	SCFO fees 2.4 and 2.5 CCFO fees 2.4 and 2.5
	(1) on notice – £60	SCFO fee 1.2
	(2) without notice – £30	CCFO fee 1.3
	(3) otherwise – £130 or £180	
Forms	Form N244 may be used.	CPR PD23, para 2.1

Procedural Guide 4
Construction of documents

Legal background – CPR Part 8

The most usual form of proceedings for an application to court for the construction of a document will be that provided for by CPR Part 8. The Part 8 procedure may be used by a claimant who seeks the court's decision on a question which is unlikely to involve a substantial dispute of fact.

Which court	The claim may be brought in the High Court or in a county court.	
Form	Part 8 Claim Form (N208)	CPR PD8. Alternative procedure for claims, para 2.2
Statement of truth	The claim form and any particulars of claim must be verified by a statement of truth.	CPR, r 22.1(1)
Contents of claim form	The claim form must state: (1) that Part 8 applies; (2) the question which the claimant wants the court to decide or the remedy which the claimant is seeking and the legal basis for the claim to that remedy; (3) if the claim is being made under an enactment, what that enactment is; (4) if the claimant is claiming in a representative capacity, what that capacity is; and (5) if the defendant is sued in a representative capacity, what that capacity is.	CPR, r 8.2
Acknowledgement of service	A defendant who wishes to respond to a Part 8 claim form should file and serve on all other parties an acknowledgement of service not more than 14 days after service of the claim form.	CPR, r 8.3
	The acknowledgement of service must state whether the defendant contests the claim and, if the defendant seeks a different remedy from that set out in the claim form, what that remedy is.	
	The acknowledgement of service must also be signed by the defendant or his legal representative and include the defendant's address for service.	CPR, r 10.5

Evidence	The claimant must file any written evidence on which he intends to rely when he files his claim form.	CPR, r 8.5(1)
	The claimant's evidence must be served on the defendant with the claim form.	CPR, r 8.5(2)
	A defendant who wishes to rely on written evidence must file and serve that evidence at the same time as his acknowledgement of service.	CPR, r 8.5(3) and (4)
	There is provision for the claimant to serve evidence in reply, if required, within 14 days of service of the defendant's evidence.	CPR, r 8.5(5) and (6)
Allocation	A claim under Part 8 will be treated as allocated to the multi-track.	CPR, r 8.9(c)
Directions	The court may give directions immediately the Part 8 claim form is issued either on the application of a party or on its own initiative.	CPR PD8. Alternative procedure for claims, para 4.1
	Where the court does not fix a hearing date when the claim form is issued, it will give directions for the disposal of the claim as soon as is practicable after the defendant has acknowledged service of the claim form, or if no acknowledgement is served, after the period for acknowledging service has expired, including fixing a case management conference or a pre-trial review or both.	CPR PD8. Alternative procedure for claims, para 4.2 and CPR, r 29.2(1)(b)
	The court will fix the trial date or the period in which the trial is to take place as soon as is practicable.	CPR, r 29.2(2)
General	If the papers are in order, the court may not require an oral hearing, but will be able to deal with the matter on paper, either by making a final order or by directing a hearing before a judge.	Chancery Guide, para 2.20

Legal background – s 48 of the Administration of Justice Act 1985

By virtue of s 48 of the Administration of Justice Act 1985, the order of the court can be obtained on any question of construction of a will or trust without argument or attendance before the judge if an opinion of a person who has a High Court qualification of at least 10 years within the meaning of the Courts and Legal Services Act 1990 has been obtained.

Which court	The claim must be brought in the High Court and will be assigned to the Chancery Division.	SCA 1981, Sch 1, para 1(c),(d)
Form	Part 8 Claim Form (N208)	CPR PD64, para 5
Statement of truth	The claim form and any particulars of claim must be verified by a statement of truth.	CPR, r 22.1(1)
Service	The claim form may be issued without naming a defendant.	CPR PD64, para 5
Evidence	The claim form must be supported by a witness statement or affidavit to which the following must be exhibited: (1) copies of all relevant documents; (2) instructions to counsel (or other appropriate person instructed); (3) counsel's (or other appropriate person's) opinion; and (4) draft terms of the desired order.	Chancery Guide, para 26.37
	The witness statements or affidavit (or its exhibits) must state: (1) the names of all persons who are, or may be, affected by the order sought; (2) all surrounding circumstances admissible and relevant in construing the document; (3) the date of call of counsel (or date of qualification of other appropriate person) and his experience in the construction of trust documents; (4) the approximate value of the fund or property in question; and (5) whether it is known to the applicant that a dispute exists and, if so, details of such dispute.	Chancery Guide, para 26.38
General procedure	The file will be placed before the Master, who will consider whether the evidence is complete. If it is complete, he will send the file to the judge.	Chancery Guide, para 26.39
Subsequent procedure	The judge will consider the papers, and, if necessary, direct service of notices under CPR, r 19.8A or request such further information as he may desire.	Chancery Guide, para 26.40

If the judge is satisfied that the order sought is appropriate, he will make the order and it will be sent to the applicant.

If the judge directs service of notices under CPR, r 19.8A, and any acknowledgement of service is received, the applicant must apply to the Master (on notice to the parties who have filed acknowledgements of service) for directions. If the applicant wishes to pursue the claim, the Master will usually direct that the claim should proceed as a normal Part 8 claim.

Chancery Guide, para 26.41

If, when the claim is heard by the judge, the judge is of the opinion that any party who has entered an acknowledgement of service has no reasonably tenable argument contrary to counsel or the qualified person's opinion, he may, in the exercise of his discretion, order that party to pay any costs thrown away, or part of them.

Chancery Guide, para 26.42

Procedural Guide 5
Mortgage possession claims

Legal background

CPR Part 55 and PD55 provide a mandatory code for possession claims by a mortgagee. In both the High Court and county court, proceedings must be commenced using the prescribed Form N5 (claim form) and Form N120 (particulars of claim). This guide sets out the various procedural steps from issue to judgment. It should be noted that possession claims are no longer brought under Part 8. Unless specifically disapplied, the normal provisions of the CPR in relation to a Part 7 claim will therefore apply.

Definitions	'a possession claim' means a claim for the recovery of possession of land (including buildings or parts of buildings).	CPR, r 55.1(a)
	'mortgage' includes a legal or equitable mortgage and a legal or equitable charge and 'mortgagee' is to be interpreted accordingly.	CPR, r 55.1(c)
Jurisdiction	A county court has jurisdiction to hear and determine any action for recovery of land.	CCA 1984, s 21(1)
	The county court has exclusive jurisdiction in all mortgage claims in relation to dwelling-houses situated outside Greater London.	CCA 1984, s 21(3)
	The claim must be started in the county court for the district in which the land is situated unless CPR, r 55.3(2) applies.	CPR, r 55.3(1)
	The claim may be started in the High Court if the claimant files with his claim form a certificate stating the reasons for bringing the claim in that court verified by a statement of truth.	CPR, r 55.3(2)
	Only exceptional circumstances justify starting a claim in the High Court.	CPR PD55, para 1.1
	Circumstances which may, in an appropriate case, justify starting a claim in the High Court are if:	CPR PD55, paras 1.3 and 1.4
	(1) there are complicated disputes of fact; or	
	(2) there are points of law of general importance. The value of the property and the amount of any financial claim may be relevant circumstances, but these factors alone will not normally justify starting the claim in the High Court.	
	Where a mortgage possession claim is issued in the High Court it is assigned to the Chancery Division	CPR, PD55, para 1.6 Chancery Guide, para 21.3

	Where proceedings are commenced in the wrong county court, the claim may be transferred to the court in which they should have been started or struck out or may be dealt with in the court where the claim was issued.	CPR, r 30.2(2)
	If the claimant starts a claim in the High Court and the court dcides that it should have been started in the county court, the court will normally either strike the claim out or transfer it to the county court on its own initiative. This is likely to result in delay and the court will normally disallow the costs of starting a claim in the High Court and any transfer.	CPR PD55, para 1.2
Statements of case	The claimant must use a Form N5 claim form and a Form N120 particulars of claim.	CPR PD55, para 1.5 and PD4, Table 1
	The particulars of claim must contain the particulars required by the Practice Direction to the CPR Part 55, including the required particulars in relation to mortgage claims.	CPR PD55, para 2.1 CPR PD55, para 2.5
	A copy of the mortgage must be attached to or served with the particulars of claim	CPR PD16, para 7.3(1)
	The defence must be in Form N11M	CPR PD55, para 1.5
Costs	Where the court assesses the costs, the costs are, unless the mortgage expressly provides otherwise, presumed to be costs which (a) have been reasonably incurred; and (b) are reasonable in amount.	CPR, r 48.3(1)

Procedural Guide 6
Contentious probate

Procedure		
Which court	The claim must be brought in the Chancery Division in London or in one of the District Registries having Chancery jurisdiction.	CPR, r 57.2(2), (3) CPR, PD57, para 2.2
	A probate claim can be brought in the county court with a chancery district registry or the Central London County Court provided that the net estate of the deceased does not exceed £30,000.	CCA 1984, s 32
Which form	Form N1, containing a statement of the interest of the claimant and the defendant in the estate of the deceased.	CPR, rr 57.3, 57.7(1)
Parties	Every person entitled or claiming to be entitled to administer the estate of the deceased must be joined.	CPR, r 57.6
	Notice should be served on all persons who might be affected by the probate claim, whether as a beneficiary or otherwise.	CPR PD57, para 4
Lodgment of grant	In cases of revocation of the grant, if the claimant is in possession of the grant, he must lodge it in the relevant office on the issue of the claim form. If it is in the possession of a defendant, he must lodge it in the relevant office when he acknowledges service.	CPR, r 57.6(2), (3)
Acknowledgement of service	Within 28 days of the service of the claim form or particulars of claim if separate.	CPR, r 57.4(2)
Testamentary scripts	By the claimant when the claim form is issued or by the defendant when he acknowledges service.	CPR, r 57.5(2)
Particulars of claim	(1) With the claim form; or (2) within 14 days after service of the claim form.	CPR, r 7.4
Defence	In any other event, 28 days from the date of service of the claim form, or 14 days if the defendant does not acknowledge service.	CPR, r 15.4(1)

Procedural Guide 7
Applications under the Inheritance (Provision for Family and Dependants) Act 1975

Legal background

Under I(PFD)A 1975 (as amended by the Law Reform (Succession) Act 1995) certain persons may make a claim for financial provision out of the estate of a deceased person, on the ground that the disposition effected by the deceased's will and/or under the laws of intestacy is not such as to make reasonable financial provision for the applicant. Section 2 of I(PFD)A 1975 sets out the court's powers in making an order. The matters which the court must take into account are set out in s 3 and differ, depending upon who is making the application.

The procedure is governed by CPR, r 57.16, in the county court as well as in the High Court (RSC Ord 99, r A1).

Procedure

Who may apply	(1) The spouse of the deceased. (2) The former spouse of the deceased. (3) A cohabitant of the deceased. (4) A child of the deceased. (5) Any person who was treated as a child of the family. (6) Any other person who immediately before the death of the deceased was being maintained by him.	I(PFD)A 1975, s 1
Which court	High Court (Chancery Division, or Family Division) or county court. The county court has unlimited jurisdiction.	CPR, r 57.15, CLSA 1990, ss 1(1) and 120, HCCCJO 1991, art 2(1)
Application	In the High Court and county court: Part 8 claim form. The claim form should state that it is issued under Part 8 and should be entitled 'In the estate of X, deceased' and 'In the matter of the Inheritance (Provision for Family and Dependants) Act 1975'.	CPR, 57.16 CPR Part 8 CPR, r 8.2
	The claim form must be issued within 6 months of the date on which representation is taken out. Any application to extend this period should be included in the claim form.	I(PFD)A 1975, s 4
Documents	The claimant must file written evidence in support, exhibiting an official copy of the grant of representation to the deceased's estate and of every testamentary document admitted to proof.	CPR , r 57.16
	The claimant's written evidence must be filed and served with the claim form.	CPR, r 57.16

Defendants	(1) Personal representatives.	CPR, r 19.2
	(2) Beneficiaries who may be affected by any provision ordered by the court.	
	(3) Other persons affected by the claim.	
	(4) Any other person directed by the court to be added.	
Service	Acknowledgement of service must be filed within 21 days after service of the claim form and served on the claimant and any other party.	CPR, r 57.16(4)
	A failure to file an acknowledgement of service within the prescribed period means that the defendant may take part in the hearing of the claim only with the court's permission.	CPR, r 8.4
Evidence in answer	A defendant who is a personal representative and who wishes to remain neutral in respect to the claim and agrees to abide by the court's decision should state this in section A of the acknowledgement of service form.	CPR, PD57, para 15
	The witness evidence filed by a personal representative must state to the best of the witness's ability:	
	A defendant who is a personal representative of the deceased must, and any other defendant may, file a witness statement or affidavit in answer within 21 days after service of the claim form on him, inclusive of the day of service.	CPR, r 57.16(4)
	The written evidence filed by a personal representative must state to the best of the witness's ability:	
	(1) full particulars of the value of the deceased's net estate, as defined in s 25(1) of the Act;	CPR, r 57.16(5)
	(2) details of those beneficially interested in the estate and (in the case of those who are not already parties) the addresses of all living beneficiaries and the value of their interests;	CPR, PD57, para 16
	(3) if such be the case, that any living beneficiary is a child or patient; and	CPR, PD57, para 16, CPR, r 21.1(2)
	(4) any facts known to the witness which might affect the exercise of the court's powers under I(PFD)A 1975.	CPR, PD57, para 16
Service of answer	A defendant who wishes to rely on written evidence must file it when he files his acknowledgement of service and at the same time serve a copy of it on all other parties.	CPR, r 8.5(3), (4)

Further evidence	The claimant may serve further written evidence in reply within 14 days of service of the defendant's evidence on him. If he does so he must also, within the same time-limit, serve a copy of his evidence on the other parties.	CPR, r 8.5(5) and (6)
Directions	A directions hearing may be requested at the same time as issuing the claim form.	CPR PD8, para 4.1
	In other cases the court will give directions as soon as practicable after the defendant has acknowledged service of the claim form or after the period for acknowledgement has expired.	CPR PD8, para 4.2
Orders which may be made	(1) Periodical payments.	I(PFD)A 1975, s 2(1)(a)
	(2) Lump sum.	I(PFD)A 1975, s 2(1)(b)
	(3) Transfer of property.	I(PFD)A 1975, s 2(1)(c)
	(4) Settlement of property.	I(PFD)A 1975, s 2(1)(d)
	(5) Acquisition, transfer and settlement of property.	I(PFD)A 1975, s 2(1)(e)
	(6) Variation of antenuptial and post-nuptial settlement.	I(PFD)A 1975, s 2(1)(f)
	(7) Treatment of deceased's former beneficial interest in joint property as part of his estate and not passing by survivorship.	I(PFD)A 1975, s 9
	(8) Variation or discharge of secured periodical payments.	I(PFD)A 1975, s 16
	(9) Variation or revocation of maintenance payments.	I(PFD)A 1975, s 17
	(10) Order relating to disposition intended to defeat a claim under the I(PFD)A 1975.	I(PFD)A 1975, ss 10, 11 and 12
Fee	£180	SCFO fee 1.2
	£130	CCFO fee 1.3
Appeals	High Court	CPR Part 52 / CPR PD52
	County court	CPR Part 52 / CPR PD52

Procedural Guide 8
Partnership proceedings

Which court	*High Court*	
	Partnership actions are assigned to the Chancery Division.	SCA 1981, s 61(1) and Sch 1
	County court	
	The county court has jurisdiction in proceedings for the dissolution or winding-up of any partnership where the partnership assets do not exceed £30,000 or where the partners consent in writing to jurisdiction.	CCA 1984, ss 23(f) and 24(2)(g) County Courts Jurisdiction Order 1981, SI 1981/1123 (as amended by SI 1991/724)
Which part	Part 8 procedure if there is no substantial dispute of fact. Part 7 procedure in all other cases and optional when there is no substantial dispute.	CPR, r 8.1(2)(a) and CPR PD8, para 1.1 Chancery Guide, para 4.10
Statement of case	For Part 8 claims, give a brief statement of the facts and then set out the relief sought.	
	For Part 7 claims, give a concise statement of the facts on which the claimant relies; usually the formation and terms of the partnership, the partnership business and the event of dissolution and/or the justification for dissolution by the court, and set out the relief sought.	CPR, r 16.4(1)(a)
	In both cases, cross-refer to and annex relevant documents, unless they are bulky.	Chancery Guide, para 4.8
Defendant's response	*Part 8 claim*	
	(1) If he wants to put evidence forward, he must file any written statement with his acknowledgement of service, and serve the other parties at the same time.	CPR, r 8.5(3) and (4)

	(2) If he does not want to put evidence forward, he should write to the court when he sends in his acknowledgement of service to say he will file none.	Chancery Guide, para 4.13
	(3) If he thinks there is a substantial issue of fact, he must state his reasons when he files his acknowledgement of service.	CPR, r 8.8(1)
	Part 7 claims	
	Defence in the usual way.	
	Counterclaims	
	Unnecessary unless a substantial issue of fact is involved.	
General approach	If accounting is the only remedy, there will be no trial and the account will be taken by the Master or district judge.	Chancery Guide, para 22.1
	If there is a substantial dispute, there will be a two-stage process of trial before the judge, who will order accounting to follow.	Chancery Guide, para 22.2
Applications	Follow Part 23 procedure with application notice with evidence in the statement of case, in the notice itself or in a witness statement, served as soon as is practicable after issue and no less than 3 clear days before the return date.	CPR, r 23.4(1) CPR, r 23.7(3)
	Applications can be made as desired to the judge or to the Master or district judge. The exception is applications for an injunction, which can only be before the Master or district judge by consent, or in the county court to the district judge where he would have jurisdiction to try the main action.	CPR PD25 – Interim Injunctions, para 1.3

| Accounting | The court will give directions. The standard practice is that one party applies, the opposing party puts forward a schedule of the transactions ascertained to be in issue and the first party gives notice which items he objects to, with detail of how the account is said to be inaccurate and what should be added or taken away. Disclosure and then adjudication follow. | CPR PD40, paras 3.1 and 3.2 |
| | The notice must contain a statement of truth or be verified by witness statement or affidavit. | CPR PD40, para 3.3 |

Procedural Guide 9
Determination of an interim rent under section 24A
of the Landlord and Tenant Act 1954

Who can apply?	Both the landlord and the tenant can apply for the determination of an interim rent.	LTA 1954, s 24A(1)
	Neither the landlord nor the tenant may make an application for the determination of an interim rent if the other has made an application and has not withdrawn it.	LTA 1954, s 24A(2)
Time-limit for application	No application for the determination of an interim rent will be entertained by the court if it is made more than 6 months after the termination of the relevant tenancy.	LTA 1954, s 24A(3)
Where proceedings have already been commenced under s 24(1) or s 29(2)	Where proceedings have already been commenced the application for the determination of an interim rent must be made in those proceedings: 1. In the claim form. 2. In the acknowledgement of service. 3. By an interim application under CPR Part 23.	CPR PD56, para 3.17
Where proceedings under s 24(1) or s 29(2) have yet to be commenced, or where such proceedings have been disposed of.	A party who wishes to make a claim for an interim rent must commence proceedings in accordance with CPR Part 8.	CPR PD56, para 3.19
The claim form	The claim form must include details of: 1. The property to which the claim relates. 2. The particulars of the relevant tenancy (including date, parties and duration) and the current rent (if not the original rent). 3. Every notice or request given or made under ss 25 or 26 of the LTA 1954.	CPR PD56, para 3.19

	4. If the current tenancy has terminated, the date and mode of termination.	
	5. If the relevant tenancy has been terminated and the landlord has granted a new tenancy of the property to the tenant:	
	(a) particulars of the new tenancy (including date, parties and duration) and the rent; and	
	(b) in a case where s 24C(2) of the LTA 1954 applies, but the claimant seeks a different rent under s 24C(3), particulars and matters on which the claimant relies as satisfying s 24C(3).	
Where an order for a new tenancy is not proceeded with or is revoked	If a court makes an order for the payment of an interim rent under s 24C, but the order for the grant of a new tenancy is not acted upon by the landlord and the tenant, or the order is revoked under s 36(2) of the LTA 1954, then the landlord or tenant can apply to the court to determine an interim rent in accordance with s 24C(1) and (2).	LTA 1954, s 24D(3)
	If such an application is made, it must be made on an application under CPR Part 23 in the original proceedings, and not by the commencement of new proceedings.	CPR PD56, para 3.18

Procedural Guide 10
Application for a new tenancy under section 24(1)
of the Landlord and Tenant Act 1954

Application to the court for a new tenancy by either the tenant or the landlord	Application must be made before the end of the 'statutory period' which is a period ending, where a s 25 notice has been served, on the date specified in the s 25 notice, and where a s 26 request has been made, immediately before the date specified in the s 26 request.	LTA 1954, ss 24(1), 29A(1)(a) and (2)
	Where a s 26 request has been made, the application cannot be made before the expiry of 2 months after the date the request was made unless a s 26(6) notice has been served.	LTA 1954, s 29A(3)
Agreed extension of time for making the claim	The time within which the application can be made may be extended by agreement between the parties made before the end of the statutory period, and further extended by agreement between the parties provided any further agreements are made before the end of the previously extended period.	LTA 1954, s 29B(1), (2) and (3)
Where the is more than one application under s 24(1) or s 29(2)	Where more than one application to the court under s 24(1) or s 29(2) is made, the following rules apply:	CPR PD56, para 3.2
	1. Once an application to the court under s 24(1) has been served on a defendant, no further application to the court in respect of the same tenancy whether under s 24(1) or s 29(2) may be served by that defendant without the permission of the court.	CPR PD56, para 3.2(1)

	2. If more than one application to the court under s 24(1) in respect of the same tenancy is served on the same day, any landlord's application is stayed until further order of the court.	CPR PD56, para 3.2(2)
	3. If applications to the court under both ss 24(1) and 29(2) in respect of the same tenancy are served on the same day, any tenant's application under s 24(1) is stayed until further order of the court.	CPR PD56, para 3.2(3)
	4. If the defendant is served with an application under s 29(2) which was issued at a time when an application to the court had already been made by that defendant in respect of the same tenancy under s 24(1), the service of the s 29(2) application shall be deemed to be a notice under CPR Part 7, r 7.7 requiring service or discontinuance of the s 24(1) application within a period of 14 days after service of the s 29(2) application.	CPR PD56, para 3.2(4)

Claim form and date of service		
Unopposed claim	Where the claim is an unopposed claim, the claimant must use the CPR Part 8 procedure save that:	CPR, r 56.3(3)(a) and PD56, para 2.1
	1. The claimant is not required to file his written evidence with the claim form, and the defendant, as a consequence, does not have to file his written evidence in reply.	CPR, r 56.3(3)(a)(i), excluding CPR, r 8.5
	2. As a result, the prohibition on the reliance on evidence not served in accordance with CPR, r 8.5 has no application.	CPR, r 56.3(3)(a)(i) excluding CPR, r 8.6
	The claim form must be served within 2 months after the date of issue and CPR, rr 7.5 and 7.6 are modified accordingly.	CPR, r 56.3(3)(b)

Opposed claim	Where the claim is an opposed claim, the claimant must use the CPR Part 7 procedure, but the claim form must be served within 2 months after the date of issue, and CPR, rr 7.5 and 7.6 are modified accordingly.	CPR, r 56.3(4)(a), (b) and PD56, para 2.1A(1)
Form of claim form	The claim is made using Form N208. This claim form must be used even if the CPR Part 7 procedure is applicable because the claim is an opposed claim.	
Particulars in all claim forms	The particulars which the claim form must contain varies, but in every case the claim form must contain details of: 1. The property to which the claim relates. 2. The particulars of the current tenancy (including date, parties and duration), the current rent (if the not the original rent) and the date and method of termination. 3. Every notice or request given or made under ss 25 or 26 of the LTA 1954. 4. The expiry date of the statutory period under s 29A(2) of the LTA 1954 or any agreed extended period made under s 29B(1) or (2) of the LTA 1954.	CPR PD56, para 3.4
Additional particulars in the claim form where the tenant is the claimant	Where the tenant is making the claim, in addition to the details described above, the claim form must also contain the following details: 1. The nature of the business carried on at the property. 2. Whether the tenant relies upon ss 23(1A), 41 or 42 of the LTA 1954 and, if so, the basis on which he does so. 3. Whether the tenant relies upon s 31A of the LTA 1954 and, if so, the basis on which he does so. 4. Whether any, and if so what	CPR PD56, para 3.5

part, of the property comprised in the tenancy is occupied neither by the claimant nor by a person employed by the claimant for the purpose of the claimant's business.

5. The tenant's proposed terms of the new tenancy.

6. The name and address of:

(a) anyone known to the tenant who has an interest in the reversion in the property (whether immediate or in not more than 15 years) on the termination of the claimant's current tenancy and who is likely to be affected by the grant of a new tenancy; or

(b) if the tenant does not know of any such person, anyone who has a freehold interest in the property.

CPR PD56, para 3.6

The claim form must be served on one of the persons referred to above, as appropriate.

CPR PD56, para 3.7

Additional particulars in the claim form where the landlord is the claimant	Where the claimant is a landlord, in addition to the details described above, the claim form must contain details of: 1. The landlord's proposed terms of the new tenancy. 2. Whether the landlord is aware that the tenant's tenancy is one to which s 32(2) applies and, if so, whether the landlord requires that any new tenancy shall be a tenancy of the whole of the property comprised in the tenant's current tenancy or just of the holding. 3. The name and address of: (a) anyone known to the landlord who has an interest in the reversion in the property (whether immediate or in not more than 15 years) on the termination of the tenant's current tenancy and	

	who is likely to be affected by the grant of a new tenancy; or (b) if the landlord does not know of any such person, anyone who has a freehold interest in the property.	CPR PD56, para 3.8
	The claim form must be served on one the persons referred to above as appropriate.	
The proper defendant	Where a claim under s 24(1) is made by a tenant, the proper defendant is the competent landlord.	LTA 1954, s 44 and Sch 6, CPR PD56, para 3.3
	In addition to the competent landlord, a mesne landlord, whose consent is sought under para 4(2) of Sch 6 to the LTA 1954, must also be a defendant if an issue arises as to the reasonableness of the mesne landlord withholding consent, or imposing conditions, which issue is determined by the court pursuant to para 4(3) of Sch 6.	CPR PD56, para 4.1
	Where a landlord makes a claim under s 24(1), the defendant will be the tenant under the current tenancy.	
Acknowledgement of service in a tenant's claim under s 24(1) which is unopposed	A landlord, faced with a claim by a tenant under s 24(1), which he does not oppose, must nevertheless serve an acknowledgement of service. It must be in Form N210, and must state with particulars: 1. Whether, if a new tenancy is granted, the defendant objects to any of the terms proposed by the claimant and if so: (a) the terms to which he objects; and (b) the terms that he proposes in so far as they differ from those proposed by the tenant. 2. Whether the tenant is a tenant under a lease having less than 15 years unexpired at the date of the termination his current tenancy and, if so, the	CPR PD56, para 3.10

name and address of any
person who, to the knowledge
of the landlord, has an interest
in the reversion in the
property expectant (whether
immediate or in not more than
15 years from that date) on
the termination of the tenant's
tenancy.
3. The name and address of
any person having an interest
in the property who is likely to
be affected by the grant of a
new tenancy.
4. If the tenant's current
tenancy is one to which
s 32(2) applies, whether the
defendant requires that any
new tenancy shall be a tenancy
of the whole of the property
comprised in the tenant's
current tenancy.

Acknowledgement of service in a landlord's claim under s 24(1) which is unopposed	The tenant must serve and file an acknowledgement of service in Form N210, and which must contain the following particulars: 1. The nature of the business carried on at the property. 2. If the tenant relies on ss 23(1A), 41 or 42 of the LTA 1954, the basis on which he does so. 3. Whether any, and if so what part, of the property comprised in the tenancy is occupied neither by the tenant nor by a person employed by him for the purpose of the business. 4. The name and address of: (a) anyone known to the tenant who has an interest in the reversion in the property (whether immediate or in not more than 15 years) on the termination of the current tenancy and who is likely to be affected by the grant of a new tenancy; or (b) if the tenant does not know of any such person,	CPR PD56, para 3.11

anyone who has a freehold interest in the property.

5. Whether, if a new tenancy is granted, the tenant objects to any of the terms proposed by the landlord and, if so:

(a) the terms to which he objects; and

(b) the terms that he proposes in so far as they differ from those proposed by the landlord.

	The acknowledgement of service must be filed and served within 14 days of service of the claim form.	CPR, r 8.3, PD8, para 3
Acknowledgement of service and defence where the tenant is the claimant and the claim is opposed	In such a case, CPR Part 7 procedure must be used, and it is the landlord who is the defendant.	CPR PD56, para 3.12

The acknowledgement of service must be in Form N9 and in his defence the landlord must state with particulars:

1. The grounds of opposition, which having regard to the definition of that expression in PD56, para 3.1(3), are not limited to the statutory grounds described in s 30(1) of the LTA 1954.

2. Full details of those grounds of opposition.

3. Whether, if a new tenancy is granted, the landlord to any of the terms proposed by the tenant and if so, the terms to which he objects; and the terms that he proposes in so far as they differ from those proposed by the tenant.

4. Whether the tenant is a tenant under a lease having less than 15 years unexpired at the date of the termination of the current tenancy and, if so, the name and address of any person who, to the knowledge of the landlord, has an interest in the reversion in the property expectant (whether

immediately or in not more
than 15 years from that date)
on the termination of the
tenant's tenancy.

5. The name and address of
any person having an interest
in the property who is likely to
be affected by the grant of a
new tenancy.

6. If the tenant's current
tenancy is one to which
s 32(2) of the LTA 1954
applies, whether the landlord
requires that any new tenancy
shall be a tenancy of the whole
of the property comprised in
the tenant's current tenancy.

The acknowledgement of
service and defence must be
filed and served within 14 days
of service of the claim form.

Evidence	Where the claim is unopposed, no evidence need be filed unless and until the court directs it to be filed.	CPR PD56, para 3.14
	In opposed claims, evidence, including expert evidence, must be filed by the parties as the court directs, and the landlord, whether he is a claimant or defendant, shall be required to file his evidence first.	CPR PD56, para 3.15
	The court will give directions about the future management of the claim following receipt of the acknowledgement of service.	
Directions	When the claim is first before the court, directions will be given for its future prosecution. The nature and extent of the directions will turn on whether the claim is opposed or unopposed. As no evidence need be filed or served before the claim is before the court, directions for evidence will inevitably be made.	

If the claim is opposed, the grounds of opposition, be they the statutory grounds or otherwise, shall be tried as a preliminary issue, unless the circumstances are such that it is unreasonable to do so. An order will be made to that effect if the claim is opposed.

CPR PD56, para 3.16

Procedural Guide 11
Application for an order for the termination pursuant to section 29(2) of the Landlord and Tenant Act 1954

Application to the court by the landlord	Application must be made before the end of the 'statutory period', which is a period ending, where a s 25 notice has been served, on the date specified in the s 25 notice, and where a s 26 request has been made, immediately before the date specified in the s 26 request.	LTA 1954, ss 29(2), 29A(1)(b) and (2)
Agreed extension of time for making the claim	The time within which the application can be made may be extended by agreement between the parties made before the end of the statutory period, and further extended by agreement between the parties provided any further agreements are made before the end of the previously extended period.	LTA 1954, s 29B(1), (2) and (3)
Where there is more than one application under s 24(1) or s 29(2)	Where more than one application to the court under s 24(1) or s 29(2) is made, the following rules apply:	CPR PD56, para 3.2
	1. Once an application to the court under s 24(1) has been served on a defendant, no further application to the court in respect of the same tenancy whether under s 24(1) or s 29(2) may be served by that defendant without the permission of the court.	CPR PD56, para 3.2(1)
	2. If more than one application to the court under s 24(1) in respect of the same tenancy is served on the same day, any landlord's application is stayed until further order of the court.	CPR PD56, para 3.2(2)
	3. If applications to the court under both ss 24(1) and 29(2) in respect of the same tenancy are served on the same day, any tenant's application under	CPR PD56, para 3.2(3)

	s 24(1) is stayed until further order of the court.	
	4. If a defendant is served with an application under s 29(2) which was issued at a time when an application to the court had already been made by that defendant in respect of the same tenancy under s 24(1), the service of the s 29(2) application shall be deemed to be a notice under CPR Part 7, r 7.7 requiring service or discontinuance of the s 24(1) application within a period of 14 days after service of the s 29(2) application.	CPR PD56, para 3.2(4)
Claim form and date of service	The landlord must use the CPR Part 7 procedure, but the claim form must be served within 2 months after the date of issue, and CPR, rr 7.5 and 7.6 are modified accordingly.	CPR, r 56.3(4)(a), (b) and PD56, para 2.1A(2)
Form of claim form	The claim is made using Form N208. This claim form must be used even though the CPR Part 7 procedure is applicable.	
Particulars in claim form	The claim form must contain the following particulars: 1. The property to which the claim relates. 2. The particulars of the current tenancy (including date, parties and duration), the current rent (if not the original rent) and the date and method of termination. 3. Every notice or request given or made under ss 25 or 26 of the LTA 1954. 4. The expiry date of the statutory period under s 29A(2) of the LTA 1954 or any agreed extended period made under s 29B(1) or (2) of the LTA 1954.	CPR PD56, para 3.4
Additional particulars	In addition to the particulars described above, the claim form must also contain the following particulars:	CPR PD56, para 3.9

	1. The landlord's ground of opposition. 2. Full details of those grounds of opposition. 3. The terms of a new tenancy that the landlord proposes in the event that the application under s 29(2) fails.	
The proper defendant	The tenant under the current tenancy is the proper defendant.	
Acknowledgement of service and defence	In such cases, the tenant will be the defendant, and the acknowledgement of service must be in Form N9, and in his defence the tenant must state with particulars: 1. Whether he relies on ss 23(1A), 41 or 42 of the LTA 1954 and, if so, the basis on which he does so. 2. Whether the tenant relies on s 31A of the LTA 1954 and, if so, the basis on which he does so. 3. The terms of the new tenancy that the tenant would propose in the event that the landlord's claim to terminate the current tenancy fails.	CPR PD56, para 3.13
Evidence	Evidence, including expert evidence, must be filed by the parties as the court directs, and the landlord shall be required to file his evidence first.	CPR PD56, para 3.15
	The court will give directions about the future management of the claim following receipt of the acknowledgement of service.	CPR, r 56.3(3)(c)
Directions	When the claim is first before the court, directions will be given for its future prosecution. The nature and extent of the directions will turn on what is in issue	

between the parties. As no
evidence need be filed or
served before the claim is
before the court, directions
for evidence will inevitably be
made.

Appendix A

STANDARD DIRECTIONS FOR UNOPPOSED LEASE RENEWALS

Allocation
The case is allocated to the multi-track/fast track.
[Note: Although Part 56 claims are automatically allocated to multi-track being within Part 8, in low rent cases the Court will consider whether to re-allocate the case to fast track.]

Part 56
The Court gives permission for written evidence produced in accordance with these directions to be relied on at the hearing of this case and directs that the claimant and defendant are not also required to comply with the provisions of Rule 56.3(10) and (11).

[Transfer to the Chancery List
This case be transferred to this court's Chancery List and continue under Chancery number ...]
[Note: The parties and the court should consider whether the issues in dispute are such that the case is appropriate for transfer to the Chancery List. Even if the parties consider the matter should be transferred to the Chancery List, they should still seek to agree the other directions in case the court considers that transfer is not appropriate and/or to assist the [Chancery] judge with directions to be given.]

Stay of proceedings
If at any time the Claimant and Defendant jointly notify the Court that they wish the proceedings to be stayed for a fixed period (not exceeding three months) to enable the parties to attempt to negotiate a settlement, the periods of time for compliance with these directions shall be adjusted by such period provided that such stay shall not affect the date fixed for the trial of this case. Prior to the fixing of a date for trial, the parties may jointly apply for the trial window to be adjusted to take into account the agreed period of the stay.

Professional Arbitration on Court Terms (PACT) and ADR [optional]
[Note: The parties should consider a stay to enable the matter to be determined under the PACT scheme. If a reference to the PACT scheme is appropriate, in place of the directions set out below, the parties should use the appropriate form of PACT order – see the PACT booklet published jointly by the Law Society and the Royal Institution of Chartered Surveyors. Alternatively, the parties should consider a stay to enable mediation to take place]

Draft Lease
The Defendant shall serve on the Claimant [, either by e-mail or on computer disc, an electronic copy of] a draft lease by no later than 4.00pm on [insert date].

The Claimant shall serve on the Defendant its proposed amendments/counter-proposals to the lease [, either by e-mail or on computer disc, marked in *italics* or underlined (if the draft lease was submitted electronically) or marked in red or by schedule (if the draft lease was submitted in paper form)], by no later than 4.00pm on [insert date].

The Defendant shall by no later than 4.00pm on [insert date] notify the Claimant which amendments, if any, are disputed and specify the Defendant's additional amendments, [, either by e-mail or on computer disc, marked in *italics* or underlined (if the draft lease was submitted electronically) or marked in green (if the Claimant's amendments were marked in red) or by counter-schedule (if the Claimant's amendments were by schedule)].

Disclosure [optional]
Each party [the Claimant/the Defendant] shall give standard disclosure of documents to every other party [to the Defendant/the Claimant] by list by 4.00pm on [insert date].

The last date for service of any request to inspect or for a copy of any document is 4.00pm on [insert date].

Witness Statements of Fact [optional]
Each party shall serve on the other party the witness statements of all witnesses of fact on whom it intends to rely.

There shall be simultaneous exchange of such statements by no later than 4.00pm on [insert date].

[Disputed Lease Terms [optional]]
The parties/solicitors for the parties are to meet/speak by 4.00pm on [insert date] on a without prejudice basis with a view to narrowing the issues between the parties on the lease terms.

The parties do, by no later than 4.00pm on [insert date], prepare and serve a schedule setting out such terms of the draft lease as are not agreed. In each case, the party seeking materially to depart from the terms of the current lease of the premises must set out its reasons for so doing.]

Expert Evidence
If the terms of the new lease are not agreed between the parties, experts reports are to be exchanged no later than 4.00pm on [insert date] and agreed if possible, and if not agreed such expert evidence to be limited to one conveyancing expert for such party.

[Note: Since in many cases only rent and interim rent are in issue, permission for a conveyancing expert will only rarely be appropriate.]

If the rent [and interim rent] for the new lease is not agreed between the parties, each party is to be at liberty to call one expert valuation witness at the hearing of the Claimant's application for a new tenancy. Their reports, including lists of comparables and photographic evidence (if any) relating to the rent payable under the new lease to be exchanged by no later than 4.00pm on [insert date]. Such reports are to be agreed if possible.

[The respective experts are to meet/speak by 4.00pm on [insert date] on a without prejudice basis with a view to narrowing the issues between the parties]. The experts [the parties] are to agree a joint statement indicating those parts of the experts evidence with which they are/are not in agreement (including as to facts) with reasons, such statement to be served on all parties by no later than 4.00pm on [insert date], the description of the premises, any plans and photographs and the comparables (and any plans and photographs relating to them).

Questions to Experts [optional]

The time for service on another party of any question addressed to an expert instructed by that party is no later than [insert number] days after service of that expert's report.

Any such question is to be answered within [insert number] days of service of the question(s).

Request for information etc. [optional]

Each party shall serve any request for clarification or further information based on any document disclosed or statement served by another party no later than [insert number] days after disclosure or service.

Any such request shall be dealt with within [insert number] days of service of the request.

Dates for filing Listing Questionnaires and Trial

Each party must file a completed Listing Questionnaire by no later than 4pm on [insert date] with experts reports, statements of issues by experts, replies to any questions to experts and witness statements.

This case [including the Defendant's claim for interim rent] is to be tried as a fixture before a Circuit Judge in the period commencing on [insert date] and ending on [insert date] with a provisional time estimate of [insert estimate of length of hearing].

[Note: While the court will endeavour to fix the trial window requested by the parties, it will very much depend on the availability of court time. The dates suggested by the parties will be taken as an indication of their assessment of when they will be ready for trial.]

The trial date is to be fixed by [a Listing Officer] [the Specialist Jurisdiction manager] at a listing appointment at [insert time] on [insert date] at [13/14] [26] Park Crescent London W1 at which the parties are to attend and to have available all dates to avoid. The parties are to inform each other forthwith of the details of the listing appointment to ensure attendance at that appointment, so that it shall be effective. **NB The CLCC listing arrangements are due to change on or about 1ˢᵗ July 2002 in which case this direction will require amendment**

If a party does not attend at the listing appointment or does not then provide dates to avoid, the trial date will be fixed for such date as the Listing Officer/Specialist Jurisdiction Manager may decide, and any date so fixed shall only be varied upon an application to a judge.

Miscellaneous

The Claimant shall lodge at the court and with the Defendant an indexed bundle of documents contained in a ring binder and with each page clearly numbered no more than seven days and not less than three days before the start of the trial.

Skeleton arguments on behalf of both parties are to be lodged no later than three days before the start of the trial.

The parties shall seek to agree the contents of the trial bundle and the case summary.

Each party must inform the court immediately if the claim is settled, whether or not it is then possible to file a draft consent order to give effect to their agreement.

Costs in the case

Take notice that any party affected by this order may apply, within 10 days of service if upon him/her/it to have it varied, set aside or stayed.

Appendix B

STANDARD DIRECTIONS FOR OPPOSED LEASE RENEWALS

Preliminary Issue

The trial of the issue(s) as to whether the Defendant satisfies the ground of opposition contained in Section 30(1) [a-b-c-d-e-f-g] be tried as [a] preliminary issue(s).

[The trial of the issue of whether the Court has jurisdiction to make an order granting the Claimant a new lease of [the Premises] be tried as a preliminary issue.]

The directions referred to below shall apply to the preliminary issue(s) only, and all further proceedings herein (save in relation to the preliminary issue(s)) shall be stayed until the determination of the preliminary issue(s) or further order in the meantime.

Part 56

The Court gives permission for written evidence produced in accordance with these directions to be relied on at the trial of the preliminary issue(s) and directs that the Claimant and Defendant are not also required to comply with the provisions of Rule 56.3(10) and (11).

[Transfer to the Chancery List

This case be transferred to this court's Chancery List and continue under Chancery number ...]

[Note: The parties and the court should consider whether the issues in dispute are such that the case is appropriate for transfer to the Chancery List. Even if the parties consider the matter should be transferred to the Chancery List, they should still seek to agree the other directions in case the court considers that transfer is not appropriate and/or to assist the [Chancery] judge with directions to be given.]

Disclosure of Documents

Each party [the Defendant] shall give standard disclosure of documents relating to the preliminary issue(s) to every other party [the Claimant] by list by 4.00pm on [insert date].

The last date for service of any request to inspect or for a copy of any document is 4.00pm on [insert date].

[Note: The parties and the court should consider whether the tenant is in a position to give disclosure in any meaningful way and, if not, the order should be altered, accordingly. Disclosure by the tenant may be relevant where the landlord challenges jurisdiction or the entitlement of the tenant to a new tenancy.]

Witness Statements of Fact

Each party shall serve on the other party the witness statements of all witnesses of fact on whom it intends to rely.

There shall be simultaneous exchange of such statements by no later than 4pm on [insert date].

[There shall be consecutive service of such statements. The Defendant shall serve its statements by 4.00pm on [insert date] and the Claimant by 4.00pm on [insert date].

[*Note: The parties and the court should consider whether the tenant is in a position to adduce factual evidence in any meaningful way and, if not, the order should be altered, accordingly. Factual evidence from or on behalf of the tenant may be relevant where the landlord challenges jurisdiction or the entitlement of the tenant to a new tenancy.*]

Expert Evidence
[Party appointed experts will be the normal order]

[The parties shall exchange reports setting out the substance of any expert evidence relating to the preliminary issue(s) on which they intend to rely. Such evidence shall be limited to [number] for each party and the discipline(s) of [insert disciplines].

The exchange shall take place simultaneously no later than 4.00pm on [insert date].

Experts reports shall be agreed if possible no later than [   ] days after service.

[The respective experts are to meet/speak by 4.00pm on [insert date] on a without prejudice basis with a view to narrowing the issues between the parties.] The experts [the parties] are to agree a joint statement indicating those parts of the experts evidence with which they are/are not in agreement (including as to facts, the description of the premises, any plans and photographs and the comparables (and any plans and photographs relating to them)) with reasons, such statement to be served on all parties by no later than 4.00pm on [insert date].

Each party has permission to use an expert witness to give [oral] evidence [in the form of a report] at the trial provided that the substance of the evidence to be given has been disclosed as above and has not been agreed].

OR

[A single expert may be appropriate in respect of particular issues eg the condition of the property in relation to ground (a)]

[On it appearing to the court that expert evidence is necessary on the issue of [
     ] and that evidence should be given by the report of a [single] expert [insert profession] [instructed jointly by the parties], the [Claimant/Defendant] shall not later than 4.00pm on [insert date] inform the court in writing whether or not such an expert has been instructed].

OR

[The expert evidence on the issue of [   ] shall be limited to a single expert [insert profession] jointly instructed by the parties.

If the parties cannot agree by 4.00pm on [insert date] who that expert is to be and about the payment of his fees, either party may apply for further directions.

Unless the parties agree in writing or the court orders otherwise, the fees and expenses of such an expert shall be paid to him [by the parties equally] [by the Claimant/Defendant].

The report of the expert shall be served on all parties by no later than 4pm on [insert date]].

Questions to Experts [optional]

The time for service on another party of any question addressed to an expert whether instructed by that party or jointly instructed by the parties is not later than [insert number] days after service of that expert's report.

Any such question shall be answered within [insert number] days of service of the question(s).

Request for Information etc. [optional]

Each party shall serve any request for clarification or further information based on any document disclosed or statement served by another party no later than [insert number] days after disclosure or service.

Any such request shall be dealt with within [insert number] days of service of the request.

Dates for filing Listing Questionnaires and Trial

Each party must file a completed Listing Questionnaire no later than [insert date] with experts reports, statements of issues by experts, replies to any questions to experts and witness statements.

The preliminary issue(s) [is/are] to be tried as a fixture before a Circuit Judge in the period commencing on [insert date] and ending on [insert date] with a provisional time estimate of [insert estimate of length of hearing].

[Note: While the court will endeavour to fix the trial window requested by the parties, it will very much depend on the availability of court time. The dates suggested by the parties will be taken as an indication of their assessment of when they will be ready for trial.]

The trial date is to be fixed by [a Listing Officer] [the Specialist Jurisdiction manager] at a listing appointment at [insert time] on [insert date] at [13/14] [26] Park Crescent London W1 at which the parties are to attend and to have available all dates to avoid. The parties are to inform each other forthwith of the details of the listing appointment to ensure attendance at that appointment, so that it shall be effective. **NB The CLCC listing arrangements are due to change on or about 1st July 2002 in which case this direction will require amendment**

If a party does not attend at the listing appointment or does not then provide dates to avoid, the trial date will be fixed for such date as the Listing Officer/Specialist

Jurisdiction Manager may decide, and any date so fixed shall be varied upon an application to a judge.

Miscellaneous

The Defendant shall lodge at the court and with the Claimant an indexed bundle of documents contained in a ring binder and with each page clearly numbered no more than seven days and not less than three days before the start of the trial.

Skeleton arguments by both parties shall be lodged with the Court not less than three days before the start of the trial.

The parties shall seek to agree the contents of the trial bundle and the case summary.

Each party must inform the court immediately if the claim is settled, whether or not it is then possible to file a draft consent order to give effect to their agreement.

Costs in the case.

Take notice that any party affected by this order may apply, within 10 days of service of it upon him/her/it to have it varied, set aside or stayed.

INDEX